The Remembered Self

The Remembered Self

―◆―

Emotion and Memory in Personality

JEFFERSON A. SINGER

PETER SALOVEY

THE FREE PRESS
A Division of Macmillan, Inc.
NEW YORK
Maxwell Macmillan Canada
TORONTO
Maxwell Macmillan International
NEW YORK   OXFORD   SINGAPORE   SYDNEY

The Free Press
A Division of Macmillan, Inc.
866 Third Avenue, New York, N.Y. 10022

Maxwell Macmillan Canada, Inc.
1200 Eglinton Avenue East
Suite 200
Don Mills, Ontario M3C 3N1

Macmillan, Inc. is part of the Maxwell Communication Group of Companies.

Printed in the United States of America

printing number
1 2 3 4 5 6 7 8 9 10

Library of Congress Cataloging-in-Publication Data

Singer, Jefferson A.
    The remembered self: emotion and memory in personality/
Jefferson A. Singer.   Peter Salovey.
        p.   cm.
    Includes bibliographical references and index.
    ISBN 0-02-901581-2
    1. Personality and cognition.   2. Personality and emotions.
3. Autobiographical memory.   I. Salovey, Peter.   II. Title.
BF698.9.C63S56   1993
153.1'2—dc20   93–8017
                                                            CIP

Credits

"My Father Would Recall" by Anna Swir, translated by C. Milosz and L. Nathan, is from *American Poetry Review* (Jan.–Feb. 1989), pp. 23–26. Reprinted by permission.

"Those Winter Sundays" is reprinted from *Angle of Ascent: New and Selected Poems*, by Robert Hayden, by permission of Liveright Publishing Corporation. Copyright © 1975, 1972, 1970, 1966 by Robert Hayden.

"Core Relational Themes for Each Emotion" (table) is adapted from *Emotion and Adaptation* by R. S. Lazarus, p. 122. Copyright © 1991 by Oxford University Press, Inc. Reprinted by permission.

Portions of "In Memory of Sigmund Freud" are from *W. H. Auden: Collected Poems* by W. H. Auden, ed. by Edward Mendelson. Copyright 1940 and renewed 1968 by W. H. Auden. Reprinted by permission of Random House, Inc., and Faber and Faber Ltd.

*To Our Parents
and Our Wives
and in Memory
of Yetta Singer
(1898–1993)*

Contents

Preface

When we decided to write this book, we began not by rushing to the laboratory and conducting an experiment or even by spending late nights in the library stacks. Rather, we sat down in a room together and told each other stories about ourselves. Not just any story, however, but ones that we thought captured each of our identities—memories that were in some way *self-defining* for us:

Jeff:

> I remember when I was about ten years old. A bunch of my friends decided to start a club called the Possum Club. I was not a "charter member." But I hoped that they would include me. On one particular Saturday in the middle of winter, the Possum Club members met in the basement of a friend's house to decide whether or not I would be allowed to join. While they deliberated behind closed doors, I waited on a couch in another room. There was a another guy who also was being considered for membership. He suggested that we try to listen through the door to hear how it was going. When we went up to the door, we heard them arguing about us. And some of my friends were indicating their reluctance to have me join. When I heard this, I was so humiliated and hurt that I decided to leave the house and walk home. It was a very cold day and probably two miles to my house, but I started out down the street. Some of my friends realized I had left and ran after me, convincing me to come back. As if this weren't humiliation enough, later in the same day, we were all outside testing the ice on a frozen pond. And of all the people, I had to fall through. One of the Possum Club members pulled me out of the water. In thinking about this memory, I realize how well it expresses a continued fear I have about groups and my status within them. I've often preferred to find a few good friends than to be a member of a crowd.

Peter:

> When I was a little kid growing up in New Jersey, a bunch of us were playing in the yard of a neighborhood boy. This boy—I still remember his last name, it was, ironically, Tenderfoot—decided we should form

an army, and he appointed himself general. His father was a career military man, and so this kid knew lots of army lingo and routine. I remember he made me a sergeant, and we spent the afternoon being ordered by him to march around the neighborhood, dig a trench in his backyard, and carve a stairway in the slope of a hill (it was a busy afternoon). At some point, I couldn't take it anymore. My parents were fairly permissive, and they never told us what to do. So I was getting sick of being bossed around by some kid my age. Besides, digging backyard trenches wasn't my idea of a good time. So I told him that we had had enough of this, and it was time to let someone else be the general (not that I had anyone particular in mind). He responded by throwing me face down into a large puddle of muddy water and then announced to the group, "I'm busting you to buck private." I felt what can only be termed "righteous indignation"; people who know me now as an adult are always quick to comment on my low threshold for being told what to do by people in charge and by the ease with which I can launch into an indignant tirade.

Within these rather embarrassing personal memories are the essential elements of emotion, memory, and personality. These memories are vivid to each of us, and what makes them so vivid is that they involve intense emotional experiences, emotions that in some way are still a part of what makes us individuals, indeed what makes Jeff and Peter different from each other. Jeff, for instance, is ambivalent about groups, yet is lured back as he tries to break away. Peter's memory involves being accepted by others but with an intolerance for being a cog in a wheel.

An important facet of personality is the characteristic or unique way in which emotions are linked to autobiographical memories. Often these thoughts and feelings are organized around goals that the individual has. In each of our memories, there are the goals each protagonist desired. There are the factual outcomes that reflect on the status of the goals. There are also the *perceived* outcomes, which may in time come to dominate the "facts" of the situation. In response to the goal outcomes, emotions were experienced, both at the time of the event and in the days, weeks, months, and years after the event—right up to the retelling of it upon the page as we wrote them down. Because in each memory one or the other of the authors is also the protagonist, there is also a perception of the self within the memory, an image of who I am and how I am perceived by others. This self-perception and public perception are keys to the self-concept.

As the events of the memory unfold, there is also another process to mention, a dynamic effort by the protagonist to regulate emotion, to max-imize pleasant feelings and minimize unpleasant feelings. There is also in-evitably in each memory the expression of emotion; it is almost as if these memories could not exist if there had not been strong emotion felt and then expressed in the face, body, or gut.

What is not explicit in each of these memories, but also important, is the reason these memories exist for each of us. They link to a theme that one could extract from a set of related memories stored in a network of autobiographical memories. If this set of memories could be identified, it would tell us about an enduring set of concerns within each of us as rep-resented by this prototypic memory. The memories we have described would then contain the seeds of long-term goals, strivings, or motives that may play a role in influencing our interests and choices. Finally, above and beyond the content of these memories, there is the organization of the mem-ory itself and the style in which it is told, other elements that help define individuality.

Within these simple memories from childhood and adolescence are goals, outcomes, perceived outcomes, emotional responses that may per-sist or alter over time, images of a private and public self, a motivation to maximize positive and minimize negative feelings and to express these feelings, regardless of valence, and the possibility of a link to enduring goals or motives in the personality. Moreover, each memory is told in a par-ticular style and organized in an individualized way.

It seems astonishing that within such simple memories some of the most essential elements of personality are contained. Yet, it is that compactness or efficiency that convinces us that narratives play a major role in individ-ual difference. Narrative, through characterization, plot, and theme links the two major systems of personality—emotion and memory. The mem-ories we tell ourselves and tell to others inform us about ourselves when we attend to the emotions they generate in us and notice the recurring themes of what matters to us most now and before. They provide us with two important sources of information: they teach us about the outcome of goals we might pursue (cognitive input) and at the same time they remind us what it would feel like to attain these goals (emotional input). No other source of information processed by the mind provides such complex input in such a palatable form. By creating or finding memories in our lived ex-periences, we provide ourselves with a means for achieving self-under-standing and a guide for future behavior. In the chapters that follow, we examine the origin, evolution, and function of these narrative memories in personality.

Although they should not be held responsible for anything that we say here, this volume results from interactions with scholars whom we have been lucky enough to encounter. Prior to graduate school, Jeff's motivation to pursue the study of personality and cognition can be traced to interactions with John Kihlstrom, David McClelland, and Dan McAdams, and Peter's to David Rosenhan and Albert Bandura. We then met as classmates in graduate school at Yale University and became fast friends and frequent collaborators. Although more or less on opposite sides of the debate between the narrative versus paradigmatic modes of science discussed in the final chapter of this book, and, worse, differentially but deeply committed to the Yankees versus the Red Sox, we nonetheless feel that one of the greatest pleasures of writing this book, if not the greatest, was the opportunity to keep our twelve-year conversation flowing.

At Yale, we were profoundly influenced by several scholars in the Department of Psychology—Robert Abelson, Patricia Linville, William McGuire, Judith Rodin, Ira Roseman, Gary Schwartz, Jerome Singer, and Dennis Turk—and inspired by the seminal work on narrative by the Cognitive Science group, including Roger Schank, Brian Reiser, and, again, Bob Abelson. The ideas of these individuals are most noticeable in chapter 3. Much of our most creative time in graduate school was spent reading, discussing, and writing about the work of the late Silvan Tomkins. His script theory of personality has been the single most important force behind our efforts at understanding human personality.

This volume was originally conceived of as a book on affect and memory that we hoped would mark the fiftieth anniversary of the influential work in this area by David Rapaport. With Mahzarin Banaji and John D. (Jack) Mayer, we formulated such a book while at a delightful and stimulating Nags Head Conference on Motivation and Emotion. We are indebted to Mahzarin and Jack for their insights as the final framework for this volume took shape.

The influence, inspiration, and help of other scholars cannot go unacknowledged. The writings of Arnold Bruhn on early memories provided an indispensable framework for chapters 2 and 7. Our friendship and conversations with Robert Emmons regarding the measurement of personal strivings and its application to memory research are clearly evident throughout. Dan McAdams's work on identity as a life story served as a guiding idea for much of our thinking about the person as a whole. Finally, Jeff offers a special note of gratitude to a very close friend, Gary Greenberg, a clinical psychologist, for ongoing intellectual stimulation during the last six years. Gary's ideas, research, and challenges of the tenants of mainstream psychology played a major role in stimulating the debate described in chapter 8.

Without the support of our respective institutions, we could never have finished this book. We are both blessed with stimulating colleagues whose influence on our work has been both conscious and unconscious. Moreover, Connecticut College provided Jeff with a Fairchild Semester Leave and a Capstone Grant to support the writing of this book. Peter was provided a Senior Faculty Fellowship by Yale University for the same purpose. Peter also acknowledges the support of the National Science Foundation's Presidential Young Investigator Program, the National Cancer Institute, and the MacArthur Foundation-sponsored Program on Conscious and Unconscious Mental Processes.

We have been assisted by numerous students and staff members who have helped with background research, manuscript preparation, and copy editing, most notably Libie Attwater, John Beauvais, Theresa Claire, and Susan Greener. Kathie Halbach Moffitt and Carolyn Zittel collaborated on much of the research that we discuss. Susan Arellano, Celia Knight, and the entire team of professionals at The Free Press provided unending help and encouragement.

Finally, we dedicate this book to our parents, Dorothy G. and Jerome L. Singer, and Elaine Y. and Ronald Salovey, and to our spouses Anne and Marta for their constructive input, patience, and companionship. Jeff and Anne's two little girls, Olivia and Chloe, have promised that they will not color on these pages.

1

◆

Introduction

The field of personality psychology has undergone a quiet revolution during the last decade. Originally concerned with the study of enduring characteristics of the whole person (e.g., Allport, 1937; Murray, 1938), what followed was a period of ferment in which many of the basic assumptions of the subdiscipline were challenged (e.g., Mischel, 1968). Through the 1980s, however, there was a resurgence of interest in personality, inspired by advances that could reconcile some of the traditional problems with both trait theories and conceptual frameworks that relied exclusively on hidden drives and motives.

This resurgence has been characterized by a variety of new developments in the area of personality. For one, personality researchers have moved beyond their traditional interest in characterizing the content and structure of personality and toward an interest in personality processes unfolding in real time. This shift means researchers now pay regular attention to person—situation interactions and to the aggregation of behaviors over repeated samplings (Epstein, 1983; Larsen, 1989).

Second, advances in cognitive science have provided a language in which personality could be studied that tied it much closer than before to related areas of psychology and other disciplines. For instance, goals—as explicit, measurable cognitive constructs—became of interest to cognitive scientists studying text comprehension and social scripts (e.g., Schank & Abelson, 1977) at about the same time that they inspired a renewed interest among personality psychologists as one unit of human uniqueness (e.g., Emmons, 1986; Pervin 1989). Similarly, cognitive psychologists became very interested in what was called autobiographical or "everyday" memory (e.g., Neisser, 1978; Neisser & Winograd, 1988; Rubin, 1986), a movement that was concomitant with an increased interest among personality psychologists in understanding the memorial basis for personality constructs like the "self" (Greenwald & Pratkanis, 1984; Kihlstrom & Cantor, 1984; McGuire & McGuire, 1988).

1

Third, more manageable constructs that lay somewhere between the trait and the whole person were developed that were amenable to laboratory and field experimentation (see Buss & Cantor, 1989, pp. 1-3). Constructs like life tasks (Cantor & Kihlstrom, 1987), current concerns (Klinger, 1978), personal projects (Little, 1983), and personal strivings (Emmons, 1989) replaced or supplemented older constructs such as traits, achievement motives, needs, and sexual and aggressive drives.

Fourth, personality psychology heated up. It discovered that individuals are characterized by more than lists of traits or sets of *life* tasks. What makes a task a life task? What makes a project a personal project? What makes a striving a personal striving? The answer: emotion. Although Kelly (1955) certainly ushered in this new amalgam of cognitively oriented, middle-level constructs—and is owed a deep debt for this contribution—it is only recently that mood and emotion were studied by personality psychologists interested in integrating affect into other personality processes. Certainly, psychologists have long been interested in emotion (e.g., Ekman, Freisen, & Ellsworth, 1972; Izard, 1979; Rapaport, 1942), but only recently have personality psychologists heeded Tomkins's (1962, 1963) prescient message that emotion plays a more primary role in motivation than does drive reduction and is thus at the core of human individuality (Buck, 1985).

Fifth, personality psychology realized that much of the ongoing activity of the individual served a specific end state of the individual: the maintenance of equilibrium and the reduction of discrepancies between desires and present circumstances. Of course, earlier theorists interested in drive-reduction views of personality (e.g., Dollard & Miller, 1950) were also concerned with equilibrium and discrepancy reduction. However, modern approaches to self-regulation (e.g., Carver & Scheier, 1981, 1990; Higgins, 1987, 1989; Pyszczynski & Greenberg, 1987) emphasize the specific, idiographic goals of individuals as opposed to general drives to terminate aversive stimuli.

Finally, the study of narrative has had an increasingly important impact on personality psychology and on the social sciences in general (Sarbin, 1986; White, 1980). During the past twenty years or so, there has been increased attention to the limitations inherent in traditional, positivist psychology (Gergen, 1985). These criticisms have generally included a recognition that seemingly objective science is not impervious to the same sociocultural and psychosocial forces that bound the rationality of humans and social organizations in general (cf. March & Simon, 1958). Other critics have argued that traditional psychological experiments have often left out the phenomenological experience of the subject in favor of more precisely measured and easily aggregated rating scales and response latencies. As a result, constructs that can be operationalized become reified as the core aspects of human personality, while subtler and at times more complex human experiences are relegated to anecdotal accounts in the discussion sections of journal articles.

The study of narrative, or what Sarbin (1986) has referred to as the "storied nature of human conduct," has been proposed as a remedy to the limitations of more constrained approaches to the study of personality. By obtaining narratives from subjects about a variety of psychological and social phenomena, researchers believe they have tapped into dimensions of human experience glossed over or absent from current models of psychology. Some examples of this research are Baumeister (1989) on masochism and unrequited love (1992), McAdams's (1988) studies of agency and communion themes in the life story, Gergen and Gergen's (1988) characterization of the life course, Gilligan's (1982) work on moral reasoning, Schank's (1990) inquiries into the process of reminding and metaphoric memory, the examination of optimal experience among creative people, rock climbers and others by Csikszentmihalyi (1975, 1990), and Cohler's (1987) work on resilience and the psychoanalytic understanding of personal narratives. Some researchers have even suggested (Sarbin, 1986) that the organization of human experience into narratives consisting of plots, characters, settings, and conflicts is a "root metaphor" for psychology.

We hope this book contributes to this emerging attention to narrative. At the same time, we would like to demonstrate an integrative approach to the combining of traditional experimental methodologies with sensitivity to the phenomenological nuances of narrative, as have some of the scholars cited in the previous paragraph. Although we acknowledge the risk experimenters face when they believe too readily that their experimental controls free them completely from all bias, we are concerned that a disavowal of the scientific method is both highly premature and probably not desirable. The work that we present involves both laboratory experiments and the collection of freely generated narratives. Although the narratives are examined from a phenomenological and experiential perspective, we have also developed methods of content analysis and quantification that allow us to make meaningful comparisons across subjects.

With the advances in the field at large we have just enumerated, we believe it is an appropriate time to propose linkages among the major constructs represented by many of these advances: memory, goals, emotion, self-regulation, narrative, and the processes that connect them. In brief, we suggest that one aspect of what makes an individual unique, different from all others, is his or her set of personal memories and, in particular, what we call self-defining memories. Moreover, these memories are often organized around an individual's unique set of goals. The relation between such memories and goals often gives rise to characteristic patterns of emotions and their expression, which then require distinctive self-regulatory plans in order to manage them. This interrelationship among memory, goals, emotion, and self-regulation in undergirding personality is the focus of this book.

Lest we create the wrong impression at this point, we neither posit a new theory of personality (there are already enough grand theories) nor a tightly linked model with all necessary and sufficient variables included that could possibly account for individual uniqueness. Rather, we offer a perspective on personality, drawing heavily on the work of other personality/social psychology and clinical theorists. Our perspective represents what we consider an important direction for the field in the 1990s—the understanding of personality through the convergence of narrative memory, self-stated goals, and affect. In offering this linkage of personality processes, we seek to encourage a dialogue between personality psychology and related disciplines interested in similar problems, including the obviously closely related fields of social and clinical psychology, but also fields as disparate as cognitive science and sociology. Indeed, neither of us was trained as a mainstream personality psychologist. We didn't earn our Ph.D. degrees in personality programs. Rather, both of us were trained in clinical psychology, which one of us still considers his primary disciplinary affiliation, while the other of us is more comfortable in the company of social psychologists. In this sense, we are outsiders aligned with no particular political or theoretical camp.

But let us return to the three issues that form the core of this volume: memory, goals, and emotion. In emphasizing the relationship of memory to personality, we have followed Kihlstrom's (1981) admonition that "salient features of personality have the opportunity to influence not only what is remembered, in the sense of encoding and retrieval, but also what shape the reconstructed memory will finally take" (p. 127). Chapter 2 presents a view of memory that places it as a central repository of major conflicts and themes for the individual. Autobiographical memories may reveal repetitive affective patterns and themes that stamp an individual's most important concerns and unresolved issues. These memories, called self-defining memories, are identifiable by their affective intensity, vividness, and familiarity to the individual. In contrast to traditional dynamic perspectives on the hidden content of memories, we argue that much of what is of greatest importance about an individual may be learned from consciously selected recollections. Drawing upon Tomkins' script theory, we illustrate how these memories may embody nuclear scripts or organizing metaphors for the individual's personality. Through examples from drama, poetry, fiction, biography, and autobiography, we demonstrate how these self-defining memories play an organizing and central role in personality.

In chapter 3, we place these self-defining memories in the larger context of a system of personality that includes affect and motivation. In a recent chapter on his goal construct, the "personal striving," Emmons (1989) remarked that we may be in the midst of a "conative revolution." As Pervin (1989) suggests, after a period where cognitive models displaced motivational constructs, there has been a return in the past decade to research that asks questions about what impels an individual to act and then persist in that course of action. This renewed interest has supplanted the earlier drive models with the concept of a goal, though as one of us has pointed out (Singer, 1990a), a unified definition of what is meant by the term goal has yet to emerge. Still, Pervin is able to distinguish the goal concept from drives by specifying the importance of a "cognitive representation or image" that frees the individual from the demands of immediate stimuli (Pervin, 1989, p. 7). The goal, unlike the drive, points the individual toward possible worlds or selves in the future, as opposed to reflexive responses to one's own biology. Yet, paradoxically, and this is our particular focus in chapter 3, it is one's interest in the attainment of goals that may shape our memories and in turn be shaped by our recollection of these same memories.

With these concerns in mind, we describe our research program that has demonstrated how one's current affective response to a memory may be predicted from the relevance of that memory to attainment or nonattainment of one's most important personal goals. We also discuss how we use memories to motivate our behavior—both to encourage ourselves to pursue ends we desire and to discourage ourselves from activities that would lead to outcomes we would rather avoid. In demonstrating these links among one's personal past, current affect, and future goals, we argue for a coherence and continuity in personality across the lifespan. This "unity and purpose" within personality is best captured by McAdams's proposal that identity is organized around a narrative life story that includes major themes of intimacy and power, a narrative structure, ideological setting, nuclear episodes, major recurring characters, and an identifiable and meaningful plot. We show how self-defining memories and an individual's long-term goals fit comfortably into a larger life story of identity.

In chapter 4, we turn from the content of narrative memories to the structure of these narratives. Dating back to the original work of Rorschach and early gestalt psychology, and perpetuated by the New Look and ego psychologists, researchers have long argued that how an individual perceives and describes the world may be as important as what they see. In this spirit, we present our own and related research into the organization of autobiographical memory. Recent studies from our laboratory and others' suggest that the specificity or generality of our memories may play a role in both the origin and/or maintenance of depression. Similarly, the degree to which a memory narrative is summarized and vague versus specific and detailed may reflect a characteristic defense against the recollection of painful events from the past. As the life story of personality unfolds, the manner in which we tell our story may be just as influential as the story we tell.

Memories and goals do not arise from whole cloth in the minds of individuals. They also do not remain neatly folded and shelved away, ready for use if and when we need them. Instead, our cognitive system is an ever-active process, responding to a never-ceasing flow of external and internal stimuli. Although the first part of this book addresses the content and structure of memory and personality, the second part of this book explores the activity of the mind in the context of the world around it. In particular, we look, in chapter 5, at how affectively arousing and self-relevant material influence our remembering and thinking about aspects of our personality. Emotional arousal may make certain autobiographical memories more or less accessible (see J. A. Singer & Salovey, 1988, for a review), thus causing either selective learning or retrieval of information. Perhaps an even more fundamental role for affect is that its arousal directs attention, usually focusing it on concerns that require immediate action. Our recent work (Salovey, 1992) suggests that when affect is aroused, attention is often directed on to one's self and the content of consciousness.

In chapter 5 we explore the influence of affect on attention and memory. We discuss the arousal of affect due to both the attainment and nonattainment of goals, as well as arousal caused by stimuli external to the individual. The link between affect and memory examined in this chapter also concerns the use of memory to regulate strategically one's emotional life. Individuals often construct environments that serve to remind them of incidences from their life that arouse certain feelings. They may hang a picture on the wall of their office depicting their receipt of a national award or a recent family wedding. These are not random events. At some level, the individual is aware that these pictures provide cues for certain pleasing memories. Individuals vary in their knowledge of strategies that they can implement to regulate ongoing or future emotions. Salovey and Mayer (1990) called these individual differences emotional intelligence.

The first five chapters of this book argue that conscious memories should be assigned a more prominent role in the understanding and prediction of personality. In advancing this position, we are aware that this renewed emphasis on conscious experience is not without risk. There is obviously much merit to the psychodynamic scrutiny of self-reported experience. Chapter 6 offers an empirically based overview of the necessary cautions with which we should approach the study of conscious memories. Entitled "The Misremembered Self," this chapter reminds us that the narrative truth of autobiographical memories can often be at variance with their historical truth. Any married couple can attest to this discrepancy when they compare notes about how they first met, who created a scene at the wedding, and what each person was doing just prior to the birth of a child.

Chapter 6 delineates three perspectives on inaccuracies in autobiographical memory. The first is the familiar notion of *repression*, that memories associated with unpleasant feelings are forgotten or pushed from conscious experience. In contrast to the traditional psychoanalytic approach to repression characterized and critiqued in chapters 2 and 7, we provide a more modern discussion that recasts repression in cognitive terms. Repression can be an active and, at times, resourceful process of one's current thinking rather than simply a warehousing in the unconscious of residual conflicts from the past. The second perspective concerns so-called positive illusions, the idea that we actively create memories about ourselves that serve to bolster self-esteem, prevent depression, and, generally, keep us happy. According to this view, the distortion of autobiographical memory is not necessarily the root or cause of neurosis, as a traditional psychoanalytic approach might argue. Rather, by actively accentuating the positive and eliminating the negative, we, like Gypsy Rose Lee, can maximize our chances at happiness. The final perspective, in strong agreement with chapters 2 and 3, presents the view that the past is reconstructed through the filters of the present, as opposed to the present being merely the servant of past conflicts. In other words, our current theories about ourselves and the world can structure and recast the content of autobiographical memory.

In chapter 7, we apply our perspective on memory, affect, and personality to the interpretive process of psychotherapy. We first review traditional and contemporary positions various branches of psychoanalytic and psychodynamic therapy have taken toward memory in psychotherapy. Then, through the examination of a clinical case study, we attempt to demonstrate how our view of the remembered self can provide a useful tool for understanding a client's interpersonal patterns both within and outside the therapeutic hour. In particular, we argue that discussion of self-defining memories identified from the patient's life story may allow for a richer and more empathic understanding of transference by both the therapist and the client. This chapter concludes by linking the cognitive and affective processes involved in creating misremembered experiences to the biases encountered by therapists in clinical work.

In the concluding chapter, we return to a discussion of the importance of studying conscious thought in personality. We address what we consider an imbalance of attention that was paid to unconscious motivation by traditional positions in personality theory. We suggest that narrative memory offers a window into personality that can be accessed by both experimental and phenomenological methods. Although these two methodological and philosophical approaches have often been pitted against each other, we demonstrate through a study of memories of racial differences and prejudice that the two orientations can be integrated effectively. An emphasis on narrative memory could reduce the tension between heavily quantitative psychologists and qualitatively-oriented phenomenologists, leading to a more inclusive and complex vision of the whole person.

It is an exciting time to do research in personality, social, and clinical psychology. The willingness of researchers in these related disciplines to share ideas and models of memory, affect, and motivation has led to a healthy and blossoming cross-fertilization. We hope this book demonstrates some of the benefits of this collaborative spirit.

2

◆

Self-Defining Memories

This is a chapter about memory, but not about all aspects of human memory. In fact, it is not about the topics that have traditionally preoccupied most psychologists who study memory. It is not about how information is encoded, rehearsed, stored, or retrieved. It is also not about the other favorite subject of both cognitive and psychoanalytic psychologists—forgetting rather than remembering. Instead, this chapter is about the memories that matter most to us and the role of these memories in identity and personality. We will explore how, until very recently, psychologists have generally disregarded these memories, leaving them to the descriptive powers of novelists, biographers, and poets. It is our contention, however, that an adequate understanding of personality cannot be achieved without a systematic investigation of how our most meaningful memories influence our emotions and behaviors. Through the study of what we call *self-defining memories*, we propose that individual differences in interpersonal relationships, pursuit of long-term goals, and characteristic affective reactions may be elucidated. Recent theories of identity (McAdams, 1988, 1990a) and of personality (Bruhn, 1990a, 1990b; Tomkins, 1991, 1979, 1987) have revived the Adlerian perspective on memory (Adler, 1927, 1930, 1931; Ansbacher, 1947, 1973) that places the analysis of individuals' memories at the center of an understanding of their life goals and essential conflicts. In addition, there is now an opportunity with cognitive psychologists' increasing interest in *autobiographical* or everyday memory (Conway, 1991; Neisser, 1982; Neisser & Winograd, 1988; Robinson & Swanson, 1990; Rubin, 1986; Schank, 1982, 1990; Schank & Abelson, 1977) to integrate the study of individuals' most meaningful memories into existing paradigms and theories of cognitive psychology and cognitive science. In sum, this chapter takes to heart Ulric Neisser's (1978) famous call to psychology to study the "important questions" of memory rather than what may be most artificially and exactly controlled in the laboratory but of very little meaning, in his view, to the human being. As clinical and

9

personality psychologists, we have taken his request much farther than he might even have envisioned. We have chosen as our domain those memories that give shape to and are shaped by our lives, memories of our proudest successes and humiliating defeats, memories of loves won and lost—memories that repetitively influence our manner of intimacy or our pursuit of power—the memories that answer the question of who we are. Using both psychological theories and literary sources, we look in depth at five essential features that make up a self-defining memory. We explore both positive and negative self-defining memories and look at the different functions they may play in personality.

Let us begin with a memory:

When I was a little girl, not even four, I desperately wanted to read and would play with books all the time. My older sister noticed my interest and decided to teach me some basics. I was very proud of what I had learned and when the first day of the new school year came, I decided I would go off to school with my older brothers and sisters. I followed them to school and sat down in the classroom with the first graders. The teacher knew all the children in the town and knew me especially because my oldest brother also taught in the school. He came to my desk and said, "Yetta, you are too little to be in school, you must go home." I refused and said I was ready for school and that I knew how to read. This irritated the teacher and he said to me, "Little girls should not lie; I'll get your brother and have him bring you home." When he returned with my brother, he explained to him in front of the class that I was too little and that I was telling fibs about being able to read. My brother said to the teacher that it was not fair to assume that I was lying, that he should give me a chance to prove I could read. So the teacher gave me the lesson book for the day and asked me to read aloud. I read it without a mistake and the teacher was quite impressed. He said, "Yetta, you can read and I shouldn't have said you were lying. You may remain in the class and I hope the other older students show just one half of your determination." And that was how I started my schooling.

If you have not guessed, this is a memory told (and retold and retold) by one of our grandmothers. When psychologists use fancy experiments to demonstrate common-sense ideas, they are accused of practicing bubba psychology—proving things your grandmother could tell you. In our case, our view on memory is literally bubba psychology, our grandmother's memory contains the essence of what we mean by self-defining or meaningful memory.

Grandma Yetta loves to tell this story, and no matter how many times she tells it, she ends her tale with a savoring smile and delighted laugh at her vindication and intellectual triumph. Why does this memory and not some other have this compelling hold over her? Why can she repeat it innumerable times and the memory never loses its imagistic power or emotional charge for her? To begin to answer this question, one necessarily asks, does this memory symbolize or encapsule some important theme or issue in Grandma Yetta's own life? Is it a shorthand way of saying what matters to her? In thinking about this question, other memories of Yetta's that she would tell repeatedly over the years come to mind. With variations and twists, these memories convey the same essential theme—a young child of considerable promise, feeling overlooked or neglected, is ultimately recognized by an authority figure for her gifts.

Only the barest details of Yetta's life story are needed to see immediately the relevance of these memories to key concerns of her personality. A child of immigrants, raised in New York City, she assimilated rapidly to her new land. The youngest of her brothers and sisters, she was the only one to graduate from high school in the United States. Demonstrating the intellectual promise she highlights in her memory, she was accepted to and enrolled in Hunter College in New York City. Yet, in what was perhaps the pivotal disappointment of her life, she was forced to drop out after the first year. The United States had just entered World War I and her older brother was in danger of being drafted. With a daughter in college, the family could not make a creditable argument to the draft board that her brother was needed as a wage-earner for the family. The solution was simple—Yetta could no longer attend college.

Shortly after, she married and had a son, whom she named after an English playwright and upon whom she displaced every strain of intellectual aspiration she had ever harbored. It almost seems overdetermined that the son grew up to be a professor and that even one of the grandsons has followed suit. With even this little bit of history, one can see the power of the memory in a new light. Regardless of the veracity of the memory, it contains the fantasy of vindication that remained unrealized in Yetta's own life. Although in her adult life, her own intellectual accomplishment was thwarted and only achieved vicariously, in her memory she perpetually overcomes the obstacles to her erudition and succeeds famously. When living in the imagined world of her memory, she can relish her delicious triumph and feel again the limitless intellectual promise she embodied as the youngest and most determined student of the class. The power of this memory is that it both defines her not only as she sees herself, but also as she would want to see herself. It resolves, at least in the moments of the memory's recollection, what has remained unresolved in her own life.

The following features of Yetta's memories form the core of our understanding of self-defining memories and can be located in contemporary theories of personality (Bruhn, 1990a, 1990b; McAdams, 1988, 1990a; Tomkins, 1979, 1987, 1991):

- affective intensity
- vividness
- repetitiveness
- linkage to other memories
- focus on enduring concerns or unresolved conflicts

We propose that each person has a unique collection of autobiographical memories and that these memories can be examined in an effort to define who a person is. Imagine that each individual carries inside his or her head a carousel of slides of life's most important personal memories. These slides have been carefully selected to represent the major emotionally evocative experiences that the person has ever had. The vividness of these memories and the intense affect they evoke ensure the memorability of the original event but also make recollection of that event particularly revealing to us of what matters most. Although memory is perpetually taking snapshots of each and every experience that we encounter, there always emerges a core of slides to which we return repeatedly. This dog-eared bunch of slightly obscured or distorted images comes to form the central concerns of our personality.

The repetitive series of memories that evoke strong emotions differs dramatically from individual to individual but these memories share common attributes. First, they are by nature densely packed and consequently repetitive. By densely packed, we mean to convey the concepts of *representation* and *instantiation*. Representative images crystalize characteristic interests, motives, or concerns of an individual into a shorthand moment (the hundreds of minor embarrassing moments in school for a shy child become symbolized by that one time when she tripped in front of the school assembly). Each slide in the carousel is an intra-individual archetype. They are the slides that are mounted, framed, and left on the piano to represent "that summer out west" or "our daughter's wedding."

In this sense, these memories also have the attribute of instantiation (Schank & Abelson, 1977). They have collapsed a sequence of associated experiences into a single one. By focusing on the one representative memory, one gains access, whether implicitly or explicitly, to an extensive series of related memories. If a memory is to qualify for membership within the individual's personal carousel, it must go beyond itself to connote similarly toned experiences. It is linked to other similar memories.

Repetitiveness also emerges as a function of the memory's densely packed nature. Because the memory is associated with other similar experiences, it is likely to be retrieved in the face of external events or internal cues that evoke similar affective reactions. Each new instance in which the memory is retrieved only reinforces its saliency to the individual and its power as a symbolic representation of events that evoke similar feelings. We grow more and more attached to these particular memories as integral components of our basic responses to events in our lives. Ultimately, these memories begin to define one's basic interactions with the world.

Although these memories may contain but a kernel of their original truth and be filled with embellishments, false recollections, descriptions provided by others, and multiple events blended into seemingly singular occurrences, these characteristics in no way diminish their power in organizing who we are. In fact, the memories that affect us most strongly may be those that provide commentary about expectations that we either have yet to realize or may never hope to realize. These memories hold out to us the promise of clues to the resolution of unresolved or troubling conflicts about our identities. Conversely, they may also provide encouragement or reinforcement of an enduring concern through evidence of past success and satisfaction.

To summarize, a self-defining memory, as typified by Grandma Yetta's memory, is vivid, affectively charged, repetitive, linked to other similar memories, and related to an important unresolved theme or enduring concern in an individual's life. As we discuss later, most of these features can be incorporated into what Silvan Tomkins called *script theory*. Yet, before we discuss his theory in detail and relate it to our emerging conception of self-defining memories, it is important to examine how past psychologists have thought about similar kinds of meaningful memories.

Given the central role in personality we have assigned to these memories, one might expect they have spawned a long and extensive history of theory and research in both personality and clinical psychology. Remarkably, they have not. This fact was highlighted for us when we were in graduate school in the early 1980s. While working in an advisor's laboratory, one of us had the opportunity to conduct research on cardiovascular responses to different emotional states. Of greater interest than the changes in systolic and diastolic blood pressure was the manipulation used to obtain the emotional states. Subjects were asked to recall a particularly vivid memory that would evoke in them the specific emotional state requested by the experimenter. What astonished us about these experiments was that simply thinking of a memory caused distinct and significant changes in heart rate and blood pressure (Schwartz, Weinberger, & Singer, 1981). It was taken for granted that a memory could do this, but we felt that this ability to evoke such strong emotion was a remarkable phenomenon in its own right. How could a given memory have the affective power to induce physiological responses of such magnitude that subjects could be moved to tears, giggles, or trembling fear simply by recalling a memory? Far from taking this phenomenon for granted, we were stunned by it. Combined with our dawning awareness of the power that memory held for Yetta and, upon introspection, in our own lives as well, we were sure that these meaningful affective memories must play a major role in how psychologists have studied personality. Yet, if we were first astonished by the power of these memories, we were then equally flabbergasted by the lack of systematic attention they had received. Before we go further into our discussion of self-defining memories, it is important to try to understand why a psychological concept of such intuitive importance has only recently become a more central topic in the thinking of more mainstream academic psychologists or research-practitioners.

American psychology is a history of movements that, for the most part, have operated at best with indifference and more often in opposition to each other. The three dominant movements, *experimental psychology* (and its present incarnation as *cognitive psychology*) with its interest in perception and memory (traceable to Wundt and the first psychological laboratory in Leipzig, Germany), *behaviorism* with its focus on learning, and *psychoanalysis* with its heralding of the unconscious, each in their own way managed for most of this century to push meaningful, affective memory into a minor league existence alongside these major league topics. We should look more closely at how this has occurred.

Experimental Psychology

Since the early days of Ebbinghaus (1885/1964), laboratory researchers have sought to eliminate the effects of individual differences upon investigations of memory. As Ebbinghaus suggested, an individual's past history, moods, and goals affect their ability to recall information that held any particular personal significance or meaning for them. Because the experimenter could not control for these influences, investigators in this tradition have thought it better to study memory for stimuli in which the possibility of idiosyncratic association was minimized. Such reasoning led to the use of nonsense syllables and isolated words in memory experiments that has continued up until the present day. As Kihlstrom (1981) points out, Ebbinghaus had planned to reintegrate this study of "pure" memories with research into more personal memories once the preliminary controlled work was accomplished. Unfortunately, few researchers followed up on this part of his vision, and fifty years of list-learning experiments ensued. Although these studies revealed much about the structure and organization of memory and much about the process of remembering and forgetting (we in no way want to minimize the importance of this kind of work), they were necessarily silent about the role of particular content in memory or of that content's relationship to personality.

The striking exception in experimental research was the work of Bartlett (1932). Bartlett's book was a response to the associationist perspective that dominated the psychology of learning and memory of that period. This perspective explained learning and memory as the strengthening of associations between any two psychological units—whether an idea and a stimulus, a stimulus and a response, two stimuli, and so on (Paul, 1959)—and can be seen in present-day connectionist models of memory. Stronger bonds mean better memory, and weaker ones mean more difficult retrieval. In other words, memory follows mechanistic principles and it matters little who the individual is who is doing the remembering and what his or her mood state or motivation might be. It is notable that contemporary models of memory, though employing a computer metaphor, still rely on this associational model. In contrast to this position, Bartlett argued that memory is a reconstructive process and that recollection is heavily guided by one's current attitude and frame of reference. Along with Head (1926) and Piaget (1926/1955), Bartlett is recognized for the introduction of the term *schema*, which may be defined as a general knowledge structure about a domain, including a specification of its principal attributes, the relationship among these attributes, as well as specific examples or instances (J. L. Singer & Salovey, 1991; Taylor & Crocker, 1981). Schemas might influence the reconstructive process of memory by guiding the encoding, storage, or retrieval of an event to fit one's pre-existing knowledge and understanding of events similar to the one in question. Yet, the kind of schematic influences that were studied by Bartlett tended to be more cultural and situational rather than reflections of longstanding personality dispositions. Similarly, Piaget focused on schemas as a function of cognitive development and intellectual capacity and did not address how memory organization might be shaped by individual differences in personality.

Subsequent to these researchers, the *New Look* perceptual psychologists (Bruner & Klein, 1960; Bruner & Postman, 1947, 1949; Klein, 1970; Klein & Schlesinger, 1949) advanced the notion that perception, learning, and memory could not be studied without attention both to the context and current concerns of the individual who is perceiving, learning, or remembering. Although much of this research was again directed at more transitory influences on perception (the effects of cognitive sets, momentary frustrations, group dynamics, etc.), some perceptually oriented clinical psychologists argued that personality could be understood through the enduring cognitive styles or *ego defenses* displayed by individuals (Rapaport, Gill, & Schafer, 1945-1946; Witkin, Lewis, Hertzman, Machover, Meissner, & Wapner, 1954). George Klein (1970) sums up the thrust of this perspective:

> it is misleading to separate cognitive events from those that reflect "personality" and to speak of their "interaction." Rather, personality embodies stabilized dispositions of perception and cognition—or what we refer to as "cognitive style." Stable modes of cognitive control are thus presumed to reflect basic personality invariants. (p. 10)

Although researchers of cognitive style paid some attention to memory (Paul, 1959), the overwhelming body of their work was directed at stable perceptual differences, exemplified by the study of field dependence and independence in which individuals could be characterized by the degree to which their perceptions of the world were influenced by external rather than internal cues (Witkin, 1950). Once again, the question of the content of the stimulus was secondary in importance to the manner in which the perception of the stimulus was organized. Even in Paul's (1959) work, he continued to use experimenter-provided stories rather than self-generated memories and concerned himself more with cognitive styles of remembering than with the meaning that particular memories might hold for personality.

Overall, then, despite pockets of interest and enthusiasm regarding the relationship of memory and personality, the study of memory's content and meaning has never been part of the mainstream of experimental psychology. However, in the past fifteen years or so, a new branch of psychology, cognitive science, has begun to alter this focus (Kolodner, 1984; Schank, 1982, 1991; Schank & Abelson, 1977). Cognitive scientists are interested in creating smart computers, machines that can think like people. Their initial efforts in this regard helped to reveal how complex human intelligence is and how much information human beings process in even the simplest exchange. In their classic example, Schank and Abelson (1977) point out that if, in conversation, one person says to another, "I went to a restaurant last night," the listener implicitly understands a tremendous amount of schematic information. The listener can immediately extrapolate that the restaurant-goer was seated, presented with a menu, ordered a meal, received food, asked for and obtained a check, paid, and left. If a computer is going to understand in the same way as the listener, it must be able to have this same implicit understanding (imagine how much must be understood implicitly when one person says "I love you" to another and how idiosyncratic that understanding must be for each individual). What these researchers concluded is that computers need to avail themselves of the same "reminding" process that human beings do (Schank, 1982). When new information is processed, it needs to be compared with previous instances from memory and evaluated accordingly. In attempting to program a computer to remind itself, Schank (1990) has come to feel that "stories" or narrative memories may be vital to much of human intelligence. Although he is not a personality psychologist, his recent book (Schank, 1990) certainly holds open the possibility of a blending of this emerging cognitive science perspective on memory with a theory of personality that puts storytelling or narrative memory at its center (see also McAdams, 1988, 1990a; Tomkins, 1979, 1987, 1991). It is not surprising that an early influence on Schank's collaborator, Robert Abelson, was Silvan Tomkins, whose personality theory is a major focus of this chapter.

Psychoanalysis

Let us next turn in our review to traditional psychoanalysis. One would expect that, with its emphasis on interpretation, meaning, and symbolism, it would be a logical place to find inquiries into the role that memory plays in personality. Chapter 7, which focuses on memory and psychotherapy, provides a much more detailed analysis of why this is not exactly so, but we give a more abbreviated account at this point.

Psychoanalysis has tended to follow the point of view set forth by Freud (1899/1973) in his first published paper on memory. Freud noted that most of our earliest childhood experiences were blanketed by an overall repression that protected us from anxiety over our infantile erotic impulses (repression is discussed in more detail in chapter 6). However, he noted the existence of seemingly *trivial* memories that still survive from this period. He dubbed these residues *screen memories* and stated they could not be treated at face value and explored for their *manifest* connection to major themes in one's life. Rather, these early memories are like dreams, which require free association and interpretation of their metaphors in order to decipher their *latent* and essential meanings for the individual.

Unfortunately, as with Ebbinghaus's successors, psychoanalysts took Freud's original construction of the screen memory in a direction he had not intended. Memory itself, not just one's earliest memories, became suspect, and no recollection at any period of one's life could be accepted on its own terms without recourse to associational and interpretive speculation. Also, because memories are more accessible to the individual's conscious attempts at revision and defensive self-justification, they were considered less a "royal road to the unconscious" than dreams. The resulting scholarship in classical psychoanalysis tended to perpetuate the concept of screen memory as the way to think about memory in psychoanalysis and gave it little attention beyond this perspective (Fenichel, 1927; Greenacre, 1949; Kennedy, 1971; Kris, 1956a, 1956b). Instead, psychoanalytic researchers and many social psychologists were more likely to show an interest in the phenomenon of *motivated forgetting* or repression (Dutta & Kanungo, 1975; Rapaport, 1942), an interest that has persisted into the present time (J. L. Singer, 1990a).

In the 1940s and 1950s, drawing upon ego psychology (Hartmann, 1939), gestalt psychology, the New Look theorists, and empirical challenges to classical drive theory, psychoanalytic revisionists, such as Rapaport (1951, 1959) and Klein (1956), encouraged reconsideration of memory's role in personality. At last, some of the new generation of ego psychologists chose to look explicitly at memory content, as well as organization, as a window into the personality and defenses of individuals. In the 1960s, Martin Mayman and Robert Langs, working independently (Langs, 1965a, 1965b; Mayman, 1968), developed scoring systems for studying the relationship between early memories recalled by subjects and corresponding major themes of their personalities. Psychoanalysis began to shift its emphasis from concealing to revealing aspects of memories; analysis of actual memory content could elucidate not only sexual or aggressive themes, but an individual's characteristic defenses as well. We discuss this work at greater length in chapter 7 on memory and psychotherapy, but for the present discussion it is only necessary to point out that despite the intelligence and creativity of their efforts, neither Mayman's nor Langs' scoring system has been adopted by other researchers, and they themselves have not continued to publish reports of further applications of their memory scoring systems. Since the late 1960s, American psychoanalysts have been more concerned with theories of object relations (Kernberg, 1976) and self psychology (Kohut, 1971), which have moved far afield from the experimental efforts of ego psychologists to integrate psychoanalysis with general psychology. Some recent attempts to reconnect object relations theories with academic personality and social psychology are promising (Westen, 1991) but have yet to reach a level of specificity regarding the function of memory content in personality.

It is a poignant and somewhat troubling historical fact that the essence of what we have to say about meaningful memory, and what Bruhn (1985, 1990a, 1990b), McAdams (1988, 1990a), and Tomkins (1979, 1987, 1991) have to say, was said by Adler (1927, 1930, 1931) in the first decades of this century. Once again, chapter 7 describes Adler's position in detail; what is important for our present discussion is that Adler, alone among all theorists in the clinical and experimental circles, argued for the centrality of memory to the understanding of personality. He proposed that one's earliest memories are merely reflections of the most valued current tendencies and life goals of the individual. Memories are revised and shaped in the service of one's enduring attitudes. Rather than veridical accounts of past experiences, they are tendentious fictions that encapsule in their manifest content what is now most important to the person. For Adler, the memory contained the projective content of personality; further free association or mining of the memory for its latent meaning was unnecessary and possibly obfuscating. As we show throughout this book, Adler's emphasis on the manifest content of memory and its relationship to the major themes within personality captures an essential argument of contemporary personality theorists. Why, then, this fifty- to sixty-year gap in mainstream attention to Adler's position?

It is important to recognize that Adlerians have continued to publish case studies and occasional experimental studies based on his perspective on memory right up to the present (see Bruhn, 1984, 1990a, 1990b for reviews), yet with only a few exceptions these articles have been published in journals clearly identified with an Adlerian approach. These journals are not available in many academic libraries and the attention paid to them by mainstream academic psychologists is minimal. One must question why such important insights on memory as those offered by Adler and his followers would be relegated to a marginal role in American psychology. Although we have no hard data, we speculate that the following factors may have played a role. Though some of Adler's writings on memory are eloquent, there is an overall fragmentary and outmoded style to many of his essays on the topic (e.g., reference to the "soul," see Adler, 1927). Because we do not read German, we cannot be sure that Adler has suffered more than Freud in translation and in the choice of works to be translated, but we submit, without much fear of dissent, that there are genuine differences in the scholarly and literary presentations of Adler and Freud. To be blunt, Freud was a more systematic scholar and a much better writer than Adler. For sheer intellectual pleasure and dazzling prose style, the choice between Adler and Freud is not really a choice at all. We suspect that the packaging of Adler's message has had a severe impact on the attention it has received from subsequent scholars and scientists. Suffice it to say that contemporary researchers who scoff at Freud's "sloppiness" and lack of rigor would find Adler's unabashedly anecdotal, openly opinionated prose even more disconcerting.

Yet most American academic psychology departments have never been warmly receptive to theories that grew out of Freud's original psychoanalytic circle, whether his own, Jung's, or Adler's, so this indifference alone could not explain the relative neglect of Adler's ideas. We believe that Adler's break from Freud, and Freud's subsequent repudiation of Adler, may have played an equally important role in the limited attention to Adler's perspective on memory. For members of the psychoanalytic movement to accept Adler's position on memory was to acknowledge the possibility that analysis of the conscious and manifest content of a patients' reported memories in treatment could lead to a meaningful understanding of major conflicts in their personality. If this were so, the technique so prized by psychoanalysis, and what distinguished it most dramatically as a new science—the interpretation of dreams through free association— would be undermined. Why spend so many hours and travel such a winding path as dream analysis if the therapist could instead simply ask the patient to recall earliest memories and then summarily extract many of the important themes of the patient's life?

As Adler and Freud both well knew, the Adlerian position on memory was subversive and threatening to some of the basic tenets of psychoanalysis. In the battle for legitimacy as a new science and a new form of medical healing, psychoanalysis needed to establish its pre-eminence and could not truck with dissenting theories that would chip away at its developing orthodoxy. For this reason, more than any other, we suggest, the Adlerian view of memory was relegated to a marginal position within the thinking of most of this century's psychologists. Unlikely to be accepted on its own merits in academic circles, it posed an unacceptable challenge to the dominant movement within the psychotherapeutic arena, psychoanalysis. Other than the small band of Adlerians, it had no natural allies. Once again, it took until the late 1950s and early 1960s for ego psychologists like Mayman and Langs to make explicit reference and pay tribute to the seminal work of Adler. In current psychology, only the work of Bruhn (1985, 1990a, 1990b), which is discussed extensively in chapter 7, has kept the Adlerian tradition vibrant.

Behaviorism

The final force militating against attention to meaningful memory in psychology was the wholesale rejection of any meaningful mental content whatsoever—behaviorism. As espoused by Skinner (1938), dreams, fantasies, and memories are artifactual phenomena that ultimately play little or no role in the determination of behavior. In the behavioristic flood tide that dominated American psychological laboratories from the 1930s well into the early 1960s, there was little interest in any kind of memory, let alone vivid meaningful memory. To study conscious thought was to risk falling into the trap of the introspectionists of the late nineteenth century and early twentieth century; self-report from subjects could not be considered reliable data. A true science would concern itself only with observable facts that could be objectively measured and would leave the "black box" to the poets and philosophers.

It was not until the 1950s and the so-called cognitive revolution that a resurgence of concern with human memory and learning took place. Yet this movement took as its central metaphor the information-processing model of the digital computer, leaving little room for imagistic and affective memory in its theories. Although it effectively dealt a death blow to the dominance of behaviorism over American academic psychology, cognitive psychology was in its own way every bit as associational and mechanistic as its predecessor. Through the pioneering work of Tomkins (1962, 1963, 1991), followed by other affect theorists (Ekman, Freisen, & Ellsworth, 1972; Izard, 1979), the late 1970s and early 1980s finally saw the emergence of attempts to introduce "hotter" cognitive activity into the computer model metaphor (Bower, 1981; Lazarus, 1980, 1984; Mandler, 1975, 1984; Zajonc, 1980, 1984). Simultaneously, the work of J. L. Singer (1966, 1974a, 1974b, 1975) on daydreaming, fantasy, and the stream of consciousness demonstrated that active ongoing thought could be measured scientifically and need not be relegated to the category of epiphenomena. Further, J. L. Singer's work suggested that the private personality (J. L. Singer & Bonanno, 1990) could be known not only through the arcane secrets of the unconscious, but also through the accessible aspects of an individual's fantasies and daydreams.

Script Theory

As this overview of psychology's approach to self-defining or meaningful memory indicates, a convergence of interest in this topic did not take place until the late 1970s; it then began to gather speed in the mid to late 1980s. Concern with the role of emotion in human beings, increasing interest in consciousness, recognition of the limitations of drives as the central motivating forces in human nature, the focus on human beings' efforts to reduce the complexity of incoming stimuli into meaningful patterns, and the new field of cognitive science were all pulled together in a new perspective on human personality called *script theory* (Tomkins, 1979, 1987, 1991). Although script theory did not address the topic of self-defining memory explicitly, it provides a framework from which memories like the one that began this chapter can be understood and studied. Its language and metaphors are also easily compatible with the cognitive science theories mentioned previously. Script theory recognizes the powerful influence of cognition and the need to reduce ambiguity into patterned meaning. Finally, it is dynamic without being determinist.

Silvan Tomkins (1911–1991) was one of the most brilliant and unorthodox psychologists of the twentieth century. When we were both in graduate school, Tomkins was a notorious hero to us. Psychologist after psychologist would speak with awe and affection about the influence he had had upon their work. Carroll Izard, Paul Ekman, affect theorists; Robert Abelson, a cognitively oriented social psychologist; Irving Alexander, Rae Carlson, and Dan McAdams, personality psychologists; and Jerome L. Singer, a clinical psychologist, each prominent figures in their respective fields, all have acknowledged a debt to the inventive ideas of Tomkins. Yet when we delved into the literature to read his work for ourselves, we were somewhat surprised. There were some important books and papers on TAT (thematic apperception test) interpretation written in the 1940s and 1950s, but this was not what these Tomkins enthusiasts had recommended to us.

We next found the first two volumes of his unfinished work, *Imagery, Affect, Consciousness* (Tomkins, 1962, 1963), which were profound in their argument that affect is at the center of motivation rather than drives (the third and fourth volumes have been recently published, one just prior to his death and the second posthumously). Tomkins proposed that there are ten fundamental affects and that the human being acts on behalf of these affects to maximize positive affect and minimize negative affect, to express affect whenever possible, and to control affect whenever necessary. The two volumes go on to present evolutionary arguments and some empirical evidence for the universality and unique patterning of these fundamental affects. Although these two volumes on their own represent a major contribution to psychology, we still wondered about the level of reverence accorded their author. After all, by the late 1970s, volume 3, which was listed in the table of contents of the original 1962 book had not yet appeared, and researchers like Izard and Ekman had published a series of empirical studies that had both verified and extended the relatively small data base upon which Tomkins had drawn.

However, in 1979, Tomkins (1979) published a paper, which he had delivered at the 1978 Nebraska Symposium on Motivation, that placed us firmly among his list of admirers. In this dense and complex theoretical presentation, Tomkins offered a cognitive-affective perspective on personality that he dubbed *script theory*. Tomkins's (1979, 1987, 1991) script theory is a grand attempt to integrate models of perception, cognition, memory, affect, action, and feedback theory (Tomkins, 1979). The unit of this integration is the scene, which consists of at least one affect and at least one object of that affect (see Kernberg, 1976, for a similar starting point in a theory of personality). Scenes are linked through the process of *psychological magnification*. Psychological magnification is the linking of one scene to another through the connection of the same affective pattern shared across scenes. *Transient scenes* are scenes that contain brief bursts of affect but do not link to other scenes. Examples might be momentary startlement when one stumbles at a crossing or a flash of pain when one cuts oneself chopping vegetables. *Habitual scenes* are recurrent and linked scenes that lack affect. Examples might be crossing the street without incident or setting the table each night. Neither transient nor habitual scenes are magnified.

Magnified scenes are linked through the basic human desire to increase positive affect and minimize negative affect. Scenes containing positive affect lead to the imagining and seeking out of similar scenes that will link to and reinforce this aspect in memory. Importantly, these positive affect scenes should not be exactly the same or else there would be an eventual attenuation of the pleasure one took from them. Psychological magnification of positive scenes is *variant magnification* — the finding of pleasant differences in scenes that are at the core quite similar (e.g., a symphony's subtle variations on the same musical theme). On the other hand, psychological magnification of negative affect scenes is *analog magnification* — the finding of similar negatively toned experience in what is essentially a different event (e.g., one meets a stranger at a party who reminds one of a childhood bully).

Tomkins is rather cryptic about why positive and negative affect scenes rely upon different forms of magnification, but we would suggest the following mechanism. Individuals seek to find positive affect wherever they may uncover it and therefore are always trying to generate new variations or possibilities of pleasant experience. The creative process embellishes the familiar with heretofore undetected nuances that give new enjoyment to the individual. If one loves the movie *Casablanca* and has seen it numerous times, there is still enjoyment to be found in watching each of the supporting characters do their comic turns without upstaging the drama of the main plot.

With negative affect scenes, we are motivated to avoid situations that would bring further negative affect. Yet, paradoxically, we also unconsciously seek out negative affect scenes in order to work through and master them. This unconscious motivation to return to unresolved conflicts in order to master them was one component of Freud's concept of the *repetition compulsion* (Freud, 1914/1973, 1920/1973) and is certainly the premise behind most analytic thinking about negative transference.

The patient imagines the therapist to be a frustrating parent (the similarity in the difference), although the therapist may look, speak, and act utterly differently from the patient's actual parent. The finding of similar negative affect in ostensibly different scenes is a means of gaining control over the bad scenes that haunt and distort our internal and external worlds. By projecting these scenes onto new situations, the unconscious renews the possibility that we can create a different and more satisfying ending to the scene. At the same time, the individual faces the risk that the scene will remain unresolved and the negative affect will be further reinforced.

Over the course of extensive repetition (magnification) of positive and negative scenes, an abstraction process takes place much akin to Tulving's (1972) episodic/semantic distinction. Scenes that are imagined as specific events or episodes in memory become blended into *scripts*. The script may be defined as "an individual's rules for predicting, interpreting, responding to, and controlling a magnified set of scenes" (Tomkins, 1979, p. 217). The following conditions are necessary for a set of scenes to form a script:

- Intense and enduring affect across a set of scenes.
- Sharp changes from one affect to another.
- Continued repetition of this affective pattern.

The sharp alteration in affect prevents the scenes from becoming habitual, while the repetition of affect patterns saves them from transience. The script is the abstracted template for a series of well-learned expectations, affective responses, and behaviors. In script formation, the scenes, through their shared patterns, create the rules and conditions of the script. Later on, after the script has formed, the script will shape and influence the structure and experience of new scenes.

Although Tomkins (1987, 1991) has more recently described a variety of themes around which scripts may form (e.g., ideology, commitment, addiction), the script he has discussed most extensively is the *nuclear script*. Nuclear scripts grow out of *nuclear scenes*, which possess the intense, alternating, and patterned affect of other magnified scenes. However, nuclear scenes also contain an incident in which a wish or conflict, though capable of short-term amelioration, is related to larger, recurrent themes that are unresolvable (i.e., Oedipal wishes, fear of death, feeling adequately cared for or understood, etc.). What defines the unique nuclear scenes and, ultimately, nuclear scripts for a given individual is the frequency of repetition of incidents that share one or more of these major life conflicts. This frequency will be a function of both chance encounters and the individual's tendency through analog magnification to recreate unconsciously the conditions of previous nuclear scenes.

In a crucial departure from psychoanalytic models or other stage theories of development (e.g., cognitive or moral), Tomkins does not subscribe to a genetic determinism. He does not believe that the initial interactions of an infant with its mother in the first few years of life will lock in the nuclear scenes to be lived out for the rest of the individual's life. Although early interactions may create the parameters of what nuclear scenes and scripts might emerge, magnification of particular scenes into scripts will only be determined by the ongoing experiences of an individual's life that involve the repetition of similar thematic and affective patterns. Though the individual may project expectations onto new situations, new situations have the power, according to Tomkins, to violate and modify those expectations, resulting in reorganizations of the basic affective or narrative structure of nuclear scenes. Similar to Piagetian notions of assimilation and accommodation, nuclear scenes both shape and are shaped by new situations. In fact, an important question for this theory is to develop specifications for when nuclear scenes will absorb new scenes or have their structure modified by these scenes.

Tomkins's proposal that early experiences are not sufficient to lead to nuclear scenes or scripts expands the thinking about the traditional Adlerian emphasis on early memories. Why should the themes or affects associated with early memories be any more important or nuclear than the those attached to experiences from adolescence or adulthood? Because a series of scenes would be linked by their shared affective pattern, any one of the magnified scenes could lead to the instantiation of the nuclear script. This granted, one would need to investigate not simply the early memories of individuals but memories from diverse periods of their lives. To demonstrate the existence of a nuclear script, one would need to find evidence of it in memories at virtually every stage of an individual's life. Accordingly, in our empirical studies of the remembered self (chapters 3 and 4), we almost always examine memories from across a lifetime and not simply the earliest years of life.

Script theory has only begun to receive experimental attention (Carlson & Carlson, 1984; Demorest & Alexander, 1992; McAdams, 1988), while Carlson has provided some initial support through a nonclinical case study (Carlson, 1981) and an analysis of historical figures (Carlson, 1982). There is only one published attempt (J. A. Singer & J. L. Singer, 1992) to apply script theory to a series of memories generated by patients in the course of psychotherapy.

In script theory, we find a psychological theory that can account for the power of Grandma Yetta's school memory in her life. The memory, which constitutes a nuclear scene for her, combined with similar memories from her youth and young adulthood, yields a script that captures her life theme of intellectual achievement thwarted and then vindicated. What are the elements that make this memory a nuclear scene? They were already enumerated in the beginning of this chapter: affective intensity, vividness, repetitiveness, linkage to other similar memories, and focus on an unresolved conflict. Now, however, we can see that the linkage to other memories is really Tomkins's concept of psychological magnification.

It is important to note that not all self-defining memories are nuclear scenes. A nuclear scene, by definition, will be organized around an unresolved conflict, most often stemming from childhood and usually of a psychodynamic nature (Oedipal conflict, dependency needs, aggression, etc.). This criterion is not essential for a self-defining memory. The self-defining memory, while including the nuclear scene, need only be experienced as important and definitional to the individual; in this respect, its content could concern the satisfaction or achievement of an enduring desire for the individual. Although the memory of winning a fifth-grade spelling bee may be highly self-defining for an achievement-oriented individual, it would not necessarily fit the criterion of a nuclear scene, because achievement may be an enduring concern rather than an unresolved conflict.

Tomkins's theory accounted for the fact that not all affectively powerful scripts or scenes would be nuclear. As mentioned earlier, in his expansion of the theory (Tomkins, 1987), he gave other examples of scripts that individuals form, including addictive and ideological ones. There is a second subtle difference, however, between Tomkins's scenes and scripts and the concept of self-defining memory as we have begun to employ it here. Working in a psychodynamic and projective testing tradition, Tomkins did not emphasize the individual's awareness of the importance of a particular scene memory for their personality. In contrast, we put much more stock in the individual's self-knowledge about the meaning or influence of this memory in their lives. As shown in the next chapter, we explicitly ask subjects in our studies to identify and tell us about their most important, self-defining memories. Although the therapist may still draw inferences from these memories that might not be accessible to the patient, there is a recognition that the individual's selectivity and reflection on the remembered events provide a crucial window to their dynamic meaning. Although this point of view is not in opposition to script theory, it is also not an explicit tenet of Tomkins' approach.

The Features of Self-Defining Memories

To clarify the meaning of each of the features of the self-defining memory, we have drawn upon examples from novels, poetry, autobiography, and biography. Thus far, as we have indicated, the psychological literature has been silent on the qualities these memories possess and the influence they may play in personality. It is necessary to draw upon these other sources to highlight our argument and demonstrate the urgency of these memories in individuals' lives. As we demonstrate, while psychologists labored in endless hours of memory experiments to determine the priming effects of phonemes, writers of this century have attempted to convey through words the lightning power of memory to illumine and, at times, to shatter our lives.

Affective Intensity

Perhaps the most well-known and recognized chronicler of memory in fiction is Marcel Proust. His eight-volume work, *Remembrance of Things Past* (1913/1930, 1927/1932) is in part an attempt to understand the emotional power memory held over him. The work of 1,240,000 words, twice the length of Tolstoy's *War and Peace* (Thody, 1988), is framed by two discussions of involuntary memory, first in *Swann's Way* and again the last section of the last volume, *The Past Recaptured*. By involuntary memory (Salaman, 1970), Proust meant memories that seize one suddenly due to a cue in the present time that reminds one of the previous experience. If one were to attempt to will the memory back into consciousness, it would not come back easily, if at all. It would also lack the affective intensity that would accompany its unexpected revival. Although the concept of the involuntary memory is slightly different from the self-defining memory or nuclear scene (neither of these is necessarily limited to this type of involuntary recollection), there is no question that Proust grasped in his writing the passionate intensity a memory may hold for an individual upon recollection. In the most famous instance of involuntary memory, Proust's narrator, Marcel, is taking tea with his mother and lifts his spoon holding a tea-soaked crumb from a "madeleine" to his lips. At that moment:

> No sooner had the warm liquid, and the crumbs with it, touched my palate than a shudder ran through my whole body, and I stopped, intent upon the extraordinary changes that were taking place. An exquisite pleasure had invaded my senses, but individual, detached with no suggestion of its origin. . .
>   Whence could it have come to me, this all-powerful joy? I was conscious that it was connected with the taste of tea and cake, but that it infinitely transcended those savours, could not, indeed, be of the same nature as theirs. Whence did it come? What did it signify? How could I seize upon it and define it? (Proust, 1913/1930, p. 55)

Attempting to hold on to this intense and unexpected pleasure, he takes a second and a third spoonful of tea and cake, but the feeling and sense of insight begin to fade. Feeling a deep sense of longing for this sudden joy, he tries to recreate in his mind the moment of the first spoonful and the exact physical and emotional sensation it engendered for him. As he performs this mental exercise, the feeling begins to resurface:

> And suddenly the memory returns. The taste was that of the little crumb of madeleine which on Sunday mornings at Combray (because on those mornings I did not go out before church-time), when I went to say good day to her in my bedroom, my aunt Leonie used to give me, dipping it first in her own cup of real or of lime-flower tea. (p. 57)

His joy may be traced to a childhood memory of quiet Sundays with his aunt in his pastoral birthplace of Combray. As the novel proceeds, we come to understand the symbolic role that Combray plays for the narrator; it is the secure and value-based center of his life in comparison to the hypocrisy and intrigues of Parisian social life. The joy he feels at that moment is for a recovery of the innocence he feels he has lost and the artistic integrity he believes he has betrayed in his quest for pleasure and status in the big city.

What is important to notice from the standpoint of the self-defining memory and nuclear scene is the depth of emotion attached to the memory. The emotion cued by the taste and texture of the madeleine emerges even before the memory takes shape. Some writers have referred to Marcel's memory as a *screen memory* (Miller, 1956) because it takes "its essential significance from the shallow well of a cup's inscrutable banality" (Beckett, 1987, p. 30). Yet as the narrator begins to relive his memory through his concerted effort at imagining the original sensation of the tea and cake, more than the madeleine comes to mind. In fact, "the vast structure of recollection" returns:

> so in that moment all the flowers in our garden and in M. Swann's park, and the water-lilies on the Vivonne and the good folk of the village and their little dwellings and the parish church and the whole of Combray and of its surroundings, taking their proper shapes and growing solid, sprang into being, town and gardens alike, from my cup of tea. (p. 58)

As Shattuck (1963) has pointed out, far from being a screen memory, the narrator's initial memory of the madeleine contains within its "vast structure" the remaining volumes of the novel to come; indeed, the joy that signalled it represents more than the pleasure of lost innocence. This feeling marks the awakening of an artistic imagination that, taking its impetus from involuntary memory, will apply its purpose to the crafting and recreation of this paradise lost in Combray and now fleetingly regained.

Although Proust clearly identifies emotion as the fulcrum for remembered experiences, psychologists have paid the connection between memory and emotion sporadic attention. We review this literature and the recent renewed interest in chapter 5, but it is worth noting that after a flurry of early work documented by Rapaport (1942) in a major and exhaustive review, little empirical work was directed at emotion and memory until seminal experiments by Alice Isen and her colleagues (Isen, Shalker, Clark, & Karp, 1978) and an important paper by Gordon Bower (1981). In his network theory of affect (reviewed in J. A. Singer & Salovey, 1988), Bower considers emotion a central node in an interconnected network of memory. The node of joy or of sadness has attached to it a series of remembered events that share this essential emotional experience. New experiences that invoke this emotion have the capacity to "light up" the emotion node in memory and summon up related experiences that shared the same emotional quality; these experiences are then more accessible to consciousness and therefore more easily retrieved by memory. In the narrator's memory, the sensual pleasure of tasting the madeleine is enough to cause a pleasure node in memory to fire and activate a related experience of pleasure (the Sunday teas in Combray).

As we discuss in chapter 5, this associational account (reminiscent of the connectionist perspective referred to earlier) of how emotion and memory are linked is satisfying up to a point and may be a useful framework to explain how involuntary memory works. Yet Proust would have waited many lifetimes if all the events and experiences that form *Remembrance of Things Past* were retrieved in this fashion. What is lacking from this model is a motivational framework that would explain how individuals seek out and summon emotional memories to soothe, excite, and encourage them in pursuit of their desired goals. We discuss this issue at length in the next chapter when reviewing the relationship of self-defining memories to motives and long-term goals. For now, we can conclude by noting that self-defining memories invariably have the capacity to invoke strong emotion. Memories that share this emotion are linked together by it, so that any one of the linked memories could be cued by internal or external activation of this shared emotion.

Vividness

Connected to the affective intensity of the self-defining memory is its ability to appear in consciousness with the vividness of an actual experience. Earlier on in the chapter, we used a metaphor that linked one's collection of self-defining memories to a carousel of slides that preserved the enduring concerns of one's personality. When discussing the vividness of these memories, it might be more accurate to consider them three-dimensional holograms or experiences created by a virtual reality machine. The virtual reality effect involves the use of goggles, headphones, and gloves to create the illusion of being in another place and reality (e.g., skiing an alpine mountain or scuba-diving in the ocean) when you are actually sitting in your own home.

To a similar extent, affective memories, along with dreams, have the capacity to insert you into the reality of the events that transpired in the past. You feel, more than remember, the experience. In her autobiographical exploration of involuntary memories and the role they play in her own and others' lives, Salaman (cited in Neisser, 1982) writes:

> But the moment which came back after fifty years was this: the dog has knocked me over, and I am actually turning my head away and burying my face in the earth while the dog is searching between my petticoats

and the long black stockings on my left leg for bare flesh to dig his teeth into. It is like a picture in slow motion. Today I am writing only a memory of a memory, but at the time it came back I was actually that child of three; the "then" was "now," and time stood still. (p. 56)

An even more powerful example occurs at the end of the play *The Glass Menagerie* by Tennessee Williams. Williams calls the play a "memory play" and the play is conceived as a series of scenes, which though telling a narrative, are meant to be self-contained memories that have continued to possess the narrator. These memory scenes tell the story of a young man, Tom, who lives with his mother and unmarried sister. The mother, who was deserted by her husband when the children were small, lives in the memories of her days as a beautiful young Southern belle. The sister, Laura, suffers from a defective leg caused by a childhood illness and is painfully shy. Unable to join the world, she increasingly withdraws into the illusory and fragile beauty of her glass animal collection. Tom, who works in a warehouse, has aspirations to becoming a writer and feels trapped by the family's seedy poverty and the two women's grim prospects for the future.

As originally conceived, the play would introduce each of its scenes of the family with a black-lettered legend projected on a screen; this legend would provide a single phrase that would highlight the major theme or point of the memory scene about to take place. In addition, the playwright called for a simple, delicate strain of music to be played at the end and beginning of each of these memory scenes. As Tom, the narrator, remarks, "In memory, everything seems to happen to music."

In the final scene of the play, as he did at the beginning, Tom speaks to the audience. He describes the circumstances in which he finally left his mother and his sister to seek adventure and his life as a writer. His leaving, which parallells his father's departure many years before, holds for him the ambivalence of both a liberation and a desertion. Pursued by guilt, he has traveled restlessly from city to city. As he recites this monologue, the mother and sister move in pantomime at center stage; some candles are lit on a table beside them. Their memory is literally alive before him, irrevocable despite distance or time:

It always came upon me unawares, taking me altogether by surprise. Perhaps it was a familiar bit of music. Perhaps it was only a piece of transparent glass—Perhaps I am walking along a street at night, in some strange city, before I have found companions. I pass the lighted window of a shop where perfume is sold. The window is filled with pieces of colored glass, tiny transparent bottles in delicate colors, like

bits of a shattered rainbow. Then all at once my sister touches my
shoulder. I turn around and look into her eyes. . . .

Oh, Laura, Laura, I tried to leave you behind me, but I am more faithful
than I intended to be!
    I reach for a cigarette, I cross the street, I run into the movies or a
bar, I buy a drink, I speak to the nearest stranger—anything that can
blow your candles out!
[*Laura bends over the candles*]
    —for nowadays the world is lit by lightning! Blow out your
candles, Laura—and so good-bye. . . .
[*She blows the candles out*]
THE SCENE DISSOLVES (Williams, 1945/1970, p. 115)

The playwright, with all the tricks of stagecraft conveys for us the urgency of memory: the use of the musical motif, the narrator speaking over
the silent recollection of mother and daughter, and finally, and perhaps most
affecting, the transition from a hypothetical situation ("Perhaps I am walking along a street at night") to the immediate moment of visitation ("Then
all at once my sister touches my shoulder. I turn around and look into her
eyes"). Once touched by this living memory, he speaks in direct address
("Oh, Laura, Laura, I tried to leave you behind me") and we feel in this encounter that this moment has happened not once, but a hundred, or even a
thousand times. No movie, alcoholic drink, or conversation can extinguish
this memory's incandescence. In fact, as with Proust, the only adequate response one can make is the act of artistic creation. In the final moment, as
Laura blows the candles out, it is the playwright's voice, more than Tom's
that says goodbye. The end of the play signals the hoped-for exorcism of
this memory, or of a real memory upon which the dramatic one is based,
from the consciousness of the playwright. The play itself has brought a kind
of resolution to the unresolved conflict that has given this repetitive memory its compelling vividness.
    In understanding the vividness of self-defining memories, it is important
to consider the work of psychologists on the stream of consciousness. In
particular, J. L. Singer (1974a, 1975) has argued that there are competing
demands for the attentional resources of consciousness. Although the external stimuli of visual and auditory cues focus attention outward and upon
the "world", there is a never-ending inner world of fantasy, daydreams,
memories, and preoccupying thoughts that tug attention inward and toward
oneself. Singer has demonstrated this phenomenon experimentally through
a series of signal detection studies (Algom & Singer, 1984-1985; Antrobus,

Coleman, & Singer, 1967; Antrobus, Singer, & Greenberg, 1966). Subjects encouraged to engage in active daydreaming show reduced eye movement, less ability to track visual stimuli, and slower reaction times to the detection of flashing lights or auditory signals. They are literally processing an interior world that interferes with their attention to the world outside them. Singer has also shown there are large individual differences in one's attentiveness to private fantasy and daydreams; the Imaginal Processes Inventory (Huba, Singer, Aneshensel, & Antrobus, 1983) is a scale for measuring individual differences in proneness to daydreaming and private imagery.

When one enters into the "as if" world of a self-defining memory, one has allowed attention to focus inward to a remarkable extent. However, it would be erroneous to think of this interior world as simply a parallel universe to the external one. When Tom feels the touch of Laura's hand upon his shoulder or when Marcel tastes a lime tea not sampled since his childhood, their experience of memory matches the sensual reality of the external world but is also something more. The memory is not simply a photographic recreation of reality, but a re-envisioning of reality within the context of the individual's own transfiguring personality. Proust (1927/1932) writes:

> An hour is not merely an hour. It is a vase filled with perfumes, sounds, plans, and climates. What we call reality is a certain relationship between these sensations and the memories which surround us at the same time (a relationship that is destroyed by a bare cinematographic presentation, which gets further away from the truth the more closely it claims to adhere to it). (p. 217)

As this passage suggests, memory is more than a photograph; it possesses what Shattuck (1963) has called stereoscopic vision; it holds images of past and present simultaneously in a "form of arrest which resists time" (p. 51). This simultaneous vision causes the inner world to present a more complex and symbolically laden world than external stimuli. Similar to the world created by dreams, the vivid world of memory holds each image within its world as both itself and a representation of crucial meanings and desires for the individual that go beyond that world. In light of this, it is understandable how one can easily become lost in thought or memory.

Repetition

As we indicated in our discussion of Yetta's memory, she found many an occasion, some relevant, some certainly less so, to tell the story of her first school day. In this regard, self-defining memories differ from traumatic memories or from involuntary memories. Self-defining memories are not like Ishi, the last Native American living in the wild, who, emerging from the dark and threatening forest, confronts one with a vision of the past that one thought was long ago tamed or at best forgotten. They are not like an old and cherished friend, fallen out of touch, whose voice surprises you late at night at the other end of the telephone. Instead, self-defining memories are almost always with you; they occupy your thoughts. The pleasant ones are like the mailbox on the corner that signals the final turnoff to your home after the long drive from work. The negative ones are more like overeager house guests who begin to insinuate themselves into your daily life and brush aside any attempt to move them on their way.

There are many possibilities to explain the repetitive and readily accessible quality of self-defining memories in one's life. Although one might propose a mechanistic explanation involving facilitation or sensitization of certain sequences of neuronal firing due to extensive connections in the semantic network of memory, we would prefer to pursue this question at a psychological level of explanation. As we have implied in the previous paragraph, positive self-defining memories may be serving a reinforcing or encouraging function. The individual may return to them frequently, either by design or inadvertently, as a means of reassurance that a particular goal or course of action is worth the effort and should not be abandoned. On the other hand, the positive self-defining memory may serve more of a nostalgic than a motivating function. It may play a soothing or escapist role for the individual who feels unable to continue direct pursuit of the memory's theme. We first consider a memory of the motivating type.

In the following poem, the late Polish poet, Anna Swir (1909–1984), describes a memory of her father's. An idealist and impoverished artist, he refused to compromise either his politics or his aesthetics and suffered accordingly. The memory is of his participation in the failed socialist revolution of 1905:

My Father Would Recall

All his life my father
Would recall the revolution
Of Nineteen Five, how he carried
tracts with his comrades,
how he was on the Grzybow Square
when it all began, how the one

who stood to his right, pulled
from under his coat
a red banner and the one to his left
a revolver.

How he marched in a demonstration
In Marszalkowska Street and suddenly the charge
Of Cossacks, above his head
horses' hooves, he was fleeing,
a Cossak cut off
his comrade's arm, it fell
on the pavement, another Cossack
cut off the head
of a woman, father was fleeing,
he had to flee
to America.

Father would sing till his death
songs from the Nineteen Five.
Now
I sing them.

—*Swir (1989, p. 23)*

In this description of her father's self-defining memory, we feel the sustaining force this memory accrued not only in the father's life, but in the daughter's as well. Though the memory is brutal and a recollection of a surface defeat, it is more deeply a testimony to the naked courage of the rebels standing up to the mounted Cossacks waving sabers from above their heads. Reading Swir's other poems that detail the disappointed expectations of her father (including the destruction of his workshop and life's work of paintings by German bombs in World War II), it is clear that this memory is a moment of solace in a defeated life, a redemptive triumph of spirit even though he is driven across the ocean into exile ("Father would sing till his death/songs from the Nineteen Five").

It is important to see how this type of memory plays a slightly different role for the individual than Yetta's school memory. The poet's father, as depicted in her poems, never gave up his ideals, despite horrendous persecution and suffering. This memory then is congruent with his life as lived and may be drawn upon to motivate future action on behalf of his ideals and integrity. Yetta's memory, in a painful way, is more prone to serve a nostalgic function than to sustain action on her own behalf. It is a safe port in the past to which one may retreat when the present confronts one with familiar, though perhaps unspoken, disappointment. A somewhat related process can be detected in the stereotypic high school athlete, whose peak of fame, popularity, and vitality came and went at age 18. From literature one can think of Rabbit in Updike's *Rabbit Run* or of the high school football player in Irwin Shaw's short story, "The Eighty-Yard Run," whose thoughts return desperately to his one touchdown run during a scrimmage, the bracing shower after, and the ride home in a convertible with his future wife. Nothing since has matched this perfect memory. One thinks, too, of Bruce Springsteen's song and video "Glory Days," in which the ex-jocks nurse their beers and recall the good old days.

Thus far, we have talked about two functions of positive repetitive self-defining memories: their role as motivators and as agents of nostalgia. Although the nostalgic memory bears upon an unresolved conflict, there is a more specific way in which the essence of a negative self-defining memory is organized around this conflict. We defer this more complicated discussion to the section of the chapter that focuses specifically on enduring concerns and unresolved conflicts.

Thus far, we have discussed memory in a way that is relatively uncommon in psychology. We have talked about the repetition of memories in functional terms. That is, we have asked and begun to answer why people return to the same memories time and time again. In doing so, we see ourselves as part of what Gardiner (1990) has called a "new functionalism," which encompasses a concern with "what memory is for, what function it serves, and wherein lies its adaptive significance" (p. 215). As we discuss in the chapter on self-defining memories and goals, a new functionalist approach to memory necessarily requires an understanding of the role that motivation plays in personality.

Linkage of Similar Memories

The key theoretical concept in Tomkins's script theory is the idea of *psychological magnification*, the linkage of similar memories through shared thematic content and affective sequence. Repetition of a particular memory in consciousness has a great effect upon us, but when this memory revives other memories that further stimulate similar thoughts and feelings, the effect helps define the central themes of personality. As detailed in chapter 7, the transference phenomenon in psychotherapy and in daily life may be understood as a form of psychological magnification (J. A. Singer & J. L.

Singer, 1992). Once memories are linked, their juxtaposition in the course of memory search and retrieval begins to create the template or abstracted skeleton that Tomkins calls a script. The script then acts upon both past and new information, assimilating any related material into its narrative themes and organization. We see the world through scripts born of our linked memories and our sight is both enhanced and limited by these filters. What scripts contribute in allowing meaning to emerge from new information, they may also take away by limiting our fullest understanding of new phenomena.

Self-defining memories may differ in their degree of magnification, but most have begun the process of linkage to similar memories. Some self-defining memories of a unique occurrence in one's life—the death of a parent, an automobile accident, a serious illness—may not link to other memories until these rare events return again into one's own life or the lives with whom one is intimate. For young adults, who comprise the initial samples from which the self-defining memories we discuss in chapter 3 are drawn, the process of script formation is still in an incipient form. However, it is likely that self-defining memories of the more nuclear kind, regarding issues of Oedipal themes, attachment, or dependence, have already begun the magnification and schematization process.

Since Tomkins's perspective on personality is essentially a dramaturgical one, it is not surprising that the concept of magnification is essential to both literary metaphor and characterization. In our earlier discussion of Proust, we mention that *Remembrance of Things Past* contains two extensive analyses of his involuntary memories. In the second discussion, which comes at the beginning of chapter 3 of *The Past Recaptured*, the narrator presents an elaborate theory of the relationship of memory both to nature and to art. At the heart of his theory is his belief that through the joining of past and present experience by metaphorical similarity, essential "truths," both natural and personal, may be uncovered. Proust writes:

> One may list in an interminable description the objects that figured in the place described, but truth will begin only when the writer takes two different objects, establishes their relationship—analogous in the world of art to the sole relationship in the world of science, the law of cause and effect—and encloses them in the necessary rings of a beautiful style, or even when, like life itself, comparing similar qualities in two sensations, he makes their essential nature stand out clearly by joining them in metaphor, in order to remove them from the contingencies of time, and links them together with the indescribable bond of an alliance of words. (Proust, 1927/1932, p. 218)

Jaeck (1990) in her discussion of metaphor in Proust's work explicates the
preceding argument in a way that seems highly applicable to the concept of
psychological magnification:

> Proust suggests that the essential mechanisms which reveal internal re-
> ality to us in natural, lived experience are superimposition or contigu-
> ity: two or more dissimilar phenomena encroach themselves one upon
> the other, and thus reveal an essential nature common to them both—
> an internal truth more real than their external differences. The
> metaphorical process, according to Proust, is the artistic means that al-
> lows the artist/writer to duplicate the superimposition or contiguity of
> dissimilars which occur spontaneously in nature. (Jaeck, 1990, p. 18)

In a similar manner, all individuals extract the "truth" of their own personality by linking their most important self-defining memories by nature
of shared theme and affects. Although this truth is inevitably a construction, or personal construct (Kelly, 1955), it holds the immediacy of a lived
reality for the individual. Until such truths are dislodged, if they ever are,
by new events powerful enough to force accommodation, the accumulated
scripts of individuals form their lives' epistemology—their essential way
of knowing themselves, others, and the world around them.

Novelists instinctively take advantage of the magnification concept to
develop the elements of characterization in a novel. A fine example occurs
in Joseph Conrad's novel *Lord Jim*, the story of a naval officer plagued by
shame over an act of cowardice committed in his youth. When we first meet
Jim, he is working as a water clerk, an advance man for the ship chandler
(supplier) in a far eastern port. We learn that he moves from position to position and to ever more obscure ports, abruptly leaving whenever a certain
fact comes to light or even when the possibility of this fact coming to light
occurs. Before we are told the circumstances of this fact, Conrad gives us
a brief review of Jim's early years. This review is necessarily selective and
serves the specific purpose of allowing us to see the trends in Jim's character that would have converged in the pivotal action of his life. We learn
that he grew up in a placid country town and was smitten with the romantic vision of life on the sea. Once he has joined the mercantile marine training ship, we see him reading the "light literature" of sea life and imagining
himself "always an example of devotion to duty, and as unflinching as a
hero in a book" (Conrad, 1900/1981, p. 11). Immediately, Conrad contrasts
this reverie of Jim's with an actual episode on the training ship. During a
fierce storm, two ships have collided and the boys are called into action to
man a cutter. As his fellow shipmates whirl by him, Jim stands frozen by

their activity; in actuality, Conrad intimates, he is paralyzed by his fear. As the cutter heads off, his spell breaks and he almost leaps over the side of the ship to join the departing boat, but is restrained by the captain, who tells him, "Better luck next time. This will teach you to be smart" (p. 13). The boys return, filled with heroic tales and pride. Envious, he derides their vanity and feels he will be ready when a more suitable test of his mettle presents itself.

With the telescoping effect of the author, we next see Jim, done with his training, working as a naval officer. Despite many voyages, he has had only one encounter with "the anger of the sea" similar to his previous time on the training ship. After being disabled by a falling spar, he is forced to spend several days on his back down below. Meantime a storm and rough seas rage above. He is secretly glad that he can remain below:

> But now and again an uncontrollable rush of anguish would grip him bodily, make him gasp and writhe under the blankets, and then the un-intelligent brutality of an existence liable to the agony of such sensations filled him with a despairing desire to escape at any cost. (Conrad, 1900/1981, p. 15)

Slow to recover from his injury, Jim recuperates in the hospital of an eastern port. Conrad shows us Jim's enjoyment of his passive life as an "invalid," his seduction by the easy languor of the "Eastern waters," suggesting "infinite repose, the gift of endless dreams" (p. 15). He meets older sailors in town who talk to him of easy duty, finding the "soft thing" in the East rather than returning to home duty and the stormy waters of the North Atlantic. Finally, he follows their lead and elects to serve as chief mate on a local steamer, the Patna, which is to carry eight hundred Muslims on a holy pilgrimage.

The fact from which Jim is running at the novel's outset now occurs. During the *Patna*'s voyage, it runs over something floating in the water, the ship shudders violently, and the hull appears to be about to give way. In the resulting chaos, the captain and the chief engineer, positive the ship is about to be sucked down a whirlpool, throw down a lifeboat and escape, abandoning the pilgrims to their death (eight hundred of them and only seven small lifeboats). Jim, standing on the deck of the *Patna*, once again frozen in the midst of crisis, ultimately leaps from the boat and joins the fleeing officers. The rain and the night obscure the great irony of their decision— the ship does not sink. Jim, along with the other two, are picked up and found guilty of abandoning ship and imperilling the lives of the passengers. Jim's heroic self-image must confront the reality of an act of cowardice.

In the remainder of the novel, we follow Jim's attempt both to justify and to escape his past. Finally, in the last third of the book, he finds some peace as the adopted protector of a small band of villagers on the remote eastern island, Patusan. Yet, a rival clan challenges his group and he is forced to fight. In the course of this struggle, he dies a brave and "heroic" death, one that allows him to reclaim for himself some semblance of the romantic honor he had always imagined his due.

In the five separate incidents described by Conrad (the three at sea, one at the hospital, and one on the island), we can see the thematic continuity and affective similarity that constitute psychological magnification. A script emerges from these incidents that would dictate the following: Jim's romantic image of himself is confronted with a real crisis; his characteristics of passivity, fearfulness, and self-absorption freeze him from action; and, in the aftermath, he hides his shame by self-justification, retreat, and resumption of his self-imaginings. This script holds true for the first four memories and is only altered in his death. Conrad offers us these events of Jim's life and then introduces a narrator, Marlow, a man who befriends Jim, as a vessel through which to explore their meaning. Marlow tries to come to terms with the "truth" that may be extracted from Jim's life. Is Jim a coward or really "one of us"? Does the complexity of one individual's motives, actions, and self-understandings belie the notion of any fixed standard of conduct that human beings may follow? Marlow highlights for the reader that the meaning of any single individual's life is found within the personal truth that an individual struggles to uncover. And how else can that truth be found but through examination and comparison of the important events of one's life? And how else can these events be known, but through the filtering process of memory?

Enduring Concern or Unresolved Conflict

In the section on repetition, we discussed how positive self-defining memories may reinforce or preserve enduring concerns for the individual. In the next chapter, we take an in-depth look at how psychologists have attempted to identify and categorize the major enduring concerns that might be linked to self-defining memories. It remains, then, in this section, to discuss how negative self-defining memories are organized around an unresolved conflict for the individual. We suggested in our discussion of Tomkins's script theory that individuals may repetitively recall unpleasant self-defining memories because they are still struggling to work through and resolve the conflict raised by the memory. Whether consciously or unconsciously, they return to these topics in memory in the interest of mastering them. Only by reviving the memories into consciousness do individuals avail themselves of an opportunity to recast the meaning of previous events or to re-imagine them in a way that is more palatable to their self-image. Similarly, they may compare current actions with those from the memory and demonstrate to themselves that they are different now, that desire has faded, or that circumstance itself has changed. The unrevived negative self-defining memory has the capacity to plague the mind, like an undercover terrorist, inflicting untraceable pain. The memory brought to light, however saddening or likely to torment, may at least be confronted and questioned. The intensity of feeling evoked by an unresolved conflict, as articulated by a negative self-defining memory, cannot be underestimated. We provide two examples of these memories that offer radically different resolutions to the conflicts expressed by the memories.

In the classic Japanese novel *Kokoro*, by Natsume Soseki (1914/1957), a lonely young student becomes intrigued by a learned teacher (Sensei), who appears to have a tragic secret. As the two spend more and more time together, the student grows extremely fond of Sensei, but Sensei is unable to let down his guard or reciprocate this intimacy to the same extent. The student notices that Sensei is also cool to his wife and cannot show her the affection and physical warmth she desires. It becomes clear as the novel progresses that Sensei is stuck in the past; he has never moved beyond some extraordinarily painful event that happened a long time ago and concerned his wife. Besides his failure to become intimate with people, he also has given up any aspirations of a formal academic career. Though he slowly finds himself growing attached to this admiring and persistent student, he has in effect lived a life of mourning most of his adult life.

Called away from Sensei because of his father's fatal illness, the student spends an extended period of time at home, only communicating with Sensei by letter and cable. In the final stages of his father's death, the student receives a cable from Sensei to come to visit him immediately. Though in conflict, the student cables an explanation that he cannot leave his father at that crucial juncture. A letter from Sensei soon follows, and the text of this letter comprises the third part of the book. An extended recollection, it tells the story of Sensei's secret and the reason for his pained and withdrawn life.

In his student days, Sensei had taken a room in the home of a widow. The older lady had a single daughter with whom Sensei quickly fell in love. Sensei's closest friend, K, also needed a place to live, and Sensei invited him to take a room with the widow as well. K was a highly disciplined and ascetic Buddhist, who sought the "true way," which requires abstinence from all kinds of physical pleasures. Sensei saw him as his superior in both intellectual and physical attainment. Unfortunately for them both, K also fell in love with the widow's daughter. Ashamed and humiliated by his weakness, he confessed his feelings to Sensei, who in turn was filled with jealousy and fear of his friend-turned-rival. He elected to reveal no hint of his own feelings to K. In a subsequent conversation, when K described his paralysis about what to do and his sense that he has lost his way, Sensei ridiculed him for going against his avowed philosophy, repeating K's own earlier words back to him:

> I said again: "Anyone who has no spiritual aspirations is an idiot." I watched K closely. I wanted to see how my words were affecting him. "An idiot. . ." he said at last. "Yes, I'm an idiot."
> (Soseki, 1914/1957, p. 215)

Through subtle probing of the guileless K, Sensei determined that K had not stated his intentions to the widow and asked for her daughter's hand. Seizing his opportunity, Sensei raised his own entreaty to the widow and received her approval of his betrothal to her daughter. K, who was already crumbling from his moral anguish, was further shaken when he heard this news from the widow. Finally, in an effort to end either his shame or his loneliness, or both, K committed suicide.

Though Sensei married the daughter, he could never show her the love he felt without an accompanying sense of shame regarding the betrayal he had committed to win her. He took to drink for a period of their marriage, and even after this phase ended, he was a withdrawn and despondent mate. As the narrative of the letter ends, Sensei writes that after the emperor's recent death, one of his two great generals, General Nogi, had committed suicide. He had suffered a defeat to the enemy thirty-five years before and had waited until his service to the emperor was complete to restore his honor. In sympathy with the nobility of this gesture, Sensei, too, has decided to take his life and end the shame his memory has never let him lay down. As the letter ends, it is clear that Sensei's life is also over.

In Sensei's life, the memory of his betrayal of K is the central defining feature of his existence. With the exception of his brief attempt to escape through drink, Sensei has lived with this memory relentlessly, allowing it to dominate his relationships, vocation, and sense of self. His continual revival of the feelings of shame and self-hatred is both in the interest of self-punishment (his conscience will not let him off the hook) and in an endless effort to redeem himself through suffering (he loyally places flowers on K's grave every month on the same day). Finally, the warrior's redemption of his honor offers Sensei a similar means to resolve his own conflict, a resolution that no other act within his life could provide.

Although the magnitude of Sensei's act of betrayal and its consequences is fitted to the proportions of a novel, many individuals carry within themselves a negative self-defining memory of more modest scope that is nevertheless haunting in what it reveals about their or an intimate other's character. These memories may be about a moment of cruelty, indifference, or dishonesty. Rather than repress them, we ceaselessly return to them. Like a phantom limb, they attract our attention and sensation long after their departure. We cannot renounce them and in some sense, do not want to because we are not done with them yet. The memory possesses a moment of our own unfinished character revealed in bold print to us. We reread these lines time after time, never quite relinquishing the hope that in recollection we will find new meaning from their message.

One possibility touched upon earlier in our discussion of Tomkins's script theory is that individuals repetitively return to negative memories in order to master the unresolved conflict that shapes the memory. As Freud suggested (1920/1973), the repetition compulsion is an unconscious effort at mastery similar to how children play peek-a-boo over and over with their mother and father. The child's game turns what is out of control and frightening (the disappearance from sight of a parent) into a event that is both initiated and controlled by the child; when passive separation becomes active separation, the child's anxiety is reduced. In the same way, we may reinvoke the themes, plots, and settings of unresolved memories to reduce their unconscious power over us and to give ourselves opportunities to create more satisfying endings.

A fine example of this process can be found in Rudi Blesh's biography of the silent film comedian, Buster Keaton (Blesh, 1971).

In the first chapter of this book, Blesh, drawing upon memories from both Keaton and his mother, describes three events from Keaton's life that happened on the same day three months before his third birthday. As Keaton himself put it:

A clothes wringer, a peach tree, and a cyclone put me on the stage. And for keeps. One way or another I've been there ever since. (Blesh, 1971, p. 7)

In one single day, Keaton caught his finger in a clothes wringer, slashed his eye throwing rocks at a peach tree, and was lifted out of his bedroom by a cyclone and set down miraculously without injury on the street. By the end of this hair-raising day, his performer parents decided the only way to keep

an eye on him was to have him join their act. The memory of this day and
its larger-than-life events became for Keaton, according to Blesh, more than
a funny anecdote, it became the expression of the pattern his life was to take.
Blesh writes:

> The fateful trio of events occurred nearly seventy years ago, and yet
> whenever Keaton speaks of them he verbally capitalizes them as if they
> had just occurred. This clues their importance in his art and in his life.
> Even then, in his first sanctioned stage appearance in 1898 and after-
> ward, he was not working for the rewards of good behavior. This was
> not what the bargain, from his point of view, meant at all. Accepting
> the good accident and the miracle, he was doing what had to do—start
> his career. This was at the age of two years and nine months, rather
> young as these things go. Here and at this time came the genesis of
> Buster Keaton's remarkable personal myth, the tripartite sense of fate
> that would henceforth dominate and eventually haunt his life, a nag-
> ging sense of the accidental in all actions and events, as often tying his
> hands as freeing them. (Blesh, 1971, p. 12)

Blesh goes on in this chapter and in the remainder of this book to trace
the roles that the Machine, the Accident, and the Miracle would play in
Keaton's life. In particular, he is able to show how central the metaphor of
the machine is to Keaton's comedies and to his own life. Keaton holds an
ambivalent relationship to machinery ("The Machine is friend or enemy,"
Blesh, 1971, p. 13); it comes to represent both Rube Goldberg gadgetry and
impersonal force. It is his beloved locomotive in *The General* and his mal-
functioning nemesis in *The Electric House*. In *The Navigator*, when Keaton
plays a spoiled dandy left to his own devices on a crewless ocean liner, the
machine becomes his sole universe and dominates the screen. First, helpless and intimidated, he eventually learns to master (with the help of a heroine, of course) this immense steel world of decks, bridges, and galleys by
rigging pulleys, automated assembly lines, and other mechanical wizardry.
In his art, Keaton is able to return to the unresolved conflict of the early
memory in which his finger caught in the roller cogwheels of the clothes
wringer. He is able to generate the challenge and fear he felt at the discovery of an inscrutable machine, but through imagination he creates a different and more satisfying ending.

Of course, as Tomkins has emphasized, if the accident with the wringer
had not been magnified by linkage to other similar incidents, it would not
have taken on the mythic quality it came to hold for Keaton. As Blesh details

in his biography, such magnification and linkage did occur. Besides his fascination and frustration with mechanical devices in his art and his life, the machine took on other meanings:

> For Keaton, The Machine can also be The Establishment with all its potential menace to the nonorganization man—the relentless pursuing police of films like the famous *Cops* or hostile wealth and management as in *Steamboat Bill Jr.* In real life, the management angle began with an acquiescent father bringing Buster onstage. Later it would become management— friendly, then hostile—first in vaudeville and later in the movies. (Blesh, 1971, p. 13)

The allusion to hostile management in the movies is highly relevant to our tracing of Keaton's essential ambivalence about the machine, as first reflected in his self-defining memory. Keaton rose to stardom in silent movies by serving as his own producer, writer, director, and star (in the Charlie Chaplin mode), but, unlike Chaplin, he did not have the power or capital to start his own independent production company. Instead, at the peak of his earnings and popularity, he was told that MGM would now take direct control of the production of his pictures; he could no longer operate in the unsupervised, autonomous fashion to which he was accustomed. Executives would decide on the scripts he should shoot and would have the last word on production values and editing. In essence, Keaton went from a self-directed creative artist to an assembly-line employee; he became a cog in the MGM machine. Within three years his pictures had become unwatchable and his drinking had gone out of control. He never recovered his stardom and it took the next fifteen to twenty years for him to regain sobriety and a modest working career as a performer. In a final irony of his lifelong struggle with the machine, MGM made a movie of his life, starring Donald O'Connor. Although the money they paid Keaton bought a fine retirement home, which gave him great happiness in the last decade of his life, the movie itself completely whitewashed the role the studio played in his demise (it portrayed the executives as understanding and willing to give him several chances to recover). So the machine, as both benevolent and malevolent, but always as a powerful and unpredictable force, was central to his life from nearly womb to tomb. And this theme is captured in the memory he portrayed to his biographer as the beginning of his art and, in a greater sense, his life. He worked with and finally through his ambivalence toward the machine in his films and his personal life, seeking through the revival of memory a mastery that somehow continued to elude him.

Conclusion

This chapter has introduced a different perspective on memory than the one traditionally studied by psychologists. This perspective looks at the self-defining memory, a memory that informs the individual and others about what are the most important conflicts and concerns in their life. It is clear from the examples cited in this chapter that self-defining memories have played a major role in the creative evolution of writers in both self-understanding and in the explication of characters within their works.

In the next chapter, we examine how self-defining memories may be collected experimentally, what kind of self-defining memories college students produce, and how these students relate these important memories to the major long-term goals of their lives. Finally, we try to show how the model of self-defining memories we have begun to sketch may be fit into a larger theory of personality that places the individual's life story at its center.

3

♦

Memory and Goals

Memory is a snare, pure and simple: it alters, it subtly rearranges the past to fit the present.

—Vargas Llosa (1990, p. 95)

In Harold Pinter's play *Betrayal*, we learn the history of a love affair by moving backward in time. Action in the play portrays earlier and earlier episodes in the relationship of two lovers, culminating in the encounter that launched their affair. The dramatic and psychological effect of this theatrical conceit is that we see the past (the particular scene we are watching at that moment) from the context of the future (scenes we have already witnessed). The lovers recall events that the playwright has yet to show us; we first know these events as memories before we watch the lovers enact them in real time. Martin Esslin comments:

> *Betrayal* continues and develops Pinter's preoccupation with memory: the way in which the passage of time changes our perception of what the past was like and what we were like—*who* we were—in that past. (cited in Tate, 1991, p. 11)

In this chapter, we pursue our interest in self-defining memories by examining the relationship of memory to present and future aspects of the self. Self-defining memories, our visions of the past, remain affectively intense and vivid to us only to the extent that they are perceived to be relevant to what matters to us in the present and the future. If what we want changes, then memories associated with our old desires may lose their immediacy and prominence for us. One wonders if Grandma Yetta's memory of her first day in school (discussed in chapter 2) would play such a repetitive and prominent role in her consciousness if she had long ago satisfied her desire for recognition of her intellectual gifts. The fact that this desire remains urgent and unfulfilled in her life may be the reason that this self-defining memory maintains its passionate hold over her psyche.

This, then, is the central question of this chapter: What makes our memories matter to us? Can we demonstrate, using the experimental tools of psychology, that individuals' unfulfilled goals—what they still want in the future—are closely linked to their enduring and affectively intense memories? Once we have established this relationship empirically, we then discuss its meaning theoretically. We argue that links among the remembered self, the present self, and the desired self may be understood within a model of personal identity that McAdams (1990a) calls the *life story*. An individual's life story, by uniting past, present, and future in a coherent narrative of the self, provides unity and purpose to that person's thoughts, feelings, and behaviors. As we show, self-defining memories, goals, and affective responses to memories and goal outcomes are simply concrete components of this more encompassing life story of identity.

Affective Responses to Autobiographical Memories and their Relationship to Long-Term Goals

The question we are asking—"What gives a memory its enduring affective quality, its ability to make one smile, blush, or become tearful long after the original event has passed—is not the traditional one asked by researchers interested in affect and memory. Influenced by the Freudian concern with repression, most investigators in this century have focused on the question of whether the affective quality or affective intensity of a memory influences its recall (Davis, 1990; Dutta & Kanungo, 1975; Gilbert, 1938; McGeogh & Irion, 1952; Meltzer, 1930; Rapaport, 1942; Robinson, 1980). The underlying hypothesis of much of this research is that painful or negatively toned memories are remembered less effectively because of our desire to defend against experiences that would cause us anxiety or conflict. As first Rapaport (1942) and later Dutta and Kanungo (1975) have detailed, the experimental evidence for this repression hypothesis is quite mixed, as we discuss in chapter 6. If any finding has emerged, it seems to be that affectively intense information, regardless of the positive or negative tone of that information, is better remembered (Dutta & Kanungo, 1975).

In light of these results, we are still left with the question of why more easily recalled memories have retained their affective intensity, while most other memories do not. It is fair to say that many experiences, which at the time caused emotional thunderstorms in our hearts and minds, are now barely remembered or are looked upon with some bemusement or perhaps even embarrassment. Yet other memories, as chapter 2 illustrates can define our lives' purpose and seem more vivid than events of the present moment.

It would be facile to say that memories are affectively intense because they are more relevant to the definition of the self. Yet, how does one differentiate between degrees of self-relevance? The most convincing way one might judge the centrality of something to the self is by the intensity of feeling one associates with that concept or object. If I were to say that "my image of myself as a father is at the center of my self-concept," am I really saying anything more than that, in comparison to other self-representations, this image of "self-as-father," matters more to me and that I feel more powerfully about it? The danger of a tautology should be apparent here. Does greater self-relevance operationally mean anything more than more affectively intense? It is difficult, if not impossible, to imagine a memory that one would judge to be highly self-relevant, but not affectively intense.

If we are to investigate empirically why certain memories become self-defining memories and retain their great affective intensity, we need to move beyond the concept of self-relevance and ask what comprises the self. It is not enough to say that strong affective memories are linked to some global entity called "the self" that remains undefined and slippery in the multitude of meanings assigned to it. In a recent article, Westen (1992) has made an ambitious attempt to draw correspondences between the psychoanalytic concept of the self and social cognitive perspectives on the self. One of us (J. A. Singer, 1992) has argued that the use of the self as an operationalized construct may be premature. As Westen has articulated his model, the individual possesses multiple self-representations that can operate simultaneously, are linked to imagery, affect, and behavioral tendencies, and contain both conscious and unconscious aspects. Given the inclusiveness of this definition, it would seem that this type of self-construct is highly complex and difficult to examine empirically, given the limitations of our current laboratory methods. Although we feel the concept of a self has an inherent experiential and metaphorical value (after all, this book is called *The Remembered Self*), we question its value as an explanatory concept or as a starting place for an empirical study of personality. Yet, what is clear throughout Westen's reading of the psychoanalytic and social cognitive literatures on the self is that any particular self-representation is known to the individual by the goals, memories, fantasies, and the corresponding affects that are linked to that representation.

Our answer, then, to the question of what makes a particular memory more self-defining and affectively intense takes us away from the higher-order concept of self into an investigation of links among the components of personality that comprise the self—specifically, for our purposes, memories, affect, and goals. What is the advantage of studying personality in

terms of goals, memories, images, fantasies, and affective states rather than
self-representations? First, individuals can more readily and more accurately answer questions like: In this situation, what did you want? Did it
make you recall any previous experiences? What did you feel as it happened? Did you have any unrealistic fantasies about the outcome? What
were you thinking about yourself? What did you think about the other person? Individuals are much more likely to have an intuitive grasp of what is
being asked of them by these prompts than if they are asked to generate a
list of typical self-representations.

Similarly, when we ask individuals for personally significant memories,
they are able to provide narrative memories that are affectively intense and
judged to be of major importance in their lives. Admittedly, these approaches that operate at the level of self-report of conscious experience lose
some of the richness invoked through psychoanalytic inference of unconscious influences upon thoughts and behavior, yet the memories we have
collected tell compelling stories that are hardly barren of meaning and depth.

To summarize our argument thus far, we are proposing that an investigation of memory's relationship to a self would pitch our inquiry at too
global and complex a level. Our preference is to begin our empirical investigation by examining how important components of the self—long-
term goals and affect—are linked to autobiographical memories. Why
goals and not some other component of the self, such as fantasies (J. L.
Singer, 1984), self-representations (Linville, 1985), visions of the ideal
versus actual self (Higgins, 1987), or of the undesired self versus the actual self (Ogilvie, 1987)? In the next sections of this chapter, we try to make
the argument, as Emmons has also suggested (Emmons, 1986, 1990), that
goals, as motivational and cognitive constructs, can offer personality, cognitive, and social psychology a unifying vision of the feeling, thinking, and
behaving person.

Affect and Goals

Although goal-based theories historically have held a place in personality
research (Allport, 1961; McDougall, 1930; Murray, 1938; Tolman, 1932),
there has been a recent resurgence of interest in goals, both in personality
(Emmons, 1986, 1989, 1990; Emmons & McAdams, 1991; Pervin, 1983,
1985, 1989; Read & Miller, 1989) and affect (Dyer, 1983; Roseman, 1984;
Roseman, Spindel, & Jose, 1990; Weiner, 1985). Similarly, researchers in
memory and artificial intelligence have identified goals as important to inferential strategies in memory retrieval (Reiser, 1983; Reiser, Black, &
Kalamarides, 1986; Schank, 1982, 1990).

Many recent theorists have suggested that how we feel about an event, whether past or present, may be a function of that event's contribution to attainment of desired goals (Abelson, 1983; deRivera, 1978; Dyer, 1983; Ortony, Clore, & Collins, 1988; Roseman, 1984; Roseman, Spindel, & Jose, 1990; Weiner, 1985). Affective states may be differentiated through knowledge of an individual's goals in a given situation, their attainment or nonattainment, and the mechanics of these outcomes (e.g., did others help or hinder the attainment of the goals?). Ira Roseman (1984; Roseman, Spindel, & Jose, 1990) has performed the most extensive test of this goal-based theory of affect. He varied the motivational states and situational outcomes, among other variables, of characters in scenarios read by subjects. The results demonstrated subjects' differential understanding of the characters' affective states depending upon the particular interactions of the active goals and outcomes depicted in the scenarios. Bernard Weiner and colleagues (Weiner, 1982, 1985; Weiner, Russell, & Lerman, 1979) have also obtained a systematic differentiation of affective states based upon goals and outcomes. From a different perspective, E. Tory Higgins and his associates (Higgins, 1987; Strauman & Higgins, 1987) have shown that attainment or nonattainment of ideal outcomes predicts both subjective and physiological affective responses.

Our experiments build upon this work and demonstrate that this goal-based theory of affect can indeed be extended to the prediction of affective responses to memory. Our central hypothesis is the following: *What we continue to feel about events long after they have occurred may be a function of how relevant these remembered events are to the attainment of long-term goals.* The more relevant a memory is to the attainment of a long-term goal, the more positively one should feel about the memory; the more relevant a memory is to the nonattainment of a goal, the more negatively one should feel about it. This hypothesis guided our first efforts at examining the relationship between affective memories and long-term goals. Yet to study this relationship, we need to define more clearly what we mean by "long-term goals." How do goals exist within our minds, and what are the goals we tend to think about most and most desire?

First Efforts at a Long-term Goal Construct

How do we identify the goals being served or frustrated in a particular memory? Robinson (1980), Holmes (1970), and Dutta and Kanungo (1975) have all demonstrated that a memory may change in its affective intensity over time. Holmes's work, especially, makes the important observation that the affective intensity associated with a memory is a function of its meaning for the individual at recall, not exposure. This difference suggests that the current goals of the individual play an important role in determining the affective intensity with which the memory is experienced. A memory may lose or gain affective intensity depending upon its connection to an individual's current goals rather than to goals originally served by the remembered behaviors.

Narrowing our emphasis to current goals, we still need to specify what types of current goals we wish to study. In a recent review, Emmons (1990) has detailed the diverse approaches researchers have taken to defining and studying goals. Despite differences in definition and level of analysis, he suggests all of the goal researchers share the following assumptions: (1) Behavior is goal-oriented and goals are end states that individuals strive to attain or avoid; (2) Goals figure prominently in the ongoing stream of thought and in our affective responses to internal and external stimuli, (3) Goals are hierarchically organized, such that lower-order goals are in the instrumental service of higher-order or more abstract goals, (4) Goals are available to consciousness, although we need not be aware of them while we are in pursuit of them (Emmons, 1990). As we shall see, each of these assumptions plays a prominent role in our empirical studies of the relationship between memories and goals.

Let us begin by looking more closely at the third assumption, which highlights the hierarchical properties of goals. Personality and behavior researchers historically have argued for a motivational hierarchy of needs, desires, or goals (Allport, 1961; Emmons, 1986, 1989; Greenwald, 1980; Maslow, 1954; McDougall, 1930; Miller, Galanter, & Pribram, 1960; Murray, 1938; Pervin, 1983; Tolman, 1932; Wicker, Lambert, Richardson, & Kahler, 1984).

Murray's (1938) concept of *subsidiation* is one important example of this hierarchical perspective. Attributes of the self or personality, such as desires, values, goals, and action patterns are organized in instrumental dependence. A desire or goal lower in the hierarchy serves a function in the service of a desire or goal higher in one's hierarchy. For example, a student desires good grades, but this desire is only instrumental to getting into a good college, or getting a good job, or, perhaps, pleasing parents. We can trace this instrumental relationship of desires at least as far back as Freud's emphasis on the development of the secondary processes from the ego's attempt to satisfy primary process needs. In current cognitive science models, some researchers have proposed that basic cognitive processes, such as narrative comprehension and textual learning, also rely upon a hierarchical organization of goals, plans, and themes in memory (Abelson,

1981; Reiser, Black, & Kalamarides, 1986; Schank, 1982, 1990; Schank & Abelson, 1977).

Looking at goals hierarchically, the lowest level of personal goals might be satisfaction of drive states or essential activities of the day (Valenstein, 1973). These goals would assuredly influence the affective intensity of an experience, but the influence would be as transitory as the drive state motivating it (similar to Tomkins's concept of the transient scene).

Eric Klinger's (Klinger, Barta, & Maxeiner, 1981) *current concerns* represent more stable personal goals. A current concern is defined as "the state of an organism between the time it becomes committed to pursuing a particular goal and the time that it either consummates the goal or abandons its pursuit and disengages from the goal" (Klinger et al., 1981, p. 162). Thus, a current concern reflects a commitment to some temporarily constrained set of plans or course of actions that lead to either the achievement or the abandonment of the goal. As Klinger et al. (1981) further state, the construct of current concern:

> Fills the gap that has traditionally remained vacant between such situationally defined motive states as central excitatory states or short-term drive states, on the one hand, and lifetime or at least very long-term motivational dispositions such as Murray-type needs on the other hand. (p. 163)

Although the current concerns tend to be more transitory than Murray's needs, they can last for years in consciousness if they remained unfulfilled or unaddressed. Yet—and this is important regarding their potential relationship to memories—they recede from consciousness once they have been resolved. Current concerns are inherently self-limiting. If the issue or conflict raised in a concern is addressed, then there is no longer a reason to devote attentional resources to it.

In sampling both students and the general population, Klinger has found the content of peoples' current concerns to be chiefly divided among thoughts about their jobs (or education), family, friends, and pastimes. Other areas occupying current concerns are love and sex, politics, religion, and physical health. Using both an interview and questionnaire format, Klinger has demonstrated that individuals are able to indicate which current concerns they think most about and which are more important than others.

At the next level of goals are sets of hierarchically linked purposeful behaviors called *personal projects* (Little, 1983, 1989; Palys & Little, 1983). One might think of a personal project as an organizing unit for related current concerns. For example, one might have the personal project of buying a new car. This project then might contain the following set of linked current concerns: The need to do research in consumer reports, worry about how to get the down-payment, going to dealers to compare prices, and getting friends' advice about car stereo systems. Personal projects help us to understand how an individual develops particular motivational preoccupations and plans of action in response to societal and cultural influences. Similar to current concerns, once the plans of action stipulated in a personal project are exhausted, the project loses its urgency and fades from consciousness.

A next level of goals are those of a longer duration than most current concerns or personal projects, but that are still focused on a specific plan or broad set of actions. Nancy Cantor and her coworkers (Cantor & Kihlstrom, 1987, 1989; Cantor & Langston, 1989; Cantor, Norem, Niedenthal, Langston, & Brower, 1987) have called these goals *life tasks* and defined them as problems to which individuals dedicate substantial energy toward solving at particular periods in their lives (Cantor & Kihlstrom, 1985). These tasks could range from adjusting to college or finding a career to starting a family or coming to terms with death; they are inevitably concerned with developmental challenges or hurdles posed by transitional periods in one's life. As Emmons (1990) points out, research on life tasks has primarily been concerned with the cognitive and problem-solving strategies individuals recruit to cope with and overcome the demands of a particular life task. For example, Zirkel and Cantor (1990) explored strategies employed by first-year students at college to cope with the unnerving initial weeks of school, in which separation from parents and sudden increased responsibility became forceful realities. Once a life task is accomplished successfully, the mind releases its preoccupation with it and moves on to the next developmental challenge.

Thus far, the goal constructs described have all shared the view that resolution of the unmet goal, whether current concern, personal project, or life task, leads to a diminution of mental and behavioral effort directed toward it. Similarly, while the temporal span it covers is quite large, each construct tends to be sensitive to particular situational contingencies that, in turn, are bound by particular moments, episodes, or epochs of one's life. However, if we are to study the relationship of goals to memories, it would be advantageous to think about long-term goals that transcended specific epochs or situational contingencies of one's life. Affectively intense memories span one's entire past and evoke themes or issues that are not always tightly constrained to a specific concern, project, or task. In order to demonstrate a correspondence between the disparate events of one's past and certain stable, enduring long-term goals, a goal construct that is more context-free and abstract would be preferred.

In our first experiments examining the relationship between memories and goals, we devised a goal measure called the *life goal* that would operate in this manner (J. A. Singer, 1990a). Emmons (1986, 1989, 1990; Emmons & King, 1988, 1989) has developed and subsequently refined a more comprehensive and elegant methodology for sampling "context-free" long-term goals. We discuss his measure and describe our subsequent research employing it in a later section of this chapter, but first it is necessary to present our initial findings examining life goals and their relationship to memories.

We defined life goals as the context-free ideas individuals hold about how their ideal life would be. One may desire a life goal because it promotes positive feeling states or aids one to avoid negative feeling states (Atkinson, 1983). Unlike current concerns or life tasks, life goals are not bound to a specific set of actions, plans, or time periods. They may evince no tangible commitment from individuals other than a persistent awareness of their desirability. Life goals bear a strong relationship to Rokeach's (1973) or Feather's (1975) *values*, though the term value connotes a normative quality that life goals need not possess (Feather, 1982, p. 82).

Life goals were designed to be the conscious expression of Murray's (1938) needs. For example, an individual high in the need for achievement might list as a life goal: "I would like to accomplish something lasting and important." It is likely that this stated goal is linked to their conscious thoughts and daydreams; it may or may not be traced to the individual's choice of certain behaviors and social interactions. The conscious expression of goals is stressed here, as opposed to unconscious needs, because, as we have argued throughout this book, it seems both prudent and efficient to investigate accessible links among components of personality before we resort to inferences about links based on unconscious processes. Our goal is to explain as much variance as possible in personality through the use of conscious measures first. When we have exhausted these efforts, we could then turn to an investigation of unconscious aspects of personality in order to account for residual variance. Referring to McClelland's (1985) distinction between motives (as unconscious needs) and incentives (or values) as conscious phenomena, we were concerned with the latter in these experiments.

In the first two experiments, subjects received a list of fifteen life goal sentences, each paraphrasing sentences written by Murray (1938) and later Edwards (1959) to convey Murray's original psychogenic needs. The life goal sentences expressed sixteen of the twenty Murray (1938) need complexes (see table 3–1). The need upon which each sentence is based may be found in parentheses after the sentence.

Eliciting Autobiographical Memories in the Laboratory

If our purpose is to study the relationship of affective responses to memories and long-term goals, it is important to find methods that will assure us of finding meaningful and affectively evocative memories. Our initial

Table 3–1 Life Goal Sentences and Corresponding Murray Need Complexes

1. I would like to be a leader and sway others to my opinion. (Need = dominance)
2. I would like to create a lasting and notable accomplishment. (Need = achievement)
3. I would like to be watched and marveled at by others. (Need = exhibition)
4. I would like to have a life of amusement filled with sports, games, parties, dances, and films. (Need = play)
5. I would like to have good and loving friendships and relationships. (Need = affiliation)
6. I would like to help and take care of others, showing gentleness whenever I can. (Need = nurturance)
7. I would like to dedicate my life to the search for truth by the application of reason. (Need = understanding)
8. I would like to honor the needs and wishes of my mother and father. (Need = deference)
9. I would like to leave the common path and blaze a new path for myself. (Need = autonomy)
10. I would like to live as sensual and erotic a life as possible. (Need = sentience and sex)
11. I would like to be able to accept my fate in life and not quarrel with destiny. (Need = abasement)
12. I would like to be a forceful person that lets no one get in my way or stop me from doing what I want. (Need = aggression)
13. I would like to avoid any kind of physical pain or danger. (Need = harm avoidance)
14. I would like to see my life orderly, organized, and balanced. (Need = order)
15. I would like to avoid failure and not attempt things I don't do well. (Need = inferiority avoidance)

Adapted from J. A. Singer, 1990a, p. 541.

approach to eliciting autobiographical memories was comparable in its simplicity to our rough life goal measure. Later, we discuss our more recent techniques of asking explicitly for self-defining memories.

Our first experiments relied upon a commonly used method for evoking autobiographical memories that dates back to Galton's (1911) association experiments and has been used more recently by Crovitz and Schiffman (1974), Fitzgerald (1980, 1981), Robinson (1976, 1980), and Rubin (1982; Rubin, Wetzler, & Nebes, 1986). These experiments consist of providing subjects with a verbal cue (usually a single word) that serves as the springboard for any kind of autobiographical memory the subject retrieves. The technique yields memories of diverse content and temporal remoteness (Robinson, 1976, p. 580).

In our first experiment, we used the life goal sentences as cues for memories, and in the second experiment, we used cues that represented more general categories of experiences (family, friends and relationships, school, and activities). Once subjects retrieved their memories, they rated them for their current affective responses in recalling them.

Relevance of Memories to Goal Attainment. Thus far, we have described how we measured subjects' life goals and how we elicited their memories and their affective responses to their memories. The one crucial variable left to be discussed is the link between these life goals and the memories. If we are to predict affective responses to memories from their relationship to long-term goals, we must have some initial method of determining how relevant a particular memory is to the attainment or nonattainment of a goal. Once subjects had recalled their memories and rated their affective responses to their memories, they went back and indicated the relevance of each memory to the attainment or nonattainment of either the goal that cued it or all fifteen life goals, depending on the experiment in which they participated. Subjects' own judgments of their memories' relevance to their goals were preferred over experimenter inferences about the memories' relevance to the goals. In this way, subjects' own interpretations of their memories' meanings were preserved.

Reciprocal Hypothesis. We have introduced measures of life goals, affective responses to memories, and the relevance of memories to goal attainment. We hypothesized that the affective quality of an autobiographical memory could be predicted from its relationship to the attainment or nonattainment of an individual's current life goals. In the studies that follow, the reciprocal hypothesis should also be kept in mind: The desirability of one's current goals may be predicted from, and shaped by, one's affect about past attainment or nonattainment of these goals.

Empirical Studies of Memories and Life Goals.   In our first experiment, participants were presented with the life goal sentences and rated them for desirability in their lives. They then retrieved one memory for each life goal sentence but were told that it was not necessary that the memory be linked to the goal sentence that inspired it. Memories could be as important or trivial as they desired. Once participants had written down their memories, they rated each memory for their current affective response to it.

After the memory task, participants rated each memory for goal attainment by asking themselves how relevant this remembered event was to the attainment or nonattainment of the goal that prompted its recall. For example, a memory of winning a spelling bee would be highly relevant to the successful attainment of the goal of "to achieving a notable accomplishment, while a memory of not being chosen for all-state chorus would be highly relevant to the nonattainment of that same goal.

Upon completion of the experiment, we checked for participants' intuition about and knowledge of the hypotheses being tested. Participants mostly believed that the experiment was intended to tell something about their personalities (i.e., what kind of people they were). They hypothesized that the experimenter would use information collected about their memories to predict which goals they found important. No subject guessed that a main purpose of the study was to predict affective responses to memories from the memories' relevance to the attainment or nonattainment of a valued goal.

We first examined participants' affective responses to their memories and the goal attainment ratings of those same memories. Our hypothesis was confirmed: the more relevant participants' memories were to goal attainment, the more positively they felt about their memories. This result was particularly true for the goals they most desired (loving relationships, notable accomplishments, helping others). In general, participants' memories cued by these goals tended to be pleasant recollections of happy romances, academic or athletic successes, or instances of generous altruism.

In contrast, when we looked at participants' avoidance goals (avoid pain, avoid failure, as well as accept fate), which tended, as a group, to be less desired by participants, we found an intriguing discrepancy. The more participants actually desired these goals, the more unpleasant their memories cued by these goals tended to be. On the other hand, when participants disliked these goals, they tended to retrieve more positive memories.

Table 3–2 looks at this effect more closely, dividing participants into those who endorsed the goal "Avoid pain or danger" and those who did not. Participants who typically seek to avoid pain or danger recalled unpleasant events in which they had failed to do so. Participants who typically reject the goal of avoiding pain or danger remembered positive experiences in which they had exposed themselves to danger or pain and triumphed. Whether participants remember events in order to justify their current stance toward avoiding pain, or whether these memories are the formative elements of their current stance (or both) remains an open and intriguing question.

Separating the Memories from the Life Goals. Although we were encouraged by the results from this first experiment, we were concerned about our use of life goals to inspire participants' memories. Our test of the role of goals in affective responses to memories would be more compelling if the memories were generated separately from the life goals. In a second experiment, we no longer used the life goals as cues for the memories. Instead, participants recalled five memories apiece in the four categories of

Table 3–2 Memories Cued by the Goal "Avoid Pain or Danger"

Subjects Who Desired the Goal	*Subjects Who Rejected the Goal*
1. Getting lost in Kennedy Airport	1. Backpacking in the Grand Canyon
2. Breaking an elbow in camp	2. After a football game, the pain and bruises were like trophies
3. A stress fracture from running Not able to compete	3. Riding a horse, jumping fences without reins or stirrups, hands over eyes
4. Taught to box; never again	4. Rock climbing at Tahoe; got hurt, but had lots of fun
5. Being chased by police	5. When Mom didn't let me go hang gliding
6. Did not jump off a very high wall into a very small pool of water	6. How good I felt after I crossed a dangerous river in Outward Bound
7. Afraid to ride horse	7. Hurting my back in fourth grade
8. A car accident when I cracked my head	8. Having my wisdom teeth out
9. Getting asthma at desert camp in Kenya	
10. Afraid to go parasailing	
11. Walking backward and hitting my head on hydrant	
12. Injuring an ankle and producing hemophiliac bleeding	
13. A boy beat me up when I was seventeen and left a lot of scars	
14. Climbing Debbie's tree to read	

Five subjects gave a neutral rating to this goal; three had memories that were uninterpretable.
Adapted from J. A. Singer, 1990a, p. 549.

family, friends and relationships, school, and activities. Participants only saw the life goal sentences after they had recalled their memories and rated their affective responses to them. Once they had rated the desirability of each life goal, participants then rated the relevance of each of their memories to the attainment or nonattainment of each of the fifteen life goals.

The findings from this second experiment once again supported our hypothesis that the more pleasant participants' memories were, the more relevant they were to goal attainment. However, this relationship was selective; goal attainment did not always predict happy memories. For example, happy and proud memories about experiences in school were highly relevant to attainment of the goals of academic accomplishment and search for truth. On the other hand, positive family memories were relevant to the attainment of the goal loving relationships, but they showed no relevance to the attainment of academic accomplishment or the search for truth. These varying relationships depending upon the match between the category of the memory and the goal domain suggest that the link between memories and goals is sensitive to content, not simply success or failure within the memory.

Once again, the relationship of avoidance goals to memories differed from the other goals. These goals may be less strongly desired, and therefore the connection between their attainment and a strong affective response may be more problematic. Alternatively, different emotional meanings may be attached to the attainment or nonattainment of an avoidance goal, compared to other goals. To avoid something that one strongly wants to avoid may not produce the same affective response as gaining something that is strongly desired. Yet, both cases are examples of goal attainment. Ortony, Clore, and Collins (1988) have written extensively about the difference between avoiding an undesirable outcome (i.e., "relief," p. 121) and achieving a desired outcome (i.e., "joy," pp. 86–87).

Self-Defining Memories and Personal Strivings

Thus far, we have provided some preliminary support for our hypothesis that a memory's relevance to goal attainment helps to predict its ability to create a strong affective response in an individual. Yet there are several important limitations to this work. In both experiments, we forced participants to make judgments about goals provided to them rather than about their own unique set of goals. Second, we offered very little guidance about the kinds of memories participants should recall. We could not be sure that the memories participants retrieved were indeed self-defining. Third, we asked participants to recall their memories and make judgments about their goals in the same experimental session. It is possible that their judgments about their goals' desirability influenced their memory ratings in the first experiment, or vice versa in the second experiment, in which goal ratings followed memory ratings. In the next experiment, we made a conscious effort to rectify each of these three methodological concerns (Moffitt & Singer, 1993).

Personal Strivings

Although Murray's list of psychogenic needs was a useful starting point, a measure that elicits self-generated goals from participants is more personally meaningful and affectively involving. Robert Emmons (1986, 1989, 1990) has developed just such a measure—the *personal striving*. Personal strivings "are idiographically coherent patterns of goal strivings and represent what an individual is typically trying to do" (Emmons, 1989, p. 92). On the one hand, personal strivings may be considered more abstract and context-free than current concerns, personal projects, or life tasks. On the other hand, they are more conscious and specific than an overarching need or motive (McAdams, 1988; McClelland, 1985). Emmons has suggested a four-level hierarchy, depicted in figure 3–1 (Emmons, 1989, p. 93). The personal striving is a general statement about what one hopes to accomplish in life. It is derived from a superordinate desire (for example, intimacy) and it leads to specific tasks, projects, and concerns that direct one's day-to-day action. Yet what is crucial to note is that a

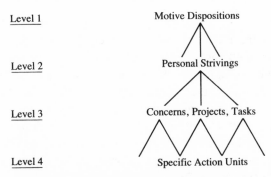

Figure 3–1 Hierarchical Model of Motivation
Adapted from Emmons, 1989, p. 9.

personal striving is not bound to specific courses of action; its goal may be satisfied in many different ways. What is important to the individual is the attainment of the striving, not so much the particular route that is taken to its fulfillment. For this reason, it is very possible that the attainment of personal strivings may be linked to diverse experiences from different time periods stored in memory.

Emmons has demonstrated several successful applications of personal strivings (Emmons, 1986; Emmons & King, 1988, 1989). Participants are asked to list in their own words the personal strivings they typically are trying to accomplish. They then rate the strivings on a variety of dimensions—for example, the happiness they would feel upon attainment of a striving, the difficulty they would encounter in attempting to achieve a striving, their past experience in attainment of the striving, and their estimate of how likely it is that they would attain the striving in the future. Participants' ratings of these strivings' characteristics have been linked to both physical and psychological well-being. Emmons (1986) showed that an individual's daily positive affect was correlated with their tendency to have valued and important strivings, as well as with their sense that they were proceeding effectively toward the attainment of their strivings. Emmons and King (1988) demonstrated that ambivalence, defined as conflict both within and between strivings, was linked to more negative affect and higher incidence of physical illness.

In our third experiment, we asked participants to generate fifteen personal strivings that would represent what they typically are trying to accomplish in their lives. Participants then rated these fifteen strivings for their importance in their lives, as well as for the estimated difficulty and probability of attaining them.

Self-Defining Memories

In the earlier experiments, participants were given minimal suggestions about the kind of memory they should retrieve. In the first experiment, memories were prompted by the life goal sentences, and in the second experiment, by broad content categories. Although many of the memories generated were rich in meaning and affectively intense, we were interested in developing a methodology that would capture the depth and quality of memories described in chapter 2. To accomplish this, we developed a new memory request task called the self-defining memory request (J. A. Singer & Moffitt, 1991–1992). This request was designed to operationalize as many as possible of the characteristics articulated in chapter 2. As table 3–3 indicates, the self-defining memory request asks for longstanding memories (at least one year old) that are especially vivid, important, affectively intense, repetitive, and that convey crucial information about one's personal identity. In our efforts to develop this approach, we have been able to demonstrate that the self-defining memory request, compared to other requests matched for detail and complexity, yields memories that participants judge to be more important to them. Raters have also found that the self-defining memory request leads to more memories that convey more themes of self-discovery. (Chapter 4 offers several examples of self-defining memories generated by participants.) In this third experiment, each subject recalled ten memories in response to the self-defining memory request.

Temporal Separation of Memory and Striving Tasks

Unlike the previous experiments, participants first recalled their self-defining memories and then, a week later, generated their personal strivings. After completion of the personal striving task including the ratings of the

---

Table 3–3 Instructions for the Self-Defining Memory Request (Excerpted)

A self-defining memory has the following attributes:

1. It is at least one year old.
2. It is a memory from your life that you remember very clearly and still feels important to you even as you think about it.
3. It is a memory that helps you to understand who you are as an individual and might be the memory you would tell someone else if you wanted that person to understand you in a more profound way.
4. It may be a memory that is positive or negative, or both, in how it makes you feel. The only important aspect is that it leads to strong feelings.
5. It is a memory that you have thought about many times. It should be familiar to you like a picture you have studied or a song (happy or sad) you have learned by heart.

    To understand best what a self-defining memory is, imagine you have just met someone you like very much and are going for a long walk together. Each of you is very committed to helping the other get to know the "Real You.". . . In the course of conversation, you describe a memory that you feel conveys powerfully how you have come to be the person you currently are. It is precisely this memory that constitutes a *self-defining memory*.

Adapted from J. A. Singer and Moffitt, 1991–1992, p. 242.

striving characteristics, participants then reviewed their memories from the previous week and rated the relevance of each memory to the attainment of each of their personal strivings. The week's time span reduced the possibility of an intermingling of participants' affective responses to memories and judgments of their memories' relevance to the attainment of their strivings.

Each of a subject's ten memories was examined for its relevance to the attainment of all fifteen of their strivings. Our findings in this experiment replicated the earlier two experiments. The happier and prouder participants' responses to their memories, the more relevant their memories were to attainment of their personal strivings. The more embarrassed, sad, and angry their responses to their memories, the more their memories reflected a failure to achieve their strivings. These results were very strong despite the fact that participants' affective responses to their memories had been generated a week before they rated the relevance of their memories to their strivings.

Regarding participants' avoidance strivings, our informal observations from the previous experiments were confirmed. The more participants valued avoidance strivings, the more their memories reflected failed avoidance and the less happy they felt about the outcomes of these memories.

General Discussion of the Three Experiments Relating Affective Responses to Memories and Long-Term Goals

We started this chapter by asking what gives a self-defining memory its enduring affective intensity. Drawing upon some current theories of affect and on a view of the self as comprised of different interwoven components (e.g., representations, fantasies, memories, goals, and affects), we decided that one possible answer to this question is that memories that still matter to us are somehow linked to our ongoing and most desired long-term goals. Across three experiments and with efforts toward an increasingly refined methodology, we were able to demonstrate empirically that an individual's affective response to a self-defining memory may be predicted from the relevance of that memory to the attainment or nonattainment of their most desired goals.

What is the psychological significance of this finding? How does it help us to understand the role of self-defining memories in personality? The relationship between affective responses to memories and goal attainment emphasizes the motivational role that memory may play in personality. Memories may motivate us, both cognitively and affectively. The relevance of a memory to the attainment or nonattainment of one's salient goals may inform an individual about the possibilities of future goal attainment. In this way, we use our memories cognitively to help us decide which long-term goals are worthy of our commitment and persistence. At the same time, just as the affect experienced with the original event may have helped to shape one's goals, the affective experience evoked by the memory may reinforce one's current attitude toward the particular goal or goals, thereby motivating one to sustain or abandon efforts at goal attainment. What we feel when we recall the memory tells us what it would feel like to have that experience of success or failure again.

This view of memory's relationship to goals might help explain why, in our first experiment, more desired goals tended to cue memories more relevant to the attainment of these goals. Individuals may selectively recall memories relevant to the attainment of desired goals as a means of self-encouragement in pursuit of these goals. Reciprocally, individuals may grow to value certain goals more as they accrue experiences of successful attainment of those goals. This kind of reciprocal reinforcement may play a part in building self-efficacy (Bandura & Cervone, 1983).

On the other hand, individuals who desire to avoid pain or failure may take a different approach in memory recall. Rather than recalling memories about times they succeeded in avoiding risky or injurious situations, they tend to retrieve memories concerned with accidents, injuries, and frightening experiences. The negative affect associated with these memories may also serve a reinforcing function to confirm them in their choice to avoid risk or challenge. Strong repetitive reinforcement of this kind may underlie some aspects of phobic behavior. Table 3–4 depicts an example of this kind of thinking from a subject in the third experiment who had a high percentage of avoidance strivings (Moffitt & Singer, 1993).

Moffitt (1991) has suggested that a similar replaying of other kinds of nonattainment memories may play a role in depression. She writes:

> According to Hyland (1987), depression may be explained within the control theory framework [Carver & Scheier, 1982] as a prolonged mismatch between peoples' goals and their perception of their environment. Thus, individuals may become depressed if they desire an active and pleasant social life but consistently fail to achieve that goal. . .
>
> [T]he replaying of personal memories relevant to failure in goals may aid in prolonging and/or reinforcing the mismatch between goals and perceptions of the environment. For example, persons who desire active and fulfilling social lives, but selectively and repetitively recall memories of unpleasant social interactions, may be at risk for prolonged negative affect. (p. 67)

Table 3–4
Personal Strivings:

I typically try to:

Avoid taking my anger out on people who don't deserve it.
Get eight hours of sleep a night
Avoid public speaking.[a]
Avoid caring about people too much.
Avoid most physical activity.[b]
Avoid being overly competitive.
Aviod being a complete cynic.
Make my family proud of me.
Avoid giving advice unless its asked for.
Avoid trusting people until they've proven many times that they deserve it.
Be loyal to my friends and especially my family.
Avoid going somewhere where I won't know anyone else.[c]
Help friends who are in trouble.
Not to be argumentative and stubborn.

Self-Defining Memories of Failure in Avoidance Strivings:

[a]"I remember having to give a demonstration speech in tenth-grade English.
I absolutely hated giving speeches. We had done several others but this was
absolutely the worst because it was the longest—ten minutes. I was
demonstrating how to make brownies; I was very nervous and was shaking
badly. When I was trying to put the tablespoon of water in the bowl it ended up
taking two tries because I shook so much half the water spilled out."

[b]"The summer after my freshman year I went to a sports camp for one week.
I wasn't in great shape and this was the type of place where you did your sport
(gymnastics) for eight hours a day. The whole week was a huge exercise in will
power trying to convince myself that I could get out of bed and my body would
make it through another day. I lasted through the week and fell asleep for
fourteen hours when I got home."

[c]"I remember driving to Florida for spring break last year. As soon as I got there
I missed my family terribly and called them every night. I was happy to be there,
but whenever it was right around dinner time I would wish I had stayed home."

Adapted from Moffitt, 1991.

These speculations about memory's role in sustaining a depressive state begin to take us away from self-defining memories into questions of how
mood, self-focus, and memory interact. Research on the effect of mood
states and self-focus of attention on memory is presented in chapter 5.

What is important for our present discussion is the dynamic aspect of memory captured by our empirical studies. Memories are not finished works, blanketed and sequestered in the museum of long-term storage, only to be dusted off and lit by a moment's recollection. They are action paintings, articulated and defined by the active mind, which shapes and reshapes their meaning and detail in the interest of desire. At the same time, future possibilities are connected to past moments as we rely upon memory to help us interpret and know how to feel about what is happening to us in the present. If our memories' relevance to what we seek to attain in the future can predict our affective responses in the present, then there is a suggested continuity in personality. This continuity stands in the face of movements in psychology that have argued against both consistency in behavior and the existence of motivated action (Emmons, 1990). Evidence for the continuity of personality is increasingly emerging, not only in personological studies, but in social cognition and social psychology research (Johnson & Sherman, 1990; Ross & Conway, 1986). These converging findings lead us to ask whether there is an overarching and organizing framework for the relationship of self-defining memories, affect, and goals. Having studied components of the self in an effort to achieve experimental control and precision, could we combine these components into a more integrated vision of the person?

Our initial thought is to return to Tomkins and script theory. Are personal strivings simply more consciously accessible and easily articulated versions of the enduring concerns and unresolved issues that are at the core of nuclear scenes as described in chapter 2? We believe this to be so, but we would also suggest that strivings and, perhaps, above them, motive dispositions (intimacy, achievement, power, etc.) guide scripts. One might consider scripts, whether nuclear, commitment, or some other variety, as commentaries on our most valued goals. For example, one could possess the nuclear script that people you look to for love always end up hurting you. This script is an individual's understanding of the result of pursuing the personal striving or long-term goal of wanting to be loved (which, in turn, is an expression of the intimacy motive). A goal and accompanying script exist in this skeletal form and then are given flesh by the nuclear scenes or self-defining memories associated with them. If an experience in one's life sparks active pursuit or consideration of the goal of wanting to be loved (e.g., the initiation of a new romantic relationship), the nuclear script with the message "I'll be hurt again" may be activated as well. Accompanying the script might be ready access to several self-defining memories that reinforce the script's position. Because the goal of being loved is very much active, recollection of these memories about painful relationships can still provoke strong affective responses. Unfortunately, the re-experience of this pain from the past may cause individuals to shut down in new relationships or to push the prospective partner away unintentionally. The resulting response of the partner may be to withdraw or become distant, only reinforcing the individual's fear that no good can come of the attempted relationship. This quotidian, but, we believe, very plausible example illustrates our argument about the interconnectedness of past, present, and future in the individual.

Yet there is a problem in this use of script theory as a starting point for a larger framework of personality. Tomkins's death in 1991 left the final integrative pages of his theory unwritten. We have no rules or guidelines to assist us in defining the parameters for the quantity of scripts an individual might possess. We have no clear explanations for the hierarchy of scripts in personality. How do we determine the relative importance of different scripts for an individual? Although we do understand how the process of psychological magnification helps turn scenes into scripts, it is not clear why a scene becomes a candidate for magnification in the first place. One could make the same point about the goals we have studied. We have little information about why individuals prefer some strivings and pursue them stubbornly, while others cannot see the worth or value in that same set of goals. The ultimate question of the origins of an individual's particular constellation of motives, goals, and memories is certainly beyond the scope of this book and perhaps beyond the grasp of psychology's current understanding of the person. Granting this, it is unsatisfying to us to imagine memories and scripts lighting up in consciousness with the randomness of fireflies in a field at night. In the final section of this chapter, we argue that placing one's memories, goals, and scripts in the larger context of a life story of identity may provide some unity and purpose to the recurrent concerns and issues of a given life.

McAdams' Life Story Theory of Identity

One of us has a two-year-old daughter who has grown to love a certain storybook called *Amazing Grace* (Hoffman & Birch, 1991). It is about a little girl named Grace who loves fantasy and ends up playing Peter Pan in the school play. It begins like this:

> Grace was a girl who loved stories.
> She didn't mind if they were read to her or told to her or made up in her own head. She didn't care if they were in books or movies or out of Nana's long memory. Grace just loved stories.

After she had heard them, and sometimes while they were still going on, Grace would act them out. And she always gave herself the
most exciting part. (p. 2)

This simple beginning of a children's book captures a fundamental truth
about human beings—we love stories. Yet we need to make this statement
more emphatic: stories are necessary to what we are as human beings. The
most successful export of the United States in this troubled economic era
is our entertainment industry—television, film, and music. All countries
and cultures, first, second, or third world, desire the telling of stories. There
is no more powerful testament to the vital importance of stories than Mario
Vargas Llosa's book, *The Storyteller* (1990). This novel tells the story of a
Peruvian writer's quest to find an old schoolmate, Saul Zuratas, who disappeared years earlier. Saul had been an outsider on several accounts: he
is Jewish, has a large colored birthmark that covers half his face, and is violently opposed to technological society. Through his anthropological studies, he developed an extreme identification with a similarly abandoned
group of people, the Machiguenga, an Amazonian tribe in the rain forest.

At the start of the novel, the writer is in a gallery in Florence, where his
eye has been caught by an exhibit of photographs entitled, "Natives of the
Amazon Forest." Suddenly, in one photograph of a man telling a story to a
circle of tribal people, the writer recognizes the distinctive face and color-
ing of his friend, Saul. The rest of the novel interweaves past and present
to explain to us how Saul gained the hallowed position of a *habladore*, or
storyteller, for the Machiguenga tribe. More importantly, we learn of the
necessity of stories to this endangered tribe, which faces extinction at the
hands of modern moneyed interests that would destroy the rain forest for
short-term economic gain. The Machiguenga are a nomadic people who
build temporary villages and move on with the changes of season. They
travel in small bands and, though sharing a common language and culture,
seldom, if ever, come together as a unified tribe. Their only link is the
habladore, who travels as a bard or minstrel among the dispersed bands.
He retells the ancient cosmological myths and reports contemporary events
such as births, deaths, marriages, and prospects for food or dwelling places.
The *habladores* give a continuity to the tribe, a collective history that provides meaning to the present and purpose to the future. As the writer
recounts:

I was deeply moved by the thought of that being, those beings, in the
unhealthy forests of eastern Cusco and Madre de Dios, making long
journeys of days or weeks, bringing stories from one group of

Machinguengas to another and taking away others, reminding each member of the tribe that the others were alive, that despite great distances that separated them, they still formed a community, shared a tradition and beliefs, ancestors, misfortunes and joys; the fleeting, perhaps legendary figures of those habladores who—by occupation, out of necessity, to satisfy a human whim—using the simplest, most hallowed of expedients, the telling of stories, were the living sap that circulated and made the Machiguengas into a society, a people of interconnected and interdependent beings. (Vargas Llosa, p. 93)

If the words of the storytellers are the living sap of society, then the stories individuals tell about their own lives are the life blood of personality. Our life stories convey the traditions, belief systems and values, family histories, and knowledge of pain and triumph that define each person's unique identity. As Henry Murray (1938) wrote in the early years of personality psychology, "The history of the organism *is* the organism" (p. 39).

Dan McAdams is the first contemporary psychologist in the field of personality to accept the telling of stories as the fundamental principle of a theory of identity. In his book (McAdams, 1988) and related chapters (McAdams, 1989, 1990a), McAdams places the problem of identity as central to an understanding of contemporary human life. In a world that often seems bereft of moral and spiritual anchors and in a century that has included two world wars, genocidal destruction, and environmental devastation, how do we find reason to continue? How do we find shape and meaning in an inchoate world? McAdams argues that the construction of identity, the building of a personal ideology and value system that both borrows from the past and invents the world anew, gives us the security and purpose to continue in a turbulent and secular society. Drawing heavily on Erikson's landmark work on identity formation, McAdams sees the individual from birth to death engaged in the forward-moving task of self-definition. From our first efforts in trusting those to whom our care has been entrusted to our final review of our life choices and of the manner in which we have cared for others, we struggle with the questions, "Who am I?" "Who might I become?" "Who have I been?" As individuals traditionally have sought to live a life in the service of a diety and his or her precepts, contemporary individuals seek a life in service of the self. The pursuit of identity, of self-knowledge, is not simply a narcissistic indulgence; it is a necessary effort to ground the individual life in a meaningful context of personal and social history. One does not create an identity solely out of immediate experiences and current surroundings. As the seekers of god turn to sacred writings and to the rituals of prayer and litany, seekers of identity must turn to the traditions of their cultures, the rituals of their families and the common stories of their communities. McAdams writes:

> The problem of identity is the problem of arriving at a life story that makes sense—provides unity and purpose—within a sociohistorical matrix that embodies a much larger story. A person's world establishes parameters for life stories. In this way identity is truly psychosocial: The life story is a joint product of person and environment. In a sense, the two write the story together. Jerome Bruner (1960) speaks of this story writing as the making of myths. He writes that the "mythologically instructed community provides its members with a library of scripts" against which the individual may judge his or her own "internal drama" (p. 281). He concludes, "Life, then, produces myth and finally imitates it" (p. 283). (McAdams, 1988, p. 18)

In the previous chapter, we described Tomkins's dramaturgical model of personality with its elements of scripts, scenes, plots, and props. McAdams takes this perspective a step further and argues that the individual is the playwright, the author, of a coherent narrative of the self.

> The central metaphor of [this] model is the life story. It is proposed that beginning in adolescence, with the advent of formal operational thinking, . . . the person becomes a biographer of self. Early biographical accounts constructed by adolescents may take the form of Elkind's (1981) personal fable—a dramatic and highly unrealistic saga of personal heroism and uniqueness. With time, the stories individuals construct may become more realistic, more tempered, as past experiences and future goals are better integrated so as to confer upon the person's life Erikson's (1963) sense of "sameness and continuity" (p. 261). At this point the individual may have "achieved" identity in Marcia's (1980) sense. Yet the story telling continues, and stories may change markedly in adulthood, corresponding to transformations in identity which occur many years after a late-adolescent stabilization. (McAdams, 1988, p. 60)

Figure 3–2, adapted from McAdams (1988, p. 61), outlines the basic components of the life story model of identity. There are four major components: *nuclear episodes, imagoes, ideological setting,* and *generativity script*. There are also two basic dimensions that carry through each component, *thematic lines* and *narrative complexity*.

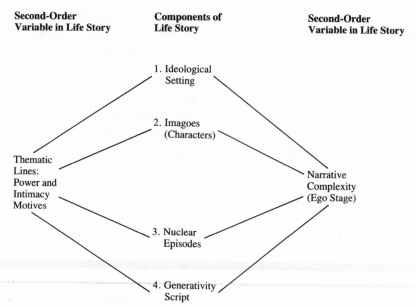

Figure 3–2 A Life-Story Model of Identity
Adapted from McAdams, 1988, p. 61.

Let us first consider these two dimensions. Thematic lines inform us about the content of the life story, and narrative complexity about its structure. McAdams writes, "Thematic lines are recurrent content clusters in stories, analogous to recurrent melodies in a complex piece of music" (McAdams, 1988, p. 62). Although there are many possible themes (for example, one might consider all of Murray's twenty psychogenic needs as potential candidates for themes), McAdams has chosen to focus on two in particular, agency and communion (McAdams, 1990a). These terms are borrowed from Bakan (1966) and embrace two basic tendencies in human life that many clinical and personality psychologists have highlighted (Blatt, 1990; Fine, 1990; Gilligan, 1982; J. L. Singer, 1988; Smelser & Erikson, 1980). Agency refers to the impulse in human beings to achieve independence, autonomy, and self-definition through separation. It refers to one's striving to be masterful, powerful, and competent. In terms of motive dispositions, agency would encompass both the power motive and the achievement motive. Communion embraces the human desire for involvement with others, for interdependence, nurturance, affection, comfort, and sharing. It evokes the image of surrender of the individual to either another person, a community, or an idea. In this surrender, individuals merge with a whole greater than themselves and transcend their own individual identity. Communion is best characterized by the intimacy motive as developed by McAdams (1980, 1984, 1988). The intimacy motive is a "recurrent preference or readiness for experiences of feeling close to and in communion with others, engaging in warm, friendly, and mutual interaction" (McAdams, 1990a, p. 158).

These two themes exist in different measures within each individual and may ebb and flow across one's lifespan. As Blatt (1990) writes, a mature identity "requires both individuation and connectedness, an integration of identity formation and interdependence, a continuity, and a separation from one's past and one's environment as well as a sense of the future and the capacity to establish new connections" (p. 302).

The second dimension of McAdams' model concerns the complexity of the life story's narrative structure. Complex stories involve many characters, plots and subplots, major and minor themes. They are more likely to contain ambiguity, contradictions, and unresolved tensions. Stories with simpler narratives proceed in a more straightforward fashion; they may be powerful and eloquent in their singularity of theme and purpose. For example, McAdams (1988) suggests that Hemingway's *The Old Man and the Sea* may be considered a story told with narrative simplicity, while Dostoyevsky's *The Brothers Karamazov* is clearly a novel filled with narrative complexity. McAdams has suggested that individuals' ego development, the level of differentiation and individuation they have achieved, might influence the complexity of their stories' narratives. To support this hypothesis, he measured participants' ego development using Loevinger's (1976) sentence-completion test and then correlated their scores on this test with measures of the complexity of their life stories. Participants with higher ego development (greater differentiation and integration of experience) supplied a greater variety of plots in the stories they told of their lives.

Although McAdams chose to operationalize narrative complexity by linking it to ego development, one could also look at other aspects of narrative structure. In chapter 4, we look at the specificity or generality of memory narratives—the extent to which an individual recounts specific details or particulars when recalling a memory. As we discuss, it is possible that a tendency to blend memories into generic stories that eschew specificity might be linked to defensiveness and/or depression. What is important to note at this juncture is that the *organization* of narrative, not simply narrative content, may be a window into personality. By arguing that narrative complexity is a basic dimension across the life story, McAdams gives structure, as well as meaning, a prominent role in the formation of identity.

These two dimensions, thematic lines and narrative complexity, weave through the four components of the life story. The first component is *ideological setting*. As adolescents gain the capacity for formal operations (Inhelder & Piaget, 1958), they begin to question their immediate world and move to consideration of the abstract, the possible, and the ideal. Able to think hypothetically, they turn their reflective powers upon themselves and ask, "Why am I here? What is my purpose on this earth? Is life even worth living? What is true and what only appears to be?" As they ponder these painful imponderables for the first time, they search for a value system, an ideology that could help to organize and guide their restless energies. Adolescents may become preoccupied with both what is Right and a right; they may seek causes, political or religious movements, and social subcultures that help them to define a moral code and value system by which to live. McAdams (1989) comments:

> By the end of adolescence or shortly thereafter, the person has consolidated an ideological setting for his or her identity story . . . The ideological setting situates the action of the person's evolving story within a particular locus of belief and value—a locus shaped by society's conventions regarding the good and the true and the individual's struggles to find meaning within or outside of conventions. (p. 165)

If we think about Jim in Conrad's *Lord Jim*, as discussed in chapter 2, he forms an ideological setting in his adolescence from which he never departs. As an early adolescent in his English village, he dreams of going to sea and living a life of honor and courage in the service of his country and fellow shipmates. As he grows into manhood and confronts the gap between his own actions and his idealized image of his behavior, he feels tremendous guilt and shame regarding his comportment as an officer in the merchant marine. Far from abandoning the ideological setting he has cast for himself, he lives the remainder of his life in the shadow of the unforgiving edifice of "proper conduct" he constructed for himself as a young man. Even his death is best understood as a "step forward from the wings" into the hero's part he had long ago written for himself in the life story he had imagined as his own. Jim's value system or ideological setting is one in which the theme of agency is central and communion secondary. For each individual, the choice of ideology involves consideration of the balance of these two life themes.

The second component of the life story is the nuclear episode. Nuclear episodes are the critical scenes that shape individuals' lives. They are the incidents or moments that people feel belong uniquely to their own lives. Although nuclear episodes may take a variety of forms, McAdams feels there are two general types: episodes of *continuity* and of *change*. Nuclear episodes of continuity are moments of truth, moments that define who individuals are and for what they stand. Episodes of continuity provide " 'proof from my past' that 'I am what I am' " (McAdams, 1989, p. 169). For example, Buster Keaton presented his infant memories of mishaps with machines (as described in chapter 2) to help explain the central role, good and bad, that machines had played in both his artistic and personal life. Episodes of continuity may be seen as stories from the past that either reveal one's true nature or help to explain how one has come to be the person one is (what McAdams calls origin myths).

Nuclear episodes of change are turning points, critical junctures in which one's life takes a new direction. In *Kokoro* (as discussed in chapter 2), when Sensei, as a young man, betrays his friend and asks the woman whom they both love to marry him, his life is changed irrevocably. It is not only the subsequent suicide of his friend but his realization of his own moral weakness in an act of betrayal that open a wound of self-hatred that time is unable to close. Sensei writes down this story from his youth for his student to read before he pays the longstanding debt of honor he believes he owes and takes his life. On the other hand, episodes of change may also be positive turning points. In Ana Swir's poem about her father (chapter 2), she describes a pivotal moment in his life—his participation in the Russian revolution. Though terrifying, this episode crystallized for him and later, through his retelling of the incident, for her the importance of moral courage and solidarity in the face of oppressive regimes.

McAdams (1982, 1988) performed some original research to demonstrate that nuclear episodes reflect dominant thematic lines in an individual's life. Participants wrote down TAT stories that were scored for their intimacy and power motives. At a subsequent time, they wrote down various memories of peak or nadir experiences and positive or negative childhood memories. Participants who scored higher in intimacy tended to have positive memories and peak memories with strong themes of love, communication, and sharing embedded in them. Alternatively, high Power participants recalled memories that were more reflective of the desire for mastery, success, and autonomy.

As the name suggests, nuclear episodes are closely linked conceptually to Tomkins's nuclear scenes and commitment scenes. Although Tomkins's nuclear scenes can be considered a particular subtype of nuclear episodes, the basic idea behind the two constructs is very similar. Prototypical past events inform our narrative knowledge of who we are. Even more, these events link to ongoing experiences and shape our interpretation of new events, placing them in the context of what has been.

There is also very little conceptual difference between self-defining memories and nuclear episodes. One might consider self-defining memories an even broader category of remembered experience than nuclear episodes. We have not yet catalogued all the various subtypes of self-defining memories, but there may be other categories of self-defining memories besides those of continuity and change already identified in nuclear episodes.

Interestingly, a cognitive scientist, Schank (1990), also has identified a narrative construct that fits into the same conceptual net as nuclear scenes, nuclear episodes, and self-defining memories. He calls them *me-goal stories* and defines them as stories we tell to others for one of five goals: to achieve catharsis, to gain attention, to receive approval, to seek advice, and to describe ourselves (p. 41). Of course, some of these intentions can be present simultaneously. The following passage, which describes me-goal stories, could just as easily be used to depict nuclear episodes:

> We tell stories like this in order to express our feelings, to get out our anger, or to explain ourselves in some fundamental way. These stories become who we are and telling them allows us to feel these feelings that define us yet again. We avoid telling stories that evoke feelings that we do not care to relive. (Schank, 1990, p. 47)

One advantage of our self-defining memory approach over these other related constructs is that it allows us to examine experimentally the specific operationalized features of individuals' narrative memories. In doing so, we have tried to fit personological concepts like the nuclear episode or nuclear scene into a framework that is compatible with current laboratory work in cognitive psychology and social cognition research. For example, we have examined the personal strivings we have collected from participants for themes of intimacy and power. At the same time, we have scored participants' self-defining memories for these same themes. The ability to show convergences of thematic lines in strivings and self-defining memories takes the work of Tomkins and McAdams into the realm of participants' conscious self-reported experience. For most of the decades since the publication of Henry Murray's *Explorations in Personality*, critics of personological approaches have dismissed their methods as too cumbersome, time-consuming, and "literary" to be of much use in advancing our scientific understanding of personality. It is our belief that these criticisms can no longer be entertained seriously. The work of Emmons (1989),

Epstein (1983), McAdams (1988), and Pervin (1983, 1989), among many others, and our own efforts presented in this book, suggest that one need not abandon a commitment to scientific rigor and precision in the quest for a more meaningful and holistic understanding of the person.

Returning to McAdams's construct of the nuclear episode, it is significant that McAdams places the individual's fledgling identification of nuclear episodes in late adolescence and young adulthood. Many writers' early novels or plays are only thinly veiled autobiographical accounts of their childhood and adolescence. Goethe's *The Sorrows of Young Werther*, *This Side of Paradise* by F. Scott Fitzgerald, Richard Wright's *Black Boy*, and Thomas Wolfe's *Look Homeward Angel* are some notable examples of this trend. A recent first collection of stories, *The Last To Go*, by the young American writer Rand Cooper (1988) offers a fine example of the crystallization of self-defining memory in one's early and mid-twenties. Set in a small city reminiscent of Cooper's hometown of New London, the fictional story of a young man coming to terms with the breakup of his parents' marriage is filled with pivotal moments of childhood and adolescence that evoke the 1960s and 1970s of the author's youth.

In a story entitled "Boy Bringing Wreaths," Cooper presents an incident of horseplay between Toby, who is the young man, but who appears in this story as a much younger boy, and his father, Dan Slattery, who is a neurosurgeon. Eventually Dan will have an affair and leave Toby's mother; this scene depicts his self-preoccupation and potential for destructiveness. At the same time, we see the admiration Toby feels for his father, which is impervious to the questionable behavior his father exhibits:

'Here Tobe,' Slattery says. 'Show ya something.' He crosses and puts his hand lightly to his son's neck, thumb on one side, index finger on the other. In his fingertips Slattery can feel the strong pulse of two carotid arteries, the vascular drumbeat of his son's life. He presses on them expertly.

'Daniel—!' Mary Ellen shouts.

He let go. Released, his son drops easily to the floor and lies there in an oxygen-thin ecstasy, mouth eerily grinning.

'Dan! What do you think you are doing?'

He is not sure what he's doing, or why. 'I'm sorry,' he says flatly. He thinks of the neck he'll rummage through next week, the arteries he'll try to scrape clear. He knows no work more delicate or more dangerous. When he did the arteriogram, the guy screamed and the needles went in. He feels like Dracula, the way necks are offered to him.

'I'm sorry,' he says again, shaking.

'Well, you should be,' his wife says. She is helping Toby to his feet. 'Oh *wow*, Dad!' his son says, smiling. 'Amazing! Just like Mr. Spock.' 'What do you mean?' Slattery says. Waves of helplessness and remorse wash over him as Toby, rubbing his face back to life, elaborates: 'The Vulcan Death Grip, Dad.' (Cooper, 1988, p. 80)

In this brief nuclear episode, Cooper has found a way of depicting an episode of change for the characters of his story. All three players, Toby, his mother, and father, have seen a side of Dan that foreshadows some of the destructiveness to come. Toby does not realize it at the time, but a seed is planted in his memory that will eventually emerge as a nuclear episode that helps define his understanding of his father. In Cooper's (whose own father is a neurosurgeon) writing about a young man's memories of his surgeon father, fictional memory and what may be the strands of actual memory converge to form a character's episode of change.

Along similar lines, it is not surprising that many young people enter psychotherapy in their late adolescence and early adulthood. Psychotherapy offers them an opportunity to examine their emerging narratives and look at the inconsistencies or tensions within them. We have seen how the writers and artists discussed in the previous chapter were all moved to artistic expression by powerful memories. Although most individuals are not writers or film makers, individuals who enter therapy may participate in the same process of articulation and resolution of nuclear episodes. Through sharing with an audience, attempting a symbolic analysis, and constructing narrative meaning, the client replicates many of the creative processes engaged in by the writer or the artist. At the very least, individuals engaged in psychodynamic therapy make this self-defining process explicit and central to their lives, at least for the duration of therapy. Chapter 7 examines extensively the role of self-defining memories and the life story metaphor in psychotherapy.

The third component of the life story model is the *imago*. Imagoes are similar to personal archetypes. They are the prototypical characters that reappear in one's nuclear episodes over and over again. McAdams suggests that a taxonomy of *Imagoes* can be created that depicts the four possible combinations of high and low agency and communion (McAdams, 1987, p. 34). For example, one's life story might contain the imago of the strong but emotionless father (high agency) or the forever nurturing and patient mother (high communion). An artist or healer imago might represent high levels of both agency and communion, while an escapist pleasure-seeker or bureaucrat imago might be low in both. McAdams (1987) has demonstrated that individuals who score high in intimacy or power on the TAT tend to tell stories of their own lives that feature imagoes with corresponding levels of agency or communion.

The fourth and final component is the *generativity script*. Generativity, another concept borrowed from Erikson, refers to individuals' concern with what the legacy of their life story will be. A legacy high in communion would be loving offspring and grandchildren who have been brought up to value family and mutual support. A legacy high in agency might be an artistic creation, a successful business, or a life lived with moral rectitude. As McAdams (1988) writes, "The generativity script is a vision of exactly what one hopes to put into life and what one hopes to get out of life before one is too old to be generative" (p. 65). The generativity script begins in adolescence and early adulthood with the barest of outlines and becomes more detailed by middle adulthood. McAdams (1988) has suggested that the midlife crisis may be more a crisis of generativity than a full reconsideration of one's entire identity.

Relating this last component to the research presented in this chapter, we submit that personal strivings are really shorthand versions of generativity scripts. The long-term goals that we acknowledge as playing a role in what we typically are trying to do are really statements to ourselves about how we want the plot of our life stories to turn out. Does the hero end up with the girl in the end? Does the heroine obtain the riches she has sought? Does the scientist uncover the hidden truth she has pursued? Does the dutiful son succeed in pleasing his parents? Personal strivings as stand-ins for the plots of our life stories are the motivating forces that carry our stories forward. McAdams (1990a) has written:

> As accounts of human intentions, stories tell what characters are *striving* to do, what they *want* and how they go about trying to get what they want over time. There is no story without intention. Further, *there may be no intention without story*. (p. 156)

Although it is easy to see that the engine of any story is its plot—we follow the efforts of the protagonist to reach some goal or end—it is harder to understand that the essence of intention is narrative. Yet, as McAdams points out, two of the most widely used methods of identifying an individual's fundamental motivations have been Freudian interpretation of dream narratives and analysis of stories created to TAT cards. To know what someone wants, we need to understand how they construct or envision the world. For individuals to know what they want, they must construct sequential thoughts that depict an agent, a course of action, and a result. In this simple construction is the beginning of narrative.

Conclusion

McAdams' life story model of identity has offered us a context for how two components of a complex self-system, memories and goals, may be linked together. If a major aspect of personality is the story we construct of our lives, then self-defining memories and personal strivings are the raw material of that story. Personal strivings or long-term goals are the outlines we sketch for our life stories to follow. Drawing primarily upon the themes of agency and communion, our strivings dictate to us how far we will take our lives in the direction of independence and/or interdependence. Our self-defining memories are the pages born of our outlined intentions. They inform us of the successes and failures we have encountered in the pursuit of our desires. In their power to evoke emotion in us by the simple act of recollection, they vivify the life story—they make the story matter. We are not only the spinners of a yarn, but through the emotional power of memory, the audience as well. One can picture Marlow, the narrator of many of Joseph Conrad's stories, sipping his brandy and telling a story to a room of white-haired English gentlemen. He is in control, masterful in his speech rhythms and his ironies. For most of us, our life stories proceed in a more tumultuous fashion. We cannot always keep a storyteller's graceful distance. Memories come upon us unawares; they grip us and demand that we read a page from a story we had written and hoped to file away. We cannot read sentences dispassionately that we ourselves have constructed from our life events. They speak to our hopes, consummated or undone. They refer us to what we imagine for the future. If we want to know how the story ends, we have only what we know of the story thus far to inform our speculation. One of life's ironies, of course, is that how we interpret the story, how we feel about past incidents of our lives, will influence the story still to come. In the act of looking back as a means to anticipate the future, we change the future. In the act of looking forward as a means to escape the past, we inevitably run into the past. The interplay of memory and desire, their reciprocal and inextricable relationship, is the life story of personality. Perhaps this is what Freud meant by the repetition compulsion. Perhaps this is what Murray meant by his aphorism about the history of the organism being the organism. Perhaps this what F. Scott Fitzgerald meant, at the end of *The Great Gatsby*, when his narrator, Nick Carraway, lamented:

And as I sat there brooding on the old, unknown world, I thought of
Gatsby's wonder when he first picked out the green light at the end of
Daisy's dock. He had come a long way to this blue lawn, and his
dream must have seemed so close that he could hardly fail to grasp it.
He did not know that it was already behind him, somewhere back in
the vast obscurity beyond the city, where the dark fields of the republic
rolled on under the night.

Gatsby believed in the green light, the orgiastic future that year by
year recedes before us. It eluded us then, but that's no matter—tomor-
row we will run faster, stretch out our arms farther. . . . And one fine
morning—

So we beat on, boats against the current, borne back ceaselessly into
the past. (Fitzgerald, 1925/1988, p. 141)

4

Memory and Personality

Those Winter Sundays

Sundays too my father got up early
and put his clothes on in the blueblack cold,
then with cracked hands that ached
from labor in the weekday weather made
banked fires blaze. No one ever thanked him.

I'd wake and hear the cold splintering, breaking.
When the rooms were warm, he'd call,
and slowly I would rise and dress,
fearing the chronic angers of that house,
Speaking indifferently to him,
who had driven out the cold
and polished my good shoes as well.
What did I know, what did I know
of love's austere and lonely offices?

—Robert Hayden (1975, pp. 113)

Although the content of this poem—the poet's recognition of his boyhood failure to see his father's silent means of caring—is certainly moving, the poem's emotional power and its message may also be found in the way the poet recalls this failure. The title, "Those Winter Sundays," tells the reader that the father's dutiful actions depicted in the poem's narrative—getting up early, stoking the fire, polishing his son's good shoes—are an amalgam of countless separate occasions. That the poet writes of a summarized memory rather than a memory of one particular Sunday gives the narrative its force. There were so many Sundays of these ritual chores, and so many Sundays in which these chores went unnoticed, that they have merged into a symbolic Sunday. The poet feels not only the weight of what

83

his father did for him, but the weight of so many missed opportunities to recognize the warmth that had surrounded him.

Precisely because the memory is told in summarized form and does not zero in on a specific event, the poet renders for the reader the tension that existed between father and son. He can know his father now only through the generality of memory; the individual and specific intimacies of these gestures are forever lost. What is ultimately most affecting about the poem is that it brings the frustrating distance between the two into the present narrative. We can feel the restrained rage of the poet pounding in repeated blows ("What did I know? What did I know?") against a wall of Sundays, so many and yet none of them can be turned into the specific moment of mutual acknowledgement that has passed and cannot be regained.

This literary example demonstrates to us the powerful effect a poet can achieve through manipulation of a memory's narrative structure. Yet, in our daily conversations, we also make exactly the same choices about how to convey information from memory. To illustrate this, let us look at a sum- marized memory generated by one of our participants in a study of self- defining memories:

> My grandfather was in a nursing home and he was barely aware of himself and my family there, although maybe deep down he was. I hated our visits but felt very strongly that they were important and I wanted to be there for him and help him in any way I could. The situa- tion of his life was so awful, I wished he would die, I could barely stand to see him that way; he said he wanted to go to heaven and was so unhappy and he loved us so much. . . . I felt after these visits that everything would be better if he were out of his misery. I've always been affected by seeing suffering and not being able to do something directly to help the sufferer.

We see here another type of summarized memory. Although it, too, blends many separate incidents into a single generic episode, it leaves out any sensory imagery or specific details of the visit. Although we hear about the narrator's emotion, the memory allows us to escape the sight, touch, or smell of the experiences that provoke her feelings. In contrast to the poet's heightening of his memory's emotion through repetition, this blended nar- rative keeps us at an abstract distance from the individual's actual encoun- ters with her grandfather in the nursing home.

Although these two summarized memories seem to vary quite a bit in their emotional quality, they share a common cognitive component. They demonstrate a tendency of the mind to group similar experiences into generic categories. If the poet were to try to recall a particular Sunday of his youth, he would have to extract it from the "Sundays when I was young" memory bin he has created. Similarly, the participant would have to reach into the memory bin she has labelled "Visits to my grandfather's nursing home." Sudden changes in fortune, milestones, or accidents—any rare events—may not lend themselves so easily to this prototyping process, but most repeated events from our lives may be codified and filed into a particular generic memory bin.

As a final introduction to this chapter, let us look at a memory that is specific and focused on a particular incident. One of our participants recalled the following self-defining memory:

> I was having a swimming lesson, and the instructor knew that I had a fear of going under deep water. She tried to solve this by sitting on the side of the pool and having me hold onto her legs and pushing me in and out of the water—so long that my head went under. I wanted to stop after a couple of minutes (I was out of breath), but she wouldn't let me—she kept pushing my head under. I panicked and tried to get out, then failing to do so, tried to pull her in. I made so much noise that eventually she let me go, and I ran outside to where my mother was waiting. I remember thinking that I was going to drown.

In contrast to the two summarized memories, the narrator gives us a specific moment in time, which she describes with frightening detail and narrative immediacy. She has chosen to tell us about a particular swimming lesson, but this certainly was not her only one. We are told that the instructor knew about her fear of deep water; we can infer from this information that they may have worked together on previous lessons. One could imagine the participant telling a summarized memory about her "Dreaded swimming lessons." Her choice to speak of a singular event may be due to the unique terror of this incident, but it may also be due to her style as a person. Is it possible that some people move from general memories to specific ones more easily than other people? Some individuals may be more comfortable with the powerful emotions that can be evoked by recalling the imagery and sensory details of a particular past experience.

Our three examples have suggested that how someone recalls and describes a memory may prove to be a rich source of information about affect, cognition, and personality. In this chapter, we attempt to identify experimentally the two types of memory narratives we have already introduced: summarized and single-event memories. In discussing memory structure, as opposed to memory content, we try to show relationships among cognitive science, personality, and clinical psychology.

From cognitive science, we borrow a hierarchical organization of autobiographical memory, emphasizing a context-plus-index model of memory retrieval (Reiser, 1983; Reiser, Black, & Kalamarides, 1986). We examine the hypothesis that in order to find specific incidents from memory, participants first generate a generic context and then isolate specific indexed events stored within that context. Drawing on personality psychology, we explore the hypothesis that the use of summary or single-event memories reflects a cognitive style embedded deep in the personality (Shapiro, 1965; J. A. Singer & Moffitt, 1991–1992). Participants prone to defensiveness may be more likely to summarize and abstract their personal memories, avoiding the emotional immediacy of a specific recollection. Finally, we present some intriguing findings from recent research in clinical psychology that suggest that depressed individuals have greater difficulty finding specific positive memories (Williams & Broadbent, 1986). We also provide a replication of this work from our own laboratory. These results add support to an emerging cognitive theory of depression that emphasizes depressed individuals' inability to repair their negative moods by recruiting positive experiences. Once again, as in the previous chapter's perspective on memory and goals, we conclude with an attempt to place our understanding of memory narrative structure in the larger context of McAdams's life story model of identity.

Hierarchical Organization of Autobiographical Memory

In this section we are concerned with how cognitive psychologists and cognitive scientists have attempted to understand the organization of autobiographical memory. Brewer (1988) defines autobiographical memory as "memory for information related to the self" (p. 26). How do we keep track of the massive amount of self-relevant information we encounter? How do we encode, store, and retrieve memories about trips we've taken, birthdays we've celebrated, loves we've won and lost, athletic triumphs and defeats we've exalted or begrudged?

For most of this century, psychologists who study memory have tended toward more mechanistic models based in an associationist philosophy (e.g., Anderson, 1983). Although these models have provided satisfactory explanations for how paired associates or lists are learned and recalled in laboratory experiments, they tend to fall short in their descriptions of more emotionally laden and personally oriented memories (Blaney, 1986;

Salovey & Singer, 1989; J. A. Singer & Salovey, 1988) Reiser, Black, and Kalamarides (1986) have written:

> Most memory models, for example, have focused on structural factors affecting the retrieval and accessibility of items in memory, such as the frequency of a target item, the discriminability of targets, the recency of encoding the item, and the strength of associations connecting items. Yet, as memory researchers now turn to studies of more natural and complex retrieval phenomena such as memory for real-world events, characterizations of the architecture of the memory system are unlikely to be sufficient. (p. 100)

These authors work out of a branch of cognitive psychology that has attempted to expand experimental psychology's approach to memory. As cognitive scientists and artificial intelligence researchers, they are concerned with modeling natural memory processes through computer simulation. For example, humans are capable of subtle inferences that allow them to understand indirect or incomplete communications, whether in written or spoken text. In the late 1970s and throughout the 1980s cognitive psychologists and cognitive scientists like Robert Abelson, John Black, Roger Schank, and Janet Kolodner attempted to build into computer programs the inferential strategies that human beings employ to understand narrative text (Black, 1984; Galambos, Abelson, & Black, 1986; Kolodner, 1983, 1984; Schank & Abelson, 1977).

A key concept that developed from this work is that human beings store information in *knowledge structures* (Galambos, Abelson, & Black, 1985), which are abstract categories that label and organize more specific remembered events. For example, Schank and Abelson (1977), in terminology overlapping with Tomkins, introduced the cognitive science concept of the *script*. Abelson defines the script in the following way:

> In sum, a script is a hypothesized cognitive structure that when activated organizes comprehension of event-based situations. In its weak sense, it is a bundle of inferences about the potential occurrence of a set of events. . . . In its strong sense, it involves expectations about the order as well as the occurrence of events. (Abelson, 1981, p. 717)

As used in this context, a script is a more narrow cognitive concept than the nuclear or commitment scripts that Tomkins discussed. Through a script's predictability and generality across similar activities, it produces a high degree of redundancy, which in turn permits inferences to be made. The most common example of the script in cognitive science terms is eating in a restaurant. Being seated, giving an order, receiving the food, eating, asking for the check, paying, leaving a tip, and exiting are all stereotypic actions that could be reproduced across a variety of restaurant experiences. Knowledge of this script allows us to infer these details if someone mentions in passing a recent night out at a restaurant. Other examples of simple cognitive scripts might be going to the bank, hosting a party, or visiting the doctor. The cognitive science approach to scripts helps to ground Tomkins's concept of psychological magnification (chapter 2) in a more general theory of memory. Magnification extracts the common properties of distinct events in time and forms a generic category in memory that serves as an abstract representation of these properties. For example, after several trips with an adult to the supermarket, a child begins to form a memory category of shopping, which includes in it a sequence of behaviors that are repeated each trip. Although in the case of Tomkins's script theory, magnification is specifically focused on meaningful affectively charged events, there is hardly any difference in the principles involved.

Brian Reiser (1983, Reiser, Black, & Abelson, 1985; Reiser, Black, & Kalamarides, 1986) has provided the best experimental tests of this hierarchical view of memory organization. He calls his approach the *context-plus-index model of autobiographical memory*. Recollection of a particular memory takes place by summoning a particular context and then making inferences to find the specific experience one seeks to recall. Within the specific generic context, the individual has indexed a variety of memories that represent subtle variations on that context. "Experiences are accessed by first retrieving the [knowledge] structures themselves, then using generic information within them to direct search through associated structures and events" (Reiser, 1983, p. 103).

By studying experimental participants' search process and the types of memories retrieved, Reiser has been able to demonstrate the indexing strategies they use to store memories. He has proposed that the most common generic context for memories is an activity (going to work, socializing with friends, eating at a restaurant, etc.) and that specific memories are indexed by details (e.g., participants, time periods, locations, motivating goals) that differentiate one particular instance of an activity from another. Although some of the subcategories of memory might be relatively nonaffective (locations or time periods, for example), the "motivating goals" subcategory (Reiser, 1983, p. 62) would tend to be more affectively charged. It would include information about how each memory linked to a particular goal was related to goal attainment or nonattainment (note the connection to topics discussed in the previous chapter).

Within the motivating goal subcategory of memory organization, one could also imagine a hierarchical arrangement of goals, as was also discussed in chapter 3. If goals can be ordered from consummatory drives all the way up to motive dispositions, it is possible that memories of increasing affective intensity and persistence are linked to these goals at each level of the hierarchy. For example, at a higher level of the motivating goal subcategory might be the personal striving to try to find a perfect love. Because this is a higher-order motivating goal, one might find memories connected to it that reflect either the euphoria or despair of romantic love. To retrieve specific memories of this kind, one would first have to access the motivating goal category of "Try to find a perfect love." From this point on, one would begin to explore more circumscribed goal subcategories, such as perfect loves in high school, or perfect loves that found me imperfect, etc.

As a first test of this hierarchical model of memory, Reiser (1983) asked participants to find specific autobiographical memories in response to cues based on common activities and actions performed in the course of these activities. The actions varied in how central they were to the particular activity. Action cues with greater centrality to the goal of the activity elicited specific memories more quickly and more often. For example, the action of mailing the box was a better cue than taping the sides for finding a memory of the activity of sending a gift. The differential effectiveness of memory cues based upon their centrality to the activity recalled suggests a hierarchical organization of memory may be in operation.

If autobiographical memories are indexed in hierarchical abstract knowledge structures of scripts, motivating goals, or time periods, one would naturally expect distortion of the original experience toward the common features of the generic knowledge structure. Blending of experience would not only be inevitable but a necessary property to avoid redundancy and to allow for effective generalization. Reiser, Black, and Kalamarides (1986) demonstrated this blurring of experience by asking a group of individuals to talk aloud as they looked for a specific memory. For example, one participant found a general context for the request, "Think of a time you went shopping and could not pay for all the items you wanted," but then had more difficulty moving to a specific instance:

Um, it happens when I go grocery shopping in Connecticut because I don't have any check-cashing privilege cards. . . . And so I have to pay with cash and I don't always calculate exactly what's in the carriage. So I'll have to put back, like, yogurt. . . . usually, yogurt's what goes. (Reiser, et al., 1986, p. 110)

Just as individual experiences blend toward the generic knowledge structure, the generic structures might subtly shift as the individual's goals and
their relative importance in a hierarchy altered over time. Shifts in how individuals think about their motivating goals might affect the accessibility
of a particular memory or even influence how it is indexed in the memory
structure. As we point out in chapter 3, changes in a memory's link to a particular goal might also change its affective value for the individual. This
argument, of course, was at the heart of Adler's views about the early memory being a reflection of one's current life attitude. However, Reiser's cognitive science framework places this Adlerian perspective in the context of
contemporary thinking about information processing.

As we have already briefly described, this same cognitive science framework sheds light on Tomkins's principle of psychological magnification.
Psychological magnification is a specific instance of how individual experiences are indexed in generic structures of autobiographical memory. In
the case of the nuclear scene, a series of events have shared a common outcome in response to a motivating goal (what began in hopeful anticipation
has ended in frustration or betrayal). Even more, these events have shared
similar affects, settings, and participants. In contrast to this type of magnification, repetitive events without much affective intensity are linked as
cognitive scripts or *habitual scenes. Transient scenes*, relatively isolated
occurrences with little psychological meaning, bear little sign of magnification.

Although there is general agreement among many researchers about the
hierarchical organization of autobiographical memory (Brewer, 1983,
1988; Neisser, 1986; Robinson & Swanson, 1990), there is not yet consensus on what the central organizing unit of autobiographical memory
might be. Barsalou (1988) has suggested that the central summarizing context for specific memories is not activities, but "extended-event time lines."
These extended event units comprise an "era" of one's life (my time in
school, the first year of my marriage, the period around my father's death,
etc.) and are less generic than a knowledge structure such as activities. They
do contain *summarized events*—repeated activities engaged in over the
course of an extended event (walking to school each morning)—but at their
lowest level of abstraction may be broken down into specific events from
within the time period of an extended event. As support for his perspective,
Barsalou recorded participants' free recall responses to an inquiry about
what they did over summer vacation. Content analysis of their replies provided evidence for their use of time periods as the organizing unit of their
memories.

It is important to consider that both Reiser and Barsalou are attempting to make inferences about memory organization from the verbal protocols produced by their study participants. Leaving aside the important methodological and philosophical question of whether the spoken or written communication of any internal product (memory, dream, self-concept, goal, etc.) transforms its original nature, there are at least three interacting factors that will influence any narrative communication: the *content*, the *context*, and the *narrator* of the communication.

Depending upon the content of a particular memory, its narrative may be more or less likely to take on a highly specific or highly abstract nature. For example, memories about one-time-only events (hitting my one and only homerun in little league) are much more likely to have a narrative specificity than memories involving repeated events in one's life (the two hundred times I struck out in little league).

Similarly, the context in which a memory is being narrated—in other words, the nature of the request for a memory—will influence its narrative form. (We explore this particular issue in depth later in this chapter.) If a physician asks, "How has your health been over the last year?", the patient may answer in the most general terms. If the same physician asks, "Tell me about your worst headache in the last year", then the answer will have a specificity that is much more likely to rely upon sensory imagery and narrative details and, in addition, be more accurate (see Salovey et al., 1992, experiment 1). Context may also involve the recipient of the memory narrative. One's choice of details, explanatory information, and summarizing comments in a memory narrative might differ greatly when telling the memory to a new friend as compared to one's long-term therapist.

Regarding the important issue of context, Brewer (1986) has reviewed many of the studies employing requests for autobiographical memory. He notes that instructions have varied as to whether the memory requested should be of a specific incident or a summary of particular time period. According to his analysis, memories generated by these studies may be broken down into categories ranging from the specific (personal memories or autobiographical facts) to the summarized or abstract (generic personal memory, semantic memory, and generic perceptual memory). As suggested by this analysis and the work of Reiser and Barsalou, there is the definite risk that researchers' inferences about memory organization may be, in part, a function of the context or instructional sets they have provided.

For example, in the experiments performed by Reiser et al. (1988), requests for a "memory about a specific time when . . ." yielded a majority of specific memory narratives compared to blended or summarized memory narratives. On the other hand, Barsalou's request that individuals recall events from their summer vacation yielded on average sixty percent summarized events and forty percent specific events. It is entirely possible that the nature of their requests, the relative generality or specificity, could have influenced their results and, inadvertently, their subsequent generalizations about memory. Although Reiser's request that participants describe their thought process as they searched for the memory (Reiser, Black, & Kalamarides, 1986) allowed for more reasonable inferences about internal processes, one cannot escape the fact that these searches were conducted in response to a particular type of memory request (e.g., "Think of a time when you felt ambitious," "Think of a time when you felt cold at an exam," etc.). This request asks participants to begin with a rather broadly stated or generic experience and then zero in on a specific instance from their own lives. With such a demand, it is not surprising that participants approached the task by generating an organizing category of activities and then searched for an instance within that category. Similarly, Barsalou's request that participants recall as many events as possible from their summer vacations is a request organized around a particular time period (summer). Participants may have approached this task by finding blocks of time within this larger period from which they could locate specific events (time at my job, my trip to Europe). Based on these responses, one might conclude that extended event time-lines or eras were a major organizing principle of memory.

Both Reiser and Barsalou's requests for memories are also notable in that they elicit memories that are not particularly self-involving or affective. There is currently much controversy in the literature over whether memories about the self are organized or processed differently from other kinds of memory (Bower & Gilligan, 1979; Greenwald & Banaji, 1989). As we have seen, there is also a long history in the clinical psychology literature of requests for memories that are highly personal and affective, such as one's earliest memory or memories about one's mother or father (Adler, 1927; Bruhn, 1984; Mayman, 1968). Would a request for memories that are highly affective and self-involving elicit memories of a different narrative type than a more neutral request for memories? For the clinical psychologist, whose inquiries during treatment often seek to invoke exactly these kinds of highly charged memories, such a question would be of considerable interest.

Finally, let us return to our earlier point that inferences about memory operations are made inevitably from verbal protocols (spoken or written) supplied by participants. Barsalou (1988) writes:

It is important to bear in mind, however, that people may employ various narrative styles when describing events from their lives. These narrative styles may in some cases be retrieval strategies that do not reflect underlying memory organization but instead reflect various cultural and linguistic conventions. (p. 217)

For this reason, it would be more accurate to refer to distinctions in memory narratives instead of presuming the verbal product is the memory itself. Along the same lines, studies in memory organization have not directly investigated the effect of writing down one's memory compared to speaking one's memory aloud. It is possible that spoken narration of memories might lead to different proportions of summary and single-event memories compared to written memories.

The pioneering work by cognitive psychologists and cognitive scientists offers an exciting challenge to personality psychologists interested in the structure of autobiographical memory. Could these distinctions in the specificity of memory narratives, which seem to be at the heart of memory organization, also play a role in personality style and mood–memory interactions? To begin to answer this intriguing question, we would need to develop a more controlled method for collecting these memory narratives and a more detailed coding system for distinguishing between summarized and single-event narratives than either Reiser or Barsalou have employed. These methodological refinements would need to address the question of context as manifest in instructional sets, written versus spoken protocols, and the degree of self-involvement elicited by a memory request. In this regard, it would be of great interest to us to explore the particular effects that our own self-defining memory request has on the structure of memory narratives. Given the personally involving and affectively laden qualities of this memory request, would it influence relative proportions of summarized and single-event memories? By first answering these various methodological questions about collecting and identifying summarized and single event memories, we could then proceed to apply our improved methods to the questions of personality style and mood–memory interactions.

Experimental Investigations of Autobiographical Memory Narratives

The theme that runs through the following four experiments we discuss is simple: how should a personality psychologist ask for an autobiographical memory from a participant (J. A. Singer & Moffitt, 1991–1992)? In the present experiments, we attempted to step back from the established word association (Robinson, 1980) and directed inquiry tactics (Reiser et al., 1986) of eliciting memories. In our first experiment, we essentially started from scratch and simply asked participants to recall and write down a memory. We then replaced these minimal instructions with a self-defining memory request in the second experiment. In a third experiment, we placed the techniques from the first two experiments side by side. By manipulating memory request in the same experiment, we hoped to demonstrate that the generality and specificity of memory narratives would be influenced. In particular, we hypothesized that a request for affective memories highly relevant to one's self-concept would produce narratives rich in both imagistic detail and summarizing abstraction. On the other hand, memory narratives elicited by a more neutral request would be less affective, less self-involving, and more circumstantial, with less evidence of generalizations or abstractions. Finally, in a fourth experiment, we again matched the self-defining memory request with a more neutral request, but this time collected spoken as opposed to written memories.

The First Experiment: Recall a Memory

Our only stipulation on our basic request to "recall a memory" was that the memory be from at least one year ago; this was to prevent participants from providing us with extremely recent or trivial memories. Participants wrote down their memories and then rated their current affective responses to the memories using the same list of emotion adjectives that we employed in the studies described in chapter 3.

Scoring the Memory Narratives. Previous articles that invoked a summary versus single-event distinction in memories were consulted to determine criteria for scoring the memory narratives. As we have seen, other researchers had noted the existence of summarized and specific memories, but no published study offered any standardized scoring guidelines for us to follow. Hanawalt and Gebhardt (1965) defined the difference simply by asking participants to recall a memory that happened only one time or repeatedly. Williams and Broadbent (1986) timed participants' latencies to find a specific memory in response to the request, "Can you think of a specific time—one particular episode?" (p. 29). Barsalou (1988) had raters divide participants' recollections of events from their summer vacations into three categories relevant to the current investigation (p. 200). The summarized event was a statement that blended two or more events of the same kind, such as going to beaches or playing golf. The specific event was a single event of no more than a day's time. Extended events were specific events that lasted longer than a day, were not continuous, and were of some significance to the participant ("I took a trip to Belgium," "I ran regularly three times a week").

We attempted to incorporate some of these previous efforts into our own scoring manual, but tried to refine them by offering more formal and precise definitions of summary and single-event memories. Table 4–1 provides an excerpt from our scoring manual. We divided the summary and single-event memories into subtypes to help identify nuances, but we did not ask our raters to make these more subtle distinctions. Each definition was accompanied by numerous examples of the particular memory narrative type in question. Across the four experiments to be presented interrater agreement averaged ninety-three percent.

Results. Using a minimal cue for memory recall, the number of single-event memory narratives (eighty-six percent) far outnumbered the summary memory narratives (fourteen percent). This finding resembles the ratio of single-event to summary memories reported by Reiser et al. (1988) and is opposite to the high number of summarized memories found by Barsalou (1988). It is possible that the omission of a request for a specific time period from which the memory should be selected reduced participants' tendency to blend together events into summarized memory narratives.

Eighty-two percent of the memories provoked emotional responses of strong intensity in the participants, with positive emotions, such as happiness and pride, predominant. In addition, eighty-six percent of the memories were rated as highly vivid. Interestingly, summary and single-event memories did not differ in affective quality or vividness of recall.

The Second Experiment: The Self-Defining Request

In the next experiment, we introduced our self-defining memory request (see chapter 3 for the excerpted instructions). We predicted that this request would yield a higher percentage of summary memory narratives than in the previous experiment. It was also hypothesized that the self-defining memory request would produce memories of greater emotional intensity and personal importance.

As in the previous experiment, participants wrote down their memories and again rated their current emotional responses to their memories. Raters then scored the memories for numbers of single-event and summary memory narratives.

Table 4–1 Excerpt from the Scoring Manual for Identifying Single-Event and Summary Memory Narratives

Single-Event Memory Narrative: A sequence of actions or images, identifiable as an unique occurrence and located in a discrete moment of time in an individual's life.

> *Two years ago I got into an awful fight with my father. I said I couldn't go to an acolyte picnic because I had to study for exams and he said I just had to go. So we fought . . . for about half an hour, until we both had forgotten about the picnic . . . it became purely a power struggle. Finally I ran across the room, came within an inch of his face and cursed him . . . and he smacked me. It didn't hurt, just surprised me. He sat down and began to cry, so did I and I felt awful because I had driven him to do it and he knew it.*

Summary Memory Narrative: The defining feature of a summary narrative is the lack of a discrete connection to a particular moment in time. It locates events in larger time frames and/or blends unique events into an amalgam meant to represent all of its constituent experiences. If a single event is mentioned, it is mentioned only in passing, without specific detail or imagery, and is subsumed by a larger generalized narrative.

There are two major types of summary memory narratives. The first is the generic narrative; for example:

> *When I was very young, four or five, my mom made me eat green beans. I could not stand to eat them. So whenever I had to, I gave an extremely horrible tantrum. Because of my reaction, my mom would rock me in the rocking chair and feed me my green beans. Today, however, I love green beans.*

The second is the eventless narrative, for example:

> *I broke up with my boyfriend about two years ago—this was very influential in my life because he was the first boyfriend I was really in love with. We dated for almost a year and shared everything together—when he left, my life completely changed.*

Adapted from J. A. Singer and Moffitt, 1991–1992, p. 239.

Results. The self-defining request slightly increased the number of summary memory narratives from fourteen percent in the first experiment to twenty-four percent in this one. Once again, summary memory narratives did not differ in affective quality or intensity from single-event memory narratives.

Participants' affective responses to their memories were not dramatically stronger in response to the self-defining memory request. However, ratings of vividness were stronger than in the previous experiment. Participants also elected to write much longer memory narratives, with an average increase of more than thirty words.

The Third Experiment: Self-Defining Memory Request Versus Autobiographical Memory Request

In addition to asking for a personally meaningful memory, the self-defining memory request of the second experiment was more detailed and specific. It may have created a set for participants to find more complex and lengthy memories, independent of the self-defining aspect of the task. Our third experiment matched an autobiographical memory request with the self-defining memory request. The autobiographical memory request made no explicit request that the memory retrieved have any particular emotional or personal significance. It was hypothesized that the self-defining memory request would still lead to more summary memory narratives than the autobiographical request. However, no difference in the length of the memory narratives for the two conditions was expected.

Half of the participants filled out the self-defining memory request and half filled out the autobiographical memory request. Each group of participants also rated their current emotional responses to the memories they recalled. The criteria for the autobiographical memory request are listed in table 4–2. We attempted to match the wording and format of the self-defining memory request as closely as possible. In contrast to the previous experiments, we also explicitly asked the participants to rate how important the memory was to them.

Table 4–2 Instructions for the Autobiographical Memory Request

The autobiographical memory should have the following attributes:

1. It is at least one year old.
2. It is not something you read about or heard about through the media. It should be a memory that happened to you and that you actually recall, not a memory from your life that a parent or older sibling may have described to you.
3. It may or may not be still important to you in your life.
4. It may be a memory that is positive or negative, or both, in how it makes you feel. On the other hand, you may have little feeling about the memory one way or another.
5. It may be a memory that you have thought about many times or rarely.

In order to find your autobiographical memory, just let your mind wander and choose the first memory that comes to mind. Do not spend a lot of time comparing or rejecting different memories. Just choose one that you can describe on the page provided.

Adapted from J. A. Singer and Moffitt, 1991–1992, p. 245.

Results.   The self-defining memory request yielded seventy-three percent single-event and twenty-seven percent summary memories. The autobiographical memory request produced ninety-two percent single event memory narratives and eight percent summary memory narratives. There was no difference in the number of words for the memory narratives generated to either request. Though the autobiographical memory request included instructions of equal detail and specificity to the self-defining memory request and produced memory narratives of equal length, the self-defining memory request yielded over three times as many summary memory narratives. Clearly, instructions given to participants may influence the kinds of memory narratives they generate.

On the other hand, when we examined the affective response ratings for the memory narratives produced by the two types of requests, there were no strong differences in emotion ratings or vividness of the memories. The only difference of note was that the self-defining memory request produced memories that were judged more important to the participant than memories evoked by the autobiographical memory request. Similarly, when we coded memories for actual references to self-discovery or self-understanding, forty percent of the self-defining memories contained explicit statements of these themes, while only five percent of the autobiographical memories made explicit mention of self-discovery.

The Fourth Experiment: Speaking the Memory Aloud

It is possible that the organization of memory narratives that we have uncovered, with a roughly eighty/twenty split in single-event to summary memory narratives, was a function of writing down a memory as opposed to describing it aloud. The constraint of writing down a memory in a paragraph or two may force participants to leave out more specific details or to stop with only a general description. The same participant, if allowed to talk about the memory, might elaborate the memory, changing it from a summary memory narrative to a summary memory narrative punctuated by a single-event example.

This mode of recalling a memory fits nicely with Reiser's ideas about the hierarchical organization of memory and the flow of memory retrieval from the general context to the specific indexed event. On the other hand, if participants, given the greater freedom of the spoken memory request, still elected on occasion to use a summary memory narrative without a single event specified, it would suggest that the distribution of the narrative types is genuine and not an artifact of the written request.

In this final test of our memory requests and scoring system, the experimenter met with each participant one at a time in a small room within our laboratory. The participant sat face-to-face with the experimenter. Participants received one of the two memory requests (self-defining versus autobiographical) and then notified the experimenter when they had retrieved a memory. Participants were allowed up to three minutes to describe the memory. After the participants had finished recalling the memory, they completed written ratings of their current affective responses to the memory as well as ratings of the memories' vividness and importance. After the memories were collected, they were transcribed from tape so that raters could apply the scoring procedures to them.

Results. As predicted, the spoken memories generated more memory narratives that blended a summarized memory narrative with mention of a single event. If a memory contained both a summary narrative and a single event, it was only scored a summary memory narrative when the summary portion dominated the narrative and the single event or specific detail was mentioned once in passing. To make this distinction clearer, table 4–3 presents a contrast between a pure summary memory narrative and a mixed summary memory narrative from the transcribed spoken memories. Both were scored as summary memory narratives of the eventless narrative type, but the mixed versus pure distinction was noted.

Table 4–3 Sample Pure Summary and Mixed Summary Memory Narratives

Pure Summary of the Eventless Narrative Type (Excerpted): Coming home for homecoming, back to my hometown, expecting to have a really good time with my friends and seeing my girlfriend in particular. . . . Got home—the weekend started off wonderfully. Saw my friends, saw my family, it was great to be back home. . . . Be away from campus life and all of it. It was a very interesting weekend, because that time my girlfriend decided that she wanted to break up, which I was not ready for or expecting.

Mixed Summary of the Eventless Narrative Type (Excerpted): It was the summer before my senior year. **I woke up in the morning and there was a note from my father** that he had taken my mother to the hospital. . . . I had known that she wasn't feeling well and that she was going to the doctor, but then it turned out that she was going to stay overnight and then that night turned into two weeks and then a month and two months and she spent the whole summer there. And she was O.K., but there were high points and low points, times when she was in intensive care. But, like, I was an only child, so that summer my father and I were running around all the time. My father was at work or in the hospital all the time.

Bold type indicates reason for narrative difference.
Adapted from J. A. Singer and Moffitt, 1991–1992, p. 250.

The self-defining request yielded sixty-two percent single-event and thirty-eight percent summary memory narratives, but the autobiographical request produced seventy-eight percent single-event and twenty-two percent summary memory narratives. The request for spoken memories encouraged slightly more summary memories for both types of memory requests. Summary and single-event memory narratives did not differ in emotional quality.

There were also no differences in emotional intensity or memory vividness for the self-defining versus autobiographical memory requests. As in the third experiment, the self-defining memory request produced memories rated as more important to the participant than memories generated in response to the autobiographical memory request. Speaking the memory aloud did not reduce the emotional quality or vividness of the memory narratives.

Discussion of the Four Experiments

First and foremost, this research program has provided us with a reliable method of identifying two different types of memory narratives. We now feel confident in applying the summary/single-event memory narrative distinction to the questions of personality style and mood–memory interactions.

Second, employing three different sets of instructions, we saw a strong tendency of participants to favor single-event memory narratives over summary memories. This tendency may be a function of the constraints of the memory task with which they were confronted. To find an autobiographical memory on demand in a matter of minutes, participants were prone to look for easy landmarks that stuck out in their memories. We received many memories about transitions (high school graduation, end of summer camp, first day of college), accidents, athletic triumphs or failures, sudden deaths or illnesses, and break ups. These one of a kind memories can be accessed more quickly and are of enough emotional intensity that they seem to satisfy the experimenter's intentions. Whether these memories are crucially self-defining is another question and is beyond the scope of this chapter. On the other hand, although there were many pure examples of single-event memory narratives, it was also clear that some participants produced memories that combined a single-event memory and the generalization of a summary memory in the same memory narrative.

This observation leads to the interesting question of what the optimal format of recollection might be. If one recalls a memory in only the vaguest and most abstract form, it could be argued that this summarization eviscerates the memory, removing both its immediacy and affective intensity. On the other hand, if one recalls the smallest details of a memory, but makes no effort to give these details a meaningful or emotional context, one may have produced a memory fragment devoid of impact. Following this line of thought, the middle-level memory, blending generalization with detail, context with specificity, might be the most meaningful and affective recollection for the individual. In cognitive psychology terminology, a memory that blends episodic elements with semantic knowledge (Tulving, 1972) gives us at least two important capacities. We can connect semantic knowledge—facts or truths about ourselves—to a specific remembered episode in our lives. We can also trace these elements of our semantic knowledge to a specific time period or situation that gives these facts a context within our personal history. Neuropsychologists and neurologists, applying yet another vocabulary of memory, have observed that the most pronounced memory deficit in amnesiac patients with severe frontal lobe destruction is a loss of this kind of context. Describing one patient called Greg, Oliver Sacks (1992) writes:

> Greg might learn a few facts, and these would be retained. But the facts were isolated, denuded of context. A person, a voice, a place would slowly become "familiar," but he remained unable to remember where he had met the person, heard the voice, seen the place. Specifically, it was context-bound (or "episodic") memory which was so grossly disturbed in Greg—as is the case with most amnesiacs. (p. 56)

Clinical and personality psychologists have also called attention to memories that lack this integration of context and specificity. As we move toward the next section of this chapter, we shall see that theorists like Shapiro (1965) have historically argued this integrative position. Between the vacuity of the hysteric and the fragmentation of the obsessive cognitive styles lies the integrative and adaptive ego. In the final section of this chapter, we make this argument in an effort to connect memory narrative to Loevinger's stages of ego development.

The existence of these combined summary/single-event memory narratives, especially in our fourth experiment, reaffirms Reiser's view that participants retrieve memories through generation of a general context, which is then made particular by a specific instance of the more general category. Interestingly, we detected two subtypes of summary memories. The *generic* summary memory narrative is a blend of many similar events repeated over a long period of time. Key phrases that signal a generic memory narrative were, "We always used to . . ." "Every summer we would . . . ," and "I can't remember how many times I . . . ," among others. The *eventless* summary memory narrative strongly resembles Barsalou's extended event memory with the exception that it does not include any specific or-detailed discussion of single incidents that happened within the time pe-riod of the extended event. The eventless memory narrative tells an imageless and detail-barren story of a sweeping episode in an individual's life (moving to a new town, breaking up with a long-term boyfriend, train-ing for the state track meet, etc.). To the degree that an eventless narrative becomes specific and imagistic, it should be considered a single-event narrative.

Finally, a few words should be said about the self-defining memory re-quest. It did produce more summary memory narratives relative to the two other memory requests used in the experiments. In retrieving a self-defin-ing memory, participants may be more likely to generate a representative grouping of similar important personal events and then stop there rather than search further for a specific instance of this grouping. They may read the self-defining request as asking for "what is typical about me" and pro-vide this typical or summary memory as opposed to a unique event. Wahler and Afton (1980) found a similar result when they asked mothers to pro-vide descriptions of their children with behavior problems; the mothers had difficulty moving beyond general descriptions that were "characterologi-cal" rather than specific in detail.

In evaluating the future potential of the self-defining memory request, one could say that the method assures the experimenter of (1) a more var-ied distribution of single-event and summary memory narratives; (2) a higher percentage of memories that are considered important to the partic-ipant; and (3) more memories concerned explicitly with themes of self-discovery and understanding. However, claims for the request's ability to invoke more vivid or affective memories than other types of requests were not substantiated. It is possible, though, that any request to participants in a psychology class to generate memories has built into it a fairly strong im-plicit demand that the memory be vivid and affective.

Although the research program we have just reviewed has provided some support for cognitive science perspectives on autobiographical memory and has demonstrated some methodological advances in the collection and identification of autobiographical memory narratives, we have yet to demonstrate its value in personality research. The next three sections of this chapter take up this challenge.

Personality Style and the Structure of Autobiographical Memory

Imagine you are a psychotherapist and during an initial interview you routinely ask your clients to tell you something about their childhoods. In one initial interview the client responds in the following way:

> Let's not beat around the bush. It was horrible. I mean, really *awful*. My father was never around, and when he did come home he was pissed off or bombed or both. My mother was miserable. I don't blame her. I used to try to stay out on the block with my friends as long as I could. Who would want to come home? You knew the next fight was just waiting for you when you got inside.

Now imagine that later in the day you are conducting another initial interview and ask the same question; this time the client responds:

> I was always uncomfortable with my parents. I never felt like my mother respected my father. I remember once when my parents found out they were moving to Indiana in a year and I was in junior high. My dad came home and told us and Mom became irate. We had lived there before, and she hated it. She started telling him she had a great job here and she wasn't going to give it up to go there where she wouldn't be able to find one. She kept telling him how stupid he was for getting transferred and how much she hated him. They fought all night. I remember his face turning red and his eyes looking down into the carpet. I went upstairs and turned up my music and ignored them.

Try to let yourself feel how each of these memory narratives affects you. Now imagine that the weeks proceed and the first client never moves to a deeper level of specificity or detail. His memories are all portrayed in long shots and medium shots. No matter what you ask or in what way you ask, he offers you no close-ups; he does not let you into the tight frame of his life where the scars and blemishes of his life might be visible. He has told you all in summary and you have felt little in return.

In contrast, the second client has gone on to describe several more memories that reflect the ongoing tension between her struggling father and frustrated mother. As you listen, you begin to feel palpably her troubled ambivalence:she loves her father and is disgusted by him; she admires her mother and despises her for her cruelty to her father. The repeated theme of going to her room and turning up the music, of going out with friends, of finding a boyfriend and losing herself in that relationship—of always escaping—emerges. You find yourself drawn into the world of the client and moved by the confusing struggle she has faced and faces.

The two cases we have just described place our summary/single-event memory narrative distinction front and center in the context of personality. We are seeing two different approaches, one highly defensive and one more open, to the threat invoked by childhood memories. The first client employs a mode of remembering that is protective; whether this is how these experiences were encoded or only how he chooses to retrieve them is unclear, but either way he is able to keep specific memories at bay.

Let us draw an analogy between the first client's use of memory and a common criticism of beginning poets. High school students often write highly wrought poems that involve many abstract nouns to represent their feelings (e.g., the use of words like despair, emptiness, solitude, etc.). Dutiful English teachers then explain how more concrete and specific words, particularly verbs, will convey greater feeling to the reader than generalized nouns. (Accomplished writers, of course, have the ability to make any word, abstract or concrete, evocative in the appropriate context.) Part of high school students' infatuation with abstract nouns has the same cause as the first client's tendency toward summary memories. These words allow for discussion of emotionally intense topics, but insure a distance from the experiences at the same time.

In the next section, we review some related research and theories that help us to understand how summary memories may serve as defenses for certain individuals.

The Defensive Use of Memory

Jerome L. Singer (1990b) has written:

> If there is any single formulation that encompasses the complex features of psychoanalysis and related psychodynamic theories, it is that a considerable portion of human thought, communication, social behavior, or psychological symptomatology involves more or less successful efforts to ward off from consciousness or from observation by others a variety of threatening conflictual cognitive contents or emotional reactions. The term Sigmund Freud used most often to represent such warding-off processes was "repression." (p. xi)

We propose that some people may use highly abstract and summarized memories as a means to ward off unwanted images and emotional reactions from their past. Rather than selective forgetting, which is the guiding idea behind most repression research, we choose to highlight a kind of selective remembering. One may not banish an experience from consciousness, but that does not mean that certain details of that experience are not smoothed over or omitted. As Erdelyi (1990) explains, repression researchers' bias in favor of the unconscious has tended to equate any defensive use of memory with full-scale loss of awareness of the item to be remembered. The mechanism of losing a specific memory in the generalities of a generic reminiscence is simply a subtler defensive strategy. Whether the use of summary memories represents conscious suppression or unconscious repression (a distinction Freud did not choose to make, Erdelyi, 1990, pp. 12–14) is less important than the idea that the organization of memory narratives, representing one aspect of a cognitive style, may be employed for defensive purposes. Weinberger (1990) makes this point well:

> Individuals with repressive coping styles are likely to use a variety
> of strategies to avoid awareness of affects and impulses that are
> incompatible with their self-images. They should not only repress
> threatening memories . . . but also recruit several neurotic-level
> defenses . . . such as intellectualization and denial. (p. 343)

Dating back to Rorschach (1921/1942), psychologists have suggested that cognitive style and defensive style may be intertwined in personality. Shapiro (1965), representing an ego psychology perspective, argued that obsessive-compulsives and hysterical personalities have different memory organizations. The obsessive-compulsive, he suggested, has an excellent memory for facts, but seldom integrates this information meaningfully. The hysterical individual remembers the global mood or feeling of an event, but little of its specifics. There is a link here between the tendency to omit meaningful details and the selective summarization of an experience (what may be considered a subtype of repression). Shapiro (1965) writes:

> If it is true that the detailed, technical cognition of the obsessive-
> compulsive and his sharply focused mode of attention are conducive
> to a "good" memory and, as I also suppose, *are not conducive to the
> repression of memory contents*, is it possible that the mode of cogni-
> tion of hysterical people is, by its nature, particularly conducive to
> forgetting and the operation of repression? (pp. 110–111)

More recently, J. L. Singer (1984) has proposed that a global and summarizing style of encoding and retrieving information may reflect a defensive strategy of handling painful or threatening information. Bruhn (1984) specifically has proposed that a tendency to collapse several distinct events into a generic or summarized memory may defend against specific single memories associated with unpleasant feelings. In an earlier study, Hanawalt and Gebhardt (1965) found that single-event memories of early childhood were rated more unpleasant than summarized memories. All of this earlier theorizing and research points to the possibility that participants prone to a defensive avoidance of negative emotion might tend to employ more summary recollections when asked to recall autobiographical memories.

We decided to test this proposition by using our self-defining memory task and our single-event/summary memory narrative scoring system. We administered the Weinberger Adjustment Inventory (WAI; Weinberger, 1989), which includes subscales that allow for the identification of a repressive personality style. As formulated by Weinberger, the *repressor* is an individual who strives for an excessive control over impulses and behavior, while at the same time denying any negative emotion or distress. Accordingly, high scores on restraint subscales and low scores on distress subscales earmark an individual for the repressor group on the WAI. In contrast to this, Weinberger has found that individuals who score relatively low on both restraint and distress scales may be characterized as a self-assured group. Self-assured individuals are more expressive of feelings and, not surprisingly, less prone to psychopathology and stress-related illnesses than the repressor group.

As described in chapter 3, participants wrote down ten self-defining memories that help them to understand themselves and to explain who they are to other people. Would the repressor group of participants generate more summary memories among their ten memories than the self-assured group? It should be mentioned that in previous research (Davis, 1990), some evidence, though not unequivocal, has been found indicating the repressor (as measured by an earlier version of Weinberger's approach) has poorer recall of negative memories than either low anxiety or high anxiety participants. Yet both the self-assured group and the repressor group report roughly equal amounts of distress, as measured by the recent version of the WAI; therefore, we could not confidently hypothesize a striking difference in memory affective content for the two groups. Regarding the affective content of their memories, the only result that would alarm us would be if the repressor group had significantly more negative memories than the self-assured group.

Fifteen of the sampled participants fit Weinberger's criteria for repressor. We matched these fifteen participants with fifteen randomly selected participants from the self-assured group. We then applied the single-event/summary memory scoring system to each participant's ten memories. The repressor group averaged thirty-four percent summary memories, over twice as much as the self-assured group's fifteen percent. This result suggests a possible difference in memory narrative style for these two different personality types.

To examine the difference in emotions for the two samples, we averaged each participant's positive and negative emotion ratings across the ten memories and compared them for the two groups. Though the repressor group showed slightly more positive emotion, they did not differ from the self-assured group for negative emotion. Both groups tended to recall more positive memories and less negative memories; we cannot therefore make a conclusive statement that the greater percentage of summary memories evidenced by the repressor group is serving to ward off negative affect. Yet the fact that we did not constrain participants to recall memories of specific affective content (i.e., "recall a positive or negative memory from your life") may have led the participants to choose more positive memories, whether they were in the repressor group or not. In previous research (J. A. Singer, 1990a), it was found over two experiments that participants presented with a free recall request tend to recall a much higher number of positive memories versus negative memories, regardless of their repressor scores. The result is a floor effect for negative memories in which the extremely narrow range of negative affect does not allow for effective discrimination between two groups of participants. In future research, one could specifically ask for a painful negative memory from childhood and then examine whether repressors recall both more summary memories and less negatively toned memories than the self-assured group. Davis (1990), as mentioned earlier, did find that repressors tend to recall fewer negative childhood memories, but she did not explore the narrative structure of the memories. There is clearly much more interesting research to do along these lines.

What is apparent even from these preliminary findings is that the repressor group showed a difference in their narrative approach to autobiographical memories. Given the accumulating research that repressors may be at greater risk for physical illness such as hypertension, asthma, and cancer (Weinberger, 1990, p. 373), the possibility of using summary memories as a marker for this personality style is intriguing. This suggestion remains a speculative one and will need further confirmation and replication of our encouraging result. Yet it points again to the importance of looking at what is remembered and how it is remembered as well as what is forgotten. It is also exciting to see that improvement in our research methods has allowed us to test some of the seminal ideas and observations recorded in Shapiro's (1965) *Neurotic Styles*. The way that we process information may be a key component to the configuration of our defenses. In ongoing research we look forward to more of this type of convergence between the ideas of the old style ego psychologists (Klein, Mayman, Shapiro, etc.) and mainstream social and personality psychology.

Finally, regarding the implications of this approach for clinical work, we wonder if, over the course of a successful psychotherapy, the first client's memories might subtly change, slowly moving the camera closer until he could allow himself to see the clearest and most painful details of his past. Assessment of therapeutic overcome could conceivably include pre-and post measures comparing percentages of single-event versus summary narrative memories. In particular, it would be fascinating to compare the same memory told in two different narrative formats—in the beginning of therapy as a summary and at the end of therapy as a single-event with appropriate summary and synthesis integrated into the narrative.

Depression and the Single Event/Summary Memory Distinction

There is another area of personality and clinical psychology where the organization of autobiographical memory may prove to be highly significant. The relationship of mood and memory has received a lot of attention in recent years and is dealt with further in the next chapter of this book (see also Blaney, 1986; Kuiken, 1989; Parrott & Sabini, 1990; J. A. Singer & Salovey, 1988). In particular, clinically oriented researchers such as Teasdale (Teasdale & Fogarty, 1979; Teasdale & Russell, 1983; Teasdale, Taylor, & Fogarty, 1980) have suggested that depressed mood may lead to a faster and more extensive retrieval of negatively toned information.

In our review of this literature (J. A. Singer & Salovey, 1988), we failed to find strong evidence for a pervasive mood congruency in the memories of individuals experiencing negative affect. In particular, research results did not strongly support the position that depressed individuals display biased recollection of negative information. On the other hand, evidence was stronger for depressed participants' reduced access to positive information. Accordingly, the mood-memory bias in depressed participants may have more to do with their inability to retrieve positive memories than with their greater access to negative memories. We have argued in that paper and elsewhere (Salovey & Singer, 1989) that the standard assumption of the mood-memory literature has been that positive and negative moods promote the learning and recall of positive and negative material, respectively. Yet, why should we assume that a normal individual who has been made temporarily sad would maintain this mood by recalling congruent negative cognitions? Even a rudimentary theory of motivation, utilizing a minimum of nonobservable variables, assumes that individuals attempt to maximize pleasurable experiences and terminate aversive ones. If this is the case, non-depressed individuals should attempt to summon thoughts incongruent with sad moods in order to remove the unpleasant state. In common parlance, we often hear the phrases "put on a happy face" or "whistle in the dark." Such expressions are exhortations to counteract negative moods with positive thoughts and actions. As we have indicated, it is this lack of positive thoughts rather than an increase in negative thoughts that is found in participants made temporarily sad in mood induction studies. Participants in sad moods might first have less access to the recall of positive memories, but, with time, would begin to draw upon reparative positive information. This process of mood restoration has been dubbed *mood repair* (Isen, 1985).

There is a fascinating link between this mood repair perspective and the organization of autobiographical memory. Williams and Broadbent (1986) reported an unexpected finding regarding depression and memory organization that they have subsequently replicated and extended (Moore, Watts, & Williams, 1988; Williams & Dritschel, 1988; Williams & Scott, 1988). In their original study, Williams and Broadbent found that individuals hospitalized for suicide attempts, when asked to recall autobiographical memories, had great difficulty in retrieving specific memories. They recalled significantly less specific memories than a matched control group and, in particular, less specific *positive* memories. Memories were judged to be not specific if they failed to refer to a time period or the time period extended beyond one day.

Williams and Dritschel (1988) replicated this finding with another group of patients hospitalized for suicide attempts, but also showed evidence of it in a group of former patients who had been discharged from three to fourteen months earlier. However, the former patients' overgeneralization of memories was not more pronounced for their positive memories. The authors suggest that these results point to a stable personality trait in depressed individuals of overgeneralization (as Beck, 1991, has proposed in his cognitive theory of depression), while the finding of less-specific positive memories in the hospitalized patients may be more a state influence of the acute depressive episode. Williams and Scott (1988) and Moore, Watts, and Williams (1988) further demonstrated that this overgeneralization effect is found in depressed individuals who have not made suicide attempts, thus ruling out the possibility that this characteristic is unique to those attempting suicide.

To explain what was initially a "serendipitous" finding (Williams & Dritschel, 1988, p. 229), Williams has developed a plausible argument based upon what should now be a familiar framework to readers of this chapter, Reiser's context-plus-index model of autobiographical memory. Depressed individuals may be less attentive to event cues either at encoding or retrieval. The subsequent unavailability of these cues reduces their capacity to move from more generalized categories of memories to specific single-events. Moore, Watts, and Williams (1988) make this point:

> Depressives' problems in retrieving specific positive memories appear to reside in their gaining access to a general level and being unable to progress beyond it. . . . Defining a general context may be an essential stage in moving down through such a hierarchy to arrive at a specific memory, and it is this search for specific instances which depressives find difficult. The result is that the cognition of depressed people is likely to be dominated by relatively abstract representations of the past rather than specific instances. (p. 276)

For the depressed individual in the midst of an acute episode, recent life events and surrounding cues would make the retrieval of more specific negative memories more likely than recall of specific positive memories. Yet the problem is not only in retrieval of specific positive memories, but in how positive information was encoded in the first place.

Williams and Scott (1988) have suggested that cognitive therapy, by encouraging increased self-monitoring (for example, through the keeping of a diary or log) promotes greater attentiveness in the depressed individual to the details and nuances of life events. The therapist makes sure that more acknowledgement is made by the patient of the positive details of ongoing events. Such improved attention provides the individual with more "tags" or descriptive labels that allow memory search to move from the general context of a memory category to a specific event indexed within that category. In particular, if the individual has encoded information of a positive and self-affirming nature with greater nuance and descriptive specificity, it will be more easily accessed when needed during a more acutely depressed time. This improved access enhances the depressed individual's capacity for mood repair.

McAdams, Lensky, Daple, and Allen (1988) offer independent support for Williams's findings, even though their work stems from a different theoretical orientation and used a different methodology. In their study, depressed and nondepressed participants generated a series of positive and negative memories and then divided up the memories into self-devised categories. Drawing on Tomkins's script theory, the authors hypothesized that nondepressed participants would tend to find multiple variations in their positive experiences (*variant magnification*), while reducing their negative experiences into a few generalized categories (*analog magnification*). McAdams found that depressed participants did just the opposite. They generated fewer and more general categories for their positive memories, while showing more nuance and variation in their categorization of negative memories. This result supports the acutely depressed participants' results in the Williams studies. Depressed participants in both the Williams and McAdams et al. studies showed greater generalization in their positive memories compared to nondepressed participants.

We decided to take these findings a step further to see if we could generalize them to a nonclinical population. Would dysphoric participants, who register only mild depression on a clinical inventory, be more prone to recall less-specific memories and, in particular, less-specific positive memories than nondysphoric participants? A positive answer to this question would give further support to the mood repair hypothesis as a model of how individuals in general, not just those who are acutely depressed, approach negative moods.

This study also achieved some other important goals (Moffitt, Nelligan, Carlson, Vyse, & Singer, 1992). It allowed us to explore the relationship between depression and memory organization using a more elaborate and systematic method of differentiating memory specificity and generality than either Williams or McAdams had employed. It also extended research on this question to written memories. All of Williams's studies used oral inquiries with participants.

Each participant filled out the Multiple Affect Adjective Checklist (MAACL-R; Zuckerman & Lubin, 1985), which consists of 132 adjectives. It yields subscales of affective states including depression. Participants checked adjectives that described their current feelings. They then recalled a positive or negative memory in response to our self-defining memory task. Unlike our previous administrations of the self-defining memory task, we specified which type of memory—positive or negative—each participant should recall. Half of the participants recalled positive memories and half negative ones.

Participants were divided into nondysphoric and dysphoric groups, according to their score on the depression subscale of the MAACL-R. We scored participants' memories for single-event/summary narratives and compared the distribution of memory narrative types for positive and negative memories. Dysphoric participants recalled a greater percentage of positive summary memories (seventy-four percent) than positive single-event memories (twenty-six percent). Nondysphoric participants recalled a greater percentage of positive single-event memories (sixty-five percent) compared to positive summary memories (thirty-five percent). These results correspond to Williams's results for participants still suffering a depressive episode and to the McAdams et al.'s results for depressed participants versus nondepressed participants. In contrast to Williams's results, no differences were found between the number of single and summary memory narratives in the negative memory request condition for dysphoric or nondysphoric participants. This last finding suggests that the sweeping overgeneralization for both negative and positive memories that Williams found in his long-term depressed patients may be related to both more chronic and severe depression. Still, using a different sample, scoring method, and medium (written versus spoken memories), we were able to find basic confirmation for the relationship of memory organization to depression. More dysphoric participants did find more general and less-specific positive memories than nondysphoric participants.

Let us step back from this research and try to put it into a possible framework for understanding how memory organization and mood repair could account for some aspects of depression. First, as the Williams studies proposed, individuals prone to depression may possess a stable tendency to overgeneralize during both the encoding and retrieval of information. Second, as a depressive episode begins, an individual's level of energy, both physical and mental, becomes compromised. Third, as the mood intensifies, it may begin to preoccupy the individual, demanding more and more attentional resources. This last point has been well-documented in research by Ellis (Ellis, 1990; Ellis & Ashbrook, 1988; Ellis, Thomas, & Rodriguez, 1984), Conway (Sullivan & Conway, 1989; Conway & Giannopoulus, 1991), and others (Potts, Camp, & Coyne, 1989; Watts & Cooper, 1989). Ellis has shown that depressed individuals have more difficulty with effortful memory tasks than nondepressed individuals, particularly during the encoding stage (Ellis & Ashbrook, 1989).

Why does depressed mood rob the individual of attentional resources and intrude upon performance of complex cognitive tasks? One possibility that Ellis suggests is that depressed individuals become more absorbed in thinking about their mood state. It is not clear what function this kind of introspective brooding serves for the individual, but it is quite possible that this self-absorption siphons attentional resources away from other internal or external stimuli. Alternatively, as Kihlstrom (1989) suggests, depression may lead to a generally lowered arousal level, causing poorer processing of any information that is not immediately salient to the individual. Either possibility, diverted or depleted attentional resources, means that the individual will be less effective at processing more challenging or difficult information.

We can link the steps of this tentative model together. Individuals prone to depression start with the tendency to process information in an overly general way, failing to encode distinctive details and nuances of stimuli or events. In particular, these individuals are less sensitive to the specifics of positive events, tending to encode them in more general terms. When life circumstances provoke a more acute depressive episode, these individuals may become preoccupied with the negative cognitions and imagery that accompany the depression. They may also feel depleted of physical and mental energy. According to the mood repair hypothesis, normal individuals would begin to search their memories for uplifting and highly positive experiences in an effort to counteract the depressive thoughts. However, chronically depressed individuals entering an acute episode are faced with two severe obstacles. Because of their summarizing style of encoding information, they have fewer specific positive memories that they can invoke in their battle against their depression. Second, because the positive events they have encoded are less numerous and richly encoded, the task of summoning them from memory is more effortful. Compounding these difficulties, depressed individuals, due either to self-absorption, fatigue, or both, have fewer attentional resources to allocate to information processing. The result, as Williams demonstrated, is that depressed individuals become stuck at the general context level of autobiographical memory. They are much slower, perhaps due to the cognitive effort it requires, to identify specific events, particularly positive ones, stored in memory. The fact that depressed individuals in some studies were able to generate more specific negative memories than positive ones may simply be a function of the saliency of negative external cues when they were depressed (particularly if they were hospitalized); the movement from the general negative memory to the specific is simply a less difficult task.

Looking at depression from this standpoint, it would seem important for therapists to work with clients on how to enhance their mood repair capacities. As indicated earlier, cognitive behavior therapies, with their emphasis on altering maladaptive patterns of encoding information as well as their efforts at creating new success experiences for these patients, directly address the need for more effective mood repair. In a similar vein, antidepressant medications may return necessary levels of energy and concentration to depressed individuals, which then allow them to search more deeply in memory and to essay more difficult processing tasks, such as encoding nonsalient or mood incongruent information. The combination of increased activation and improved strategies for encoding and retrieving positive information may play a central role in recovery from an acute depressive episode.

This tentative proposal requires thorough empirical investigation, but at the very least it demonstrates how research and ideas from cognitive science, personality and social psychology, and clinical psychology may converge to offer insight into an important clinical syndrome. As in the previous section on the defensive use of memory, we have tried to suggest that narrative structure in addition to the content of memories holds great promise as a research tool. In the last section of the chapter, we return to McAdams's life story view of identity and attempt to locate our summary/single-event memory narrative distinction within this model.

Narrative Structure and the Life Story

In the previous chapter, we detailed McAdams' life story model of identity, describing two personality variables (motives and narrative complexity) and four major components of the life story. McAdams linked individuals' narrative complexity to the status of their ego development. Individuals with less complex and more straightforward life stories, it was predicted, would show less evidence of ego integration and differentiation as measured by Loevinger's sentence completion task.

McAdams operationalized narrative complexity by analyzing participants' life story narratives for the number of generic plots present. The concept of *generic plots* was introduced by Elsbree (1982), who proposed that five core story lines tend to be repeated in stories across cultures and history. Participants high in ego development tended to have more generic plots present in their life story narratives than participants low in ego development. McAdams (1988) summarizes:

> Whereas a major plot line may involve establishing and consecrating a home for a given individual high in ego development, he or she may juxtapose that category of plot with several other plots—enduring, suffering, taking a journey, engaging in a contest, and/or pursuing consummation. The person, low in ego development, on the other hand, tends to stick with one or two basic plots, focusing on one or two fundamental narrative forms and constructing variations on each. (p. 122)

Although the number of interweaving plots participants bring to their life stories may indicate the complexity of their ego development, we have proposed in this chapter another way to approach the life story's narrative complexity. We have already suggested that the generality or specificity of a memory narrative may also be an indication of the individual's personality organization. Could these same memory narratives inform us about ego development as well? For example, at the lowest level of ego development (Loevinger's stages I-1 through I-3), Loevinger (1976) has suggested that cognitive complexity is rather minimal. Individuals engage in stereotyping and cliches, while relying on simplistic formulations of ideas and experiences. Such simplicity could be expressed in two extreme forms of memory narratives. At the extreme of memory specificity, participants might generate memory fragments. These recollections would be stray details that have no apparent meaning or greater significance in the person's life; they show no evidence of integration or connection to thematic lines of the life story. In Tomkins's terms, such memories would be merely transient scenes. An adolescent patient of ours, when asked for his earliest memory as a child, provided an excellent example of this type of memory:

> My earliest memory is of my dad driving a big tractor across my grandfather's field. That's all I can think of. Except there used to be ditches in the field, maybe irrigation ditches and they'd pour something into them; it looked like salt. That's it.

In contrast to this memory, but at a similar level of ego development, would be a stereotyped generic memory that revealed virtually nothing of uniqueness or specificity about an individual. A participant from our self-defining memory study provides an illustration:

> Everyday after school, I remember the smiling face of my mother waiting for me when I came into the house. There she was without fail, and I would have my snack of a cupcake and milk.

At the next levels of Loevinger's framework (stages I-3/4 through I-4), there is greater differentiation in participants' cognitive complexity. Participants begin to detect patterns and meanings in their behaviors. Working from the two poles of memory narratives, we might expect richer nuance and more evidence of emotion in a single-event memory narrative, but the summary memory narrative might display more attempt to relate its content to themes of importance in the individual's life. In the following single-event memory, we see more investment and personal significance invested in the memory:

When I was in seventh grade, there was a real cocky bully in my gym class. He decided one day to try and choke somebody with a jump rope after class. I saw this take place, and I came up from behind him and tore him away from his victim while people just stood around and watched. I couldn't believe everyone was that afraid that they wouldn't help the guy. The bully tried to act tough to me, but I just walked away and he never gave me any more problems. He previously had harassed me a bit. I just ignored him.

The participant describes a very specific incident from his life, but gives hints that this experience has implications for how to handle intimidating situations in his life. At the other end of the continuum, the following participant describes a summary memory that blends several events together, but also alludes to the greater significance of these events in her life:

I remember being a freshman in high school and never having thought I was particularly pretty, or ugly for that matter, and suddenly boys were calling me gorgeous! Wow. I thought it was just a fluke but then older guys started flirting with me, and I got used to it—but I'll never forget the thrill of that first "gorgeous."

Finally, at the highest level of ego development (Loevinger's stages I-5 to I-6), participants display a capacity for complex conceptual patterns, an ability to express and tolerate ambiguity, and more distance or objectivity regarding the experiences they relate. Applying these criteria, one would expect participants' memories to blend a meaningful thematic context with a highly evocative and affectively vivid single-event. Here is an example from our self-defining memory research:

It was the beginning of the fall season of my sophomore year in high school and my family had just moved to Delaware. I had been playing soccer since second grade on all-girl teams and mostly guy teams, and I found out the team was not a female soccer team. Well, I love soccer and did not really want to give up and I figured I've been playing soccer with guys all along. It was the first practice and here I was sitting in the car and all of a sudden I got really nervous and scared. It was getting to the point where I didn't want to play. All my sister said, after I told her I didn't want to play, was to just try it—you can do it. Well, I just needed that little push—I went out, made the team, had some difficulties with the guys who did not like it, but most really respected my playing and skills. Thinking about this memory, I realize I need the backing of my family and/or friends for support. I really like to know someone is behind me—but as soon as I know I just go out and try and give it everything despite what happens. Also I realize I feel that I am willing to try anything if I want it. I also feel there shouldn't be any barriers of any kind (sex, race . . .) and everyone should get a chance.

This memory demonstrates the participant's capacity to combine a highly specific single-event in her life (sitting in the car before the first day of soccer practice) with a summary memory (the remainder of the season and her ultimate success). By combining these two types of memory narratives, she is able to draw an overall meaning and self-definition from them. The fear captured by the single-event memory of her conversation with her sister highlights the subsequent determination and courage she showed in the many weeks of the season that followed. The memory successfully integrates the two ends of the narrative continuum in a way that preserves the affective immediacy of the moment and the thematic power of the summarized account. Through this integration, both the single-event and the summarized memory gain a resonance and added meaning that neither would have in isolation.

Some Concluding Remarks and Cautions

In proposing this blended summary/single-event memory as a highest stage of ego development, we are advocating, along with Loevinger and McAdams, a certain normative bias about what is optimal for human development. We are suggesting that a blend of abstraction and immediacy, of reason and emotion, makes for the fullest and most actualized adult life. In making this claim, we should call attention to its status as a claim or position rather than a biological or psychological reality. Too often, our stage theories in psychology, whether Piaget's, Kohlberg's, or Loevinger's, have been presented as if they were genetically hard-wired. We prefer to see these theories as first and foremost philosophical stances about where development should lead and what one's vision of the good life and the good man or woman should be. The certainty with which these theorists expressed their immutable sequence of stages far outstrips the empirical evidence they marshalled or that has since been marshalled to support their ideas as originally proposed.

Our own perspective on the developmental desirability of self-defining memories that blend generality and specificity has been reinforced through our clinical work. We have seen the benefits for patients when they are able to put an inchoate and terrifying memory or dream into a thematic context, which both organizes their experience and gives it meaning. In some ways, a therapist's work is about helping a patient to find a moral to confused or inexplicable thoughts, feelings, and behaviors in their lives (though this moral on occasion may be one of resigned acceptance and tolerance of the chaotic and ineffable aspects of life).

According to the *Webster's New International Dictionary* (1952) the word moral comes from the Latin *moris*, which means manner, custom, habit, way of life, or conduct (p. 1592). As a noun, moral, means "The essential moral import or instruction of or derivable from a fable, a narrative, an occurrence, an experience, etc., or the practical lesson taught" (p. 1592). As an adjective, it is "characterized by excellence in what pertains to practice or conduct; springing from, or pertaining to, man's natural sense or reasoned judgment of what is right and proper" (p. 1592). The definition goes on to say that Aristotle distinguished the "moral virtues" from the "intellectual virtues." When we examine the word virtue, we see that the moral virtues were concerned with how one conducted oneself in practical life, while the intellectual virtues pertained to wisdom and insight (p. 2849).

These distinctions seem quite appropriate in highlighting the perspective we take on personality and that we describe in regard to therapy in Chapter 7. As we have articulated our vision of personality and self-defining memory, we are emphasizing how individuals construct a coherent narrative that unifies and offers purpose to the life they have lived, are living, and hope to live. As this chapter and the preceding chapter have attempted to demonstrate, the richness and effectiveness of this narrative for individuals is found both in its content and its structure. A therapist, as we discuss in detail in chapter 7, may play a vital role for patients as a kind of narrative midwife, allowing the narrative that patients have inside of them to emerge. Crucial to this process, we argue, is the ability of individuals to connect the imagistic single-events from their lives to larger and more abstract integrative themes. They are encouraged to see the linkage of specific events in their lives to other specific events that share patterns of affective experience and meaning. (Here we see the recurring idea of Tomkins's nuclear scenes and scripts.) This blending of specificity and abstraction, is the normative demand we place upon the model of personality we embrace. Despite an obligatory nod to postmodern acceptance of incoherence and ambiguity, we still envision narrative, the ability of individuals to extract a story from their lives, as a road to healing and salvation.

We are certainly less wedded to what the content of this story should be than previous generations of psychologists, but we still posit criteria for what makes a good story. As the previous chapter indicates, the story at some point needs to address the interplay of autonomy and dependence. As this chapter has made clear, the story will be richest if it draws upon both the analytic and synthetic aspects of our nature. In other words, the moral life, the life characterized by excellence in conduct, is a life that has a moral, a lesson to be derived from the events its narrative depicts. We cannot just live, but we must step back and see the meaning, the value, of our lives. Erikson, by depicting the last stage of development, ego integrity versus despair, as encompassing a life review, certainly subscribed to this position. Yet it is a position, nonetheless, and one that places a particularly American premium on utility. We make use of our memories to help us improve our lives; our self-defining memories with their integration of summaries and scenes give us morals that reaffirm or warn us about what to do next. As Aristole's distinction suggests, they are guides to the practical life, to the day-to-day encounters with work, relationships, and family. Yet, life and therapy, though it might be hard to convince much of our culture about this, can also be about something different, though not more or less important, than love or work.

We end this chapter on memory and personality with a perspective that offers a contrast to the ideas we have presented. One of our friends, a clinical psychologist and psychotherapist, is also an avid follower of the rock-and-roll band the Grateful Dead. Although we admire their lyricism and seamless ensemble playing, we have often wondered why he would see ten concerts in a two-week stretch or follow their schedule up and down the east coast. What would make this brilliant and gentle therapist join the tie-dyed throngs of dead heads? He has tried to explain, and the best that we can understand goes something like this: When the band is "on" (and some nights they are quite off), they no longer seem to be playing the music (the music is playing them), and the distinctions of performers and audience break down. The concert is replaced by what our friend calls "intersubjectivity." It is a communal recognition of something sacred and shared, that is not at all about the individual, about the self, or about definition. In fact, it is the opposite of the ability to apply a meaning, a moral to experience. It is about the expansion of the self, to what the Hasidic mystic, Abraham Heschel called, the "meaning beyond meaning." At such moments, the memories to which this book is devoted fall away, and a memory that is larger and wholly inarticulate takes over. It is a memory of a period in human consciousness when unity dominated purpose, and the past and future, with which our theories are so concerned, were still beholden to the present.

This is where the music takes its performers, its audience, and our friend.

In presenting our view of the remembered self, we must acknowledge not only the incompleteness of our theories and methods (this is the easy part, and to do so has almost become a parody of academic modesty) but the more troubling prospect that we have neglected to ask and therefore failed to begin to answer questions about essential aspects of the person. We offer the image of our friend, admist a rhythmic and shadowy horde, eagerly swaying to the first bass notes of "Dark Star," as our cautionary tale.

5

◆

Emotion and the
Remembered Self

And memory being so hopeless bound up with emotion, the flooding im-
ages resolved into those of a single day, the most compelling day . . . of
the year.

—Sportswriter Kenny Moore reminiscing about the 1992 Olympics
held in Barcelona, Spain (1992, p. 74).

In the last three chapters, we have described the importance of self-defining memories and their link to an individual's goals and sense of self. The
present and following chapters explicate some constraints on the remembered self. This chapter is concerned with the ways in which emotions shape
what is encoded into and retrieved from memory, and the next chapter deals
with distortions in autobiographical memories that may be rooted in the
emotional system.

Imagine a theory of memory and identity suggesting that the self is collection of every single autobiographical memory of all the events in one's
life. The primary premise of such a theory is that like a perfect videotape
camcorder, we focus upon, record, and store in memory a copy of everything that happens to us, important or unimportant, profound or trivial. We
still do not know whether long-term memory works in this way, although
it is unlikely to be the case. Such a collection of autobiographic incidents
would seem to produce a rather unwieldy and inefficient amalgamation of
information. It is hard to imagine a self emerging from these boxes upon
boxes of videotaped recordings of consequential and trifling autobiographical events.

What is needed by any theory that posits the self as a collection of memories is a mechanism by which the system sets priorities. In creating the
self, how does this cognitive system decide what to focus upon, record, and

121

store? What events are not worth the videotape on which to record them? Which require intense scrutiny? And which will become the nuclear scenes and self-defining memories that undergird lifelong identity? In this chapter, we suggest that the mechanism that prioritizes memory is emotion. It is the emotions generated by events in the world that determine what we pay attention to, what we try to record in detail, and what we remember years later. We trace how emotion affects what we attend to, the direction of our attentional focus, and the encoding and retrieval of information about ourselves in memory. First, however, we should review the emotional system and its primary psychological function.

The Psychological Significance of the Emotions

Although such a view is not uniformly accepted, we believe that the primary role of emotion in humans is to alert the individual experiencing the emotion that action in some situation is necessary and to motivate or energize that action. In this sense, emotions arouse, direct, and sustain activity (Carlson & Hatfield, 1992). Or, as emotions theorist Carroll Izard (1991, p. 23) has written, "a very general and fundamental principle of human behavior is that emotions energize and organize thought and action." When we experience fear, we become vigilant for signs of danger and, perhaps, inclined to run away. When we are angry, we are motivated to attack. When joyful, we want to connect with other people. When sad, we try not to expend energy and, instead, solicit the help of others or consider changing our lives (cf. Tomkins, 1963). This view of the emotions sees them as having an important and adaptive function: They help channel thinking and behavior toward the fulfillment of goals arising in particular situations (Leeper, 1948).

A passage from William Wordsworth's *Lines Composed a Few Miles Above Tintern Abbey, on Revisiting the Banks of the Wye During a Tour: July 13, 1798* illustrates this adaptive view of emotions as a mechanism that focuses cognitive processes (Hayden, 1977, p. 358–359):

> . . . that blessed mood,
> In which the burden of mystery,
> In which the heavy and the wary weight
> Of all this unintelligible world,
> Is lightened:—that serene and blessed mood,
> In which the affects gently lead us on,—
> Until, the breath of this corporeal frame

> And even the motion of our human blood
> Almost suspended, we are laid asleep
> In body, and become a living soul:
> While with an eye made quiet by the power
> Of harmony, and the deep power of joy,
> We see the life of things.

Wordsworth describes a sense in which his feelings determine his thoughts; his "affects gently lead" him on. In this instance, the affect is one of joy whose "deep power" is to enable the individual to appreciate central purposes and existences without the burden of having to think about the mundane. In the same poem, Wordsworth also describes how such feelings may arise in the absence of specific memories about their original source. In this case, he describes the comforting emotions that are produced by pleasurable events he cannot recall, although they may have profound significance:

> And passing even into my purer mind.
> With tranquil restoration:—feelings too
> Of unremembered pleasure: such, perhaps,
> As have no slight or trivial influence
> On that best portion of a good man's life.

Our view of the emotions as adaptive and functional contrasts sharply with the way in which emotions have been treated by some thinkers, from both ancient Greece and modern American psychology. "Rule your feelings, lest your feelings rule you," advised Publilius Syrus more than 2,000 years ago (Publilius Syrus, ca. 100 B.C./1961). Emotions, in his view, are primitive, animalistic, immature, and disruptive. More recently, relatively speaking, in psychology, Young (1943) defined emotions as "acute disturbance[s] of the individual as a whole" (p. 263), and introductory psychology texts have described emotion as "a disorganized response, largely visceral, resulting from the lack of an effective adjustment" (Schaffer, Gilmer, & Schoen, 1940, p. 505). In this view, emotion is seen as causing a "complete loss of cerebral control" and containing no "trace of conscious purpose" (Young, 1936, pp. 457–458). Woodworth (1940) even suggested that a scale to measure intelligence should contain tests demonstrating not being afraid, angry, grieved, or inquisitive over things that arouse the emotions of younger children. Similar disparaging attitudes toward the function of the emotions accompany cognitive theories that assign to emotion the very limited role of interrupter or "stop rule" in ongoing cognitive activities (e.g., Simon, 1982), implying that clear thinking would continue were it not for emotional arousal. This perspective views emotions as limiting cognitive processes.

We, however, do not view emotions in this way. We begin with the idea suggested by Robert Leeper (1948) that emotions perform the adaptive function of prioritizing incoming information, focusing our attention on what is important, and motivating us to do whatever is needed—at least on first analysis—in the situation. We have described Silvan Tomkins's work extensively in previous chapters concerning nuclear scenes, scripts, and memories. In this context as well, he has influenced our thinking. Tomkins (1962) noted that emotions are triggered when someone encounters a situation that causes a change in what he called the *density of neural firing*. Although it is hard to pin down exactly what Tomkins meant by this quasiphysiological idea, J. L. Singer (1984) suggests that we translate Tomkins's neural firing construct into more cognitive terms—one of schematic match or mismatch. When the events in the environment match our expectations, positive emotions should be elicited (although consistent, perfect matches may lead to boredom). When there is a mismatch (I expected my lecture to go well today, but it did not), negative emotions are produced, with the biggest mismatches associated with intense anger and fear. Thus, in this view, the emotions are an adaptive feedback system that alerts the individual to the present status of the environment as compared with what the individual expected.

This view can also be found among investigators of stress and coping such as Richard Lazarus (1991a), who suggest, for example, that the context in which emotions should be studied is the *adaptational encounter*. In these episodes, "the fate of the business at hand, as appraised by the person, and the emotions experienced are conjoined, one being the basis for the other" (Lazarus, 1991a, p. 31). Lazarus suggests that there is a *core relational theme* for each emotion that captures the way in which the individual is appraising events in the environment or what Lazarus calls the *appraised significance* of the emotion. These themes are reprinted in table 5–1. According to Lazarus, emotions are provoked when situations unfold in which these themes are made salient. The important point for our purposes is that emotional reactions in response to these situations alert the person of the existence of the situation. Although we will not enter the debate about whether the emotional reaction precedes or is a consequence of the cognitive appraisal (see Zajonc, 1980; Lazarus, 1984), it does seem safe to say that the emotional reaction is all-encompassing, salient, and, as a result, difficult to ignore. Hence, emotions are likely to be adaptive as signals to attend and take action.

Table 5–1 Core Relational Themes for Each Emotion

Anger	A demeaning offense against me and mine
Anxiety	Facing uncertain, existential threat
Fright	Facing an immediate, concrete, and overwhelming physical danger
Guilt	Having transgressed a moral imperative
Shame	Having failed to live up to an ego ideal
Sadness	Having experienced an irrevocable loss
Envy	Wanting what someone else has
Jealousy	Resenting a third party for loss or threat to another's affection
Disgust	Taking in or being too close to an indigestible object or idea (metaphorically speaking)
Happiness	Making reasonable progress toward the realization of a goal
Pride	Enhancement of one's ego identity by taking credit for a valued object or achievement, either our own or that of someone or group with whom we identify
Relief	A distressing goal-incongruent condition that has changed for the better or gone away
Hope	Fearing the worst but yearning for better
Love	Desiring or participating in affection, usually but not necessarily reciprocated
Compassion	Being moved by another's suffering and wanting to help

Adapted from Lazarus, 1991.

Emotion and Attention

So, let us begin with the arousal of emotion as a signal to pay attention. We argue that in the creation of the remembered self, emotionally evocative experiences are more likely to be collected, remembered, and, on occasion, become self-defining because the arousing nature of these experiences cries out for further processing. Humdrum events do not capture attention. Emotionally arousing events do, and thus we provide them extra attentional resources.

What Grabs Us?

But what characteristics of events define them as potentially emotionally evocative and thus make them capture attention? Klaus Scherer and Howard Leventhal (Leventhal & Scherer, 1987; Scherer, 1984, 1986) provide a very useful theory of emotion that addresses this question. They suggest that specific emotions are aroused following a sequence of *stimulus evaluation checks* (SECs). These checks are performed as individuals scan their environment, and they occur in a particular sequence (Scherer, 1986). The first SEC is a *novelty check*. At this level, the individual simply determines (and the word determines should not imply awareness of the underlying process; which probably occurs quite automatically or unconsciously) whether there is a change in the pattern of external or internal stimulation. At this stage, the individual is exquisitely sensitive to deviations from baseline. If all is proceeding as it has been, extra attention is not required. We focus, instead, on departures from the steady state.

The next SEC is a check on *intrinsic pleasantness*. The individual must determine whether a stimulus is pleasant—and thus approachable—or unpleasant and likely to require avoidance. These pleasant versus unpleasant judgments are apt to be very gross; they are made quickly, with limited information processing, and generally are based on innate or learned reactions to specific features in the stimulus array. For instance, people are more likely to react positively to faces (even if they only catch a glimpse of them) with dilated rather than constricted pupils (Hess, 1975; Niedenthal & Cantor, 1986) or smiles of joy rather than frowns of disgust (Niedenthal, 1990).

The third SEC—and one very relevant to themes discussed in earlier chapters—concerns *goal significance*. This check determines whether a stimulus event is relevant or important to an individual's goals at the moment, whether such goals are lower level (e.g., for water or food) or higher order (e.g., to find a suitable partner for a romantic relationship, to pass a final examination). According to Scherer (1986), especially important at this level of processing is whether the external outcome is expected for this point in some goal sequence and whether it is conducive to or obstructing of progress toward the goal. This SEC moves beyond gross pleasantness or unpleasantness and focuses on a contextualized kind of gratification constrained by specific goals salient at that moment.

The fourth SEC concerns *potential for coping*. Here, the cause of the stimulus is evaluated and the individual's control over it assessed. Moreover, the individual appraises his or her power to change or avoid the stimulus. As before, this SEC moves forward in providing a more complex evaluation of the stimulus. More than just concerned with whether the events unfolding in the environment should be approached or avoided, the person now assesses whether he or she can control these events if they are approached or successfully escape them if they should be avoided.

The final SEC determines whether the event conforms to social norms and cultural conventions or whether it violates such standards. If appropriate, a similar but self-referential judgment is made: does this outcome represent a violation of a self-ideal or other self-standard?

Thus, Scherer (1986) suggests that the cognitive system continuously scans stimuli generated within the individual or the environment and executes this series of checks. An emotional reaction is the result. For example, suppose Jerome is at a concert listening to Mozart's Fortieth Symphony, a familiar and enjoyable piece of music. The SECs on these stimuli (the sounds of the symphony) reveal that novelty is relatively low, pleasantness is high, relevance to the goal of relaxing and appreciating aesthetic beauty is moderately high, coping potential is not especially relevant, and compatibility with norms and standards is high. The resulting emotion: moderate happiness. (Great joy might require higher novelty.)

Now let us say that in the middle of the symphony, the conductor, in a burst of exuberance, flings his arms into the air, looses his balance, tumbles backwards, and falls off the stage into the first row of the concert hall. Now, novelty is especially high, but pleasantness is low. The situation is relevant for goals: Jerome is unlikely to be able to continue enjoying the pleasant music following this accident. Coping potential is rather low; the situation is beyond Jerome's control. Finally, this was a violation of norms and standards; conductors are not supposed to dive off the stage. The emotions that result from these SECs are likely to include worry (at first) and perhaps irritation (especially if the conductor has not hurt himself and is perceived to have been careless or publicity-seeking).

Most important, from our point of view, is that the series of SECs revealed this situation to be one with potential emotional consequences. As a result, Jerome sat up and took notice, so to speak. Considerable attentional resources are likely to have been allocated to the ongoing event. And the event is thus likely to be stamped into long-term memory.

Can this SEC analysis be applied to more psychologically significant situations? Let us return to the memory reported by Marcel in Proust's *Remembrance of Things Past* described in chapter 2. As Marcel remembers:

> No sooner had the warm liquid, and the crumbs with it, touched my palate than a shudder ran through my whole body, and I stopped, intent upon the extraordinary changes that were taking place. An exquisite pleasure had invaded my senses, but individual, detached with no suggestion of its origin. . . . Whence could it have come to me, this all-powerful joy? I was conscious that it was connected with the taste of tea and cake, but that it infinitely transcended those savours, could not, indeed, be of the same nature as theirs. Whence did it come? What did

it signify? How could I seize upon it and define it? . . . And suddenly the memory returns. The taste was that of the little crumb of madeleine which on Sunday mornings at Combray (because on those mornings I did not go out before church-time), when I went to say good day to her in my bedroom, my aunt Leonie used to give me, dipping it first in her own cup of real or of lime-flower tea. (Proust, 1913/1930, p. 55, 57)

The memory of Sunday morning teas with Aunt Leonie is vivid because it is emotionally charged; as Kenny Moore wrote in the epigram that opened this chapter, memory is hopelessly bound up with emotion. The original situation was novel in the sense that it only occurred on Sunday mornings, and the madeleine dipped in tea (and Aunt Leonie) were both pleasant stimuli. This situation was expected every Sunday and conducive to the goal of closeness with his aunt and, at a lower level, enjoyment of a pleasurable taste. The situation required minimal coping and was compatible with social norms. Scherer (1986) would expect Marcel to experience joy; we would expect the emotional significance of the situation to account, in part, for its vividness in memory.

Emotions and Attending to the Self

Although emotionally evocative stimuli are likely to capture our attention at first, there is a second attentional process stimulated by emotions. After the stimuli instigating the arousal of emotion are identified and encoded, the emotional experience is followed by the turn of attention inward in a self-reflective state. We have called this process *mood-induced self-focused attention* (Salovey, 1992); *self-focused attention* is defined as "selectively attending to information that originates from within and concerns the self" (Carver & Scheier, 1981, p. 35).

In general, following the kindling of an emotion, we believe that individuals focus attention on themselves, unless their attentions are deliberately redirected elsewhere (Salovey & Rodin, 1985). This effect seems especially strong for more negative emotions, but is also promoted by positive emotions as well. When individuals have emotional experiences, they become self-preoccupied. Their attention turns away from external social cues and shifts inward toward themselves. There seems to be more of an inclination to search inward to clarify the emotional experience, once elicited, than outward. We speculate that during this inward focusing of attention, individuals become aware of changes in thoughts about themselves that accompany the emotion; we describe these changes in self-relevant thoughts later in the chapter.

By shifts in the focus of attention on to internal processes, we mean a reduction of the individual's concern with or awareness of cues in the external world and an increase in the processing of cues emanating from internal sources like the stream of conscious thought, mental images, or physical sensations. For example, we can become so deep in thought—that is, so self-focused—that we don't notice someone entering the room or even hear the telephone ring. Attentional capacity is limited and, more or less, the more resources devoted to internal sources of information, the less are available for the processing of external stimuli. The inverse is also true: we might be so captured by an environmental event, like a loud noise or a beautiful scene, that we lose track of our train of thought in midstream or forget that only a moment ago we were experiencing a nagging headache.

Emotion-induced self-focused attention seems rather obvious among individuals experiencing distressing affects. Sad people seem to withdraw into themselves, becoming less responsive to external cues, a phenomenon that is, perhaps, chronic among individuals suffering from depression. But even the first flush of joy or excitement may be greeted with self-focus. Upon receiving good news, we might close our eyes, smile, take a deep breath, and only then seek out others with whom to share our good fortune.

Because emotions are instigated by unexpected stimuli through the sequence of SECs described earlier, in emotionally arousing situations, one must clarify the source of the emotion and the feelings experienced by matching the incoming information with pre-existing knowledge. These processes involve self-reflective thinking, in part accounting for the turning of attention inward when emotions are experienced. Further, self-focusing in these situations intensifies the emotion, thereby allowing the feeling to be specified better and rendering it a more intelligible motivator of whatever action is necessary (Scheier & Carver, 1977; Scheier, Carver, & Gibbons, 1981). Further, emotions tend to be accompanied by physiological changes that can provide attention-catching cues—a pounding heart, churning stomach, or perspiring brow. Individuals focus attention upon themselves in response to these physiological changes in order to clarify, identify, and determine the cause of this arousal (Gibbons, Carver, Scheier, & Hormuth, 1979; Hansen, Hansen, & Crano, 1989; Wegner & Giuliano, 1980).

There is accumulating experimental evidence that depressive and anxious emotions are indeed accompanied by the tendency to focus attention upon oneself (Sedikides, 1992b; Wood, Saltzberg, & Goldsamt, 1990; see also Ingram, 1990, and Pyszczynski & Greenberg, 1987, for reviews of earlier, correlational studies). In our own experiments involving the induction of moods in the laboratory, we have found evidence that both happy and sad moods are accompanied by a shift in attentional focus onto oneself—a mood-induced self-preoccupation of sorts. For instance, in one experiment, after imagining a vivid situation from the past that evoked strong happy or sad emotions, participants were more likely to complete fill-in-the-blank sentences with first-person pronouns than were participants who imagined more emotionally neutral memories (Salovey, 1992, experiment 1). We believe that the use of first-person pronouns is a reasonable index of whether someone is reflecting on themselves versus attending to the environment while completing this task (Wegner & Giuliano, 1980).

We replicated this mood-induced self-focusing for laboratory participants experiencing induced happy and sad moods with a different measure of self-focused attention (Salovey, 1992, experiment 2). In a preliminary study, we found that when individuals think about themselves (manipulated by asking participants to stare at themselves in a mirror for a few moments), they are more likely to represent themselves mentally using more dimensions and a more intricate organization of dimensions—that is, to increase in their self-complexity (Linville, 1985, 1987). So, we asked participants to complete a measure of self-complexity (involving the sorting of trait words into piles) developed by Patricia Linville (1985) after either a happy, sad, or neutral mood induction. Sure enough, participants in the happy and sad mood conditions increased in self-complexity as compared with neutral mood participants.

Although it may be hard to introspect about changes in the focus of attention and the subsequent contents of one's mind during emotional experiences, we do engage in mood-altering experiences in order to think more clearly about certain kinds of problems, perhaps because these feelings help us to focus attention upon ourselves. For example, a psychologist we know at the University of Virginia listens to the blues on his stereo when he needs to think deeply about a scientific or personal problem. The emotions elicited by this music help him become self-preoccupied, marshalling attentional resources onto his introspections and inner dialogues. After several hours of this self-absorption, he feels better able to generate solutions. Other individuals may dance, meditate, drink alcohol, smoke a pipe, listen to Wagner, or daydream all because the emotions that accompany these behaviors facilitate the turning of attention inward. In this sense, individuals are managing their emotions strategically because the internally focused attention that follows has adaptive value.

Of course, at times, chronic, often negative emotions motivate self-focused attention that is not so adaptive. Perhaps the best example is the intense self-consciousness that accompanies many anxiety disorders. Socially anxious people are identified by their constant (internal) preoccupation with how others might be evaluating them. They are painfully aware that their actions are perceived and, perhaps, evaluated by others, and this awareness produces a chronic reflection upon or rumination about their own performance (Buss, 1980). Similarly, individuals with performance anxieties— whether about taking tests in school or engaging in sexual behavior with a lover—are often characterized by intense preoccupation with their own inner experience. They are so absorbed by monitoring the thoughts racing through their minds and the sensations experienced in their bodies that they cannot attend to the requirements of the test or experience fully the pleasures of interacting with their romantic partner (Kaplan, 1974; Wine, 1971). A vicious cycle characterizes these kinds of anxiety problems. Thoughts about poor performance and inadequacy create anxiety, and anxiety further engenders self-attending. Excessive self-preoccupation can intensify anxiety until the individual is so self-conscious that his or her worst fears of failure are realized (Salovey & Singer, 1991).

Implications for the Remembered Self

So far, we have discussed how emotions channel attention. We have described a two-step process whereby situations that give rise to emotion capture attention but then the arousal of emotion motivates a turning of attention inward. This self-preoccupation makes the contents of the mind and the sensations of the body especially salient during emotional arousal. We believe that the experience of emotion changes the way individuals organize information about and evaluate the self (Palfai & Salovey, 1992; Salovey & Rodin, 1985). This is why memory is so hopelessly bound up with emotion: because along with the arousal of emotion and the turning of attention inward, we are more likely to remember the events of our lives. We do not remember *any* event, however; some kinds of memories are more likely to come to mind than others.

Emotion and Memory

Consider the college student described by David Rosenhan and Martin Seligman (1989, pp. 307–308):

> Within a two day period, Nancy got a C on her Abnormal Psychology midterm and found out that the boy she had loved in her home town

during high school had become engaged. The week that followed her future looked empty since she believed she would now not get into graduate school in clinical psychology and that she would never find anyone she could deeply love again. She blamed herself for these failures in the two most important arenas of her life. For the first days she had trouble getting out of bed to go to class. She burst into tears over dinner one evening and had to leave the table. Missing dinner didn't much matter anyway since she wasn't hungry. After one week, the world started to look better. The instructor said that because the grades were so low on the midterm, everyone had the option of writing a paper to cancel out their midterm grade, and Nancy found herself looking forward to a blind date that her roommate had arranged for the weekend. Her usual bounce and enthusiasm for life began to return, and with it her appetite. She thought, "It will be an uphill battle, but I'm basically O.K. and I think I may find love and success."

Here is a perfectly normal young adult experiencing typical ups and downs in the two major spheres of life: love and work. As Nancy's moods swing from sadder to happier, her evaluations of herself and the world swing with them. When sad, she views herself as a failure. When happy, she is more charitable. We would expect, as well, that Nancy's recollections about her past also follow her moods. When sad, she retrieves instances of other failures, disappointments, and bad decisions. Later, when happier, she may reflect on more positive events. In the remainder of this chapter, we discuss the ways in which ongoing emotions color memory, especially memories about ourselves.

Emotion, Encoding, and Recall

Since the origins of laboratory experimental psychology at the turn of the century, investigators have explored the relationship between emotions and memory. The fundamental question concerning mood and memory during the first half of this century was the documentation of the relative ease of recall of positive memories as compared to negative ones. For example, participants in laboratory experiments who were given lists to study later could more easily recall pleasant words—flower, baby, sunshine—than unpleasant ones—death, funeral, taxes.

Interest in this phenomenon was prompted by three concurrent intellectual trends, a review of which served as a structural pillar of David Rapaport's (1942) classic volume, *Emotions and Memory*, the inspiration for our book. The first intellectual trend was rooted in Schopenhauer's pessimistic philosophy concerning the future of Western society, which had spurred much debate in the infant social sciences about the essential optimism or pessimism of the human species. Studies of individuals' differential remembering of positive or negative experiences promised one vantage point from which this idea could be tested.

Second, Freud's (1938) discussion of repression in the *Psychopathology of Everyday Life* spawned a great deal of research that sought to determine if unpleasant memories were indeed harder to recall than pleasant memories. These studies were to a large extent misguided in their translation of Freud's concern with specific unconscious memories into a blanket investigation of any conscious unpleasant memory the individual might recall; we turn our attention to these issues in the next chapter.

Spencer (1873) and Bain (1868) formulated a pleasure—pain theory of learning also in ascendance at the turn of the century. This theory was crystallized in Thorndike's (1927) *law of effect*, which stated that rewarding experiences were strongly registered in memory, while aversive ones were blocked out. This third theoretical tradition, like the other two, motivated the superficially similar prediction that pleasant experiences should be remembered more effectively and over more time than unpleasant experiences.

Rapaport (1942) also described the two major methodologies used to study the recall of pleasant and unpleasant memories. The first were association experiments, broadly divided into three types: diagnostic, feeling tone, and experience. In the diagnostic study (summarized in Jung, 1919), the investigator presents a series of words to participants who then must describe the first idea that comes to mind following each word; this procedure later became formalized as the free association technique in psychoanalytic therapy. The critical measure in research using this approach is the speed with which someone responds to a cue word. Although initially these word associations were used to identify a patient's psychopathology, later, in the feeling tone studies, (e.g., Smith, 1921; Tolman & Johnson, 1918), researchers compared response times to positively and negatively toned cues. Galton's (1892) experience studies (see also Washburn, Gian, Ives, & Pollok, 1925) represent a parallel paradigm that elicited actual experiences rather than words in response to cues. The results, although inconclusive, tended to show some influence of feeling tone on reaction time and ability to produce the required associations. Positive associations were slightly preferred and more quickly accessed than negative ones.

The second major methodology emerged from the learning laboratory.

Four primary designs were used. In the first, participants were asked to associate pleasant and unpleasant sensory experiences (usually odors) with neutral material. The ease of recall for the previously neutral material was then measured (e.g., Gordon, 1925; Ratliff, 1938). Generally, results were mixed, with no clear advantage for positively associated material. In the second experimental design, participants simply were asked to remember pleasant and unpleasant sensory material. For example, Tait (1913) asked participants to rate a series of colors for pleasantness or unpleasantness and then measured their reaction time on a color recognition test. Tait found an advantage for pleasantly rated colors. The third type of study compared the recall of positive and negative life experiences. For example Fluegel (1917, 1925) asked participants to keep a diary over a month recording the intensity, duration, and quality of their experiences. He found that participants listed more pleasant than unpleasant events. Wohlgemuth (1923) found no advantage for pleasant over unpleasant events in a study of schoolchildren's reports of vacation experiences. Finally, the fourth and most common type of study used experimenter-provided lists varying in positive and negative content and then asked participants to recall this material. For example, Tolman (1917) found that participants were better able to recall positive words from a list than negative ones. Subsequent studies found a slight advantage for positive material, although these studies were plagued by methodological and interpretative difficulties (see Holmes, 1974; Matlin & Stang, 1978).

All of the previously discussed studies required the recall of positive versus negative material. Emotion was not examined as a quality of the subject's consciousness but rather as a property of material stored in memory. Influenced by the growing gestalt movement in the study of perceptual processes, investigators soon turned to considerations of emotion as one part of the subject's "mental set" (Rapaport, 1942). Researchers in this contextual tradition emphasized that the emotional state of a subject during learning and recall would influence the quality of remembered material (Pan, 1926). In perhaps one of the first mood induction studies, Sullivan (1927) manipulated success and failure in a group of children by providing them with false good or bad performance feedback on a laboratory memory task. Children receiving failure feedback, were slower to learn subsequent material. Similarly, Barret (1938) observed by accident that participants who were anticipating a school examination recalled unpleasant material better than pleasant material. These early studies represented the influence of the emerging gestalt psychology's interest in perceptual phenomena and situational context (Bartlett, 1932; Koffka, 1935; Pear, 1922).

A later study by Postman and Brown (1952) epitomizes the convergence of gestalt ideas with laboratory research on emotions and memory. In the gestalt view, systematic shifts in situational contexts were thought to lead to changes in sensitivity to certain kinds of self-relevant percepts. Postman and Brown (1952) hypothesized that recognition thresholds for words connoting success would be lowered in the context of a recent success experience—that is, following a successful experience, individuals should recognize words related to success more quickly than other words. Parallel results were expected in the context of recent failures. In fact, participants given false feedback about their high or low achievement on a laboratory visual perception test were later more likely to recognize words congruent with that experience. In a sense, Postman and Brown's experiment was the first study to manipulate contextual factors within the framework of an associational model of memory and is thus the precursor to nearly all modern studies of the effects of emotion on memory.

Following these promising lines of investigation, interest in the impact of emotion on memory waned during the behaviorally oriented 1950s (Howes & Solomon, 1951) and on into the cognitive revolution that swept psychology in the 1960s (Broadbent, 1958; Neisser, 1967; Simon, 1967). With heavy reliance on a computer metaphor, these cognitive models included processes that were easily compartmentalized, like encoding, storage, and retrieval of information. However, the computer had no obvious analogue for emotion, and early cognitive psychologists had little use for this important but less operationalizable construct. A theory of emotion that depicted it as arousal in the service of cognition was not a surprising result of this ascendence of cognition and decline of interest in emotion (Schachter & Latané, 1964; Schachter & Singer, 1962).

It was not until the late 1970s that the mutual influences of emotion and information processing on each other began to be studied with equal respect accorded to emotion and cognition. Although several different theorists and experimentalists led this (initially) quiet revolution (e.g., Bower, 1981; Isen, Shalker, Clark, & Karp, 1978; Mandler, 1975; Zajonc, 1980), we focus primarily on Gordon Bower's (1981) *network theory of affect and memory* here.

Bower (1981; Bower & Cohen, 1982) explained the impact of emotion on remembering in terms of a semantic network and a spreading activation model of memory, which assumes that ideas are linked together in the mind in a large net and that remembering is a function of activating related ideas that then prime other ideas nearby in the network (Anderson & Bower, 1973; Collins & Loftus, 1975). More precisely, Gilligan and Bower (1984) enumerated seven postulates of network theory. First, emotions are characterized as central units in a semantic network, with many connections to related ideas, autonomic activity, muscular and expressive patterns, and events. These central units are called nodes. Second, emotion-laden material is encoded propositionally (as ideas) within the semantic network. Events are represented in terms of subject-response-object units (e.g., Jack publishes a book; Jack's mother feels happy for him). Third, thought emerges through the activation of nodes within the semantic network. Once a node is stimulated, material (other nodes) associated with it can also be primed, and, if raised above threshold, activated. This activation can spread among conceptual, emotional, and propositional nodes. Fourth, a node can be activated by internal or external sources, including thought, physiological feedback, and environmental stimuli. Fifth, spreading activation is selective, reaching out primarily to neighboring nodes and related concepts. Sixth, associations among nodes are formed during learning. When new material is learned, it is associated with nodes already active at the time. Seventh, consciousness is defined as the network of nodes activated above threshold at a given moment.

Research on the influence of emotions on memory generated by this theoretical framework (for general reviews see Blaney, 1986; Mayer & Salovey, 1988; J. A. Singer & Salovey, 1988) is organized around four psychological effects (suggested by Gilligan & Bower, 1984):

- Superior memory occurs when an individual's mood at the time of recall of a memory matches his or her mood at the time the information was first encoded (reviewed by Ucros, 1989).
- Material that is the same emotional tone as a person's mood at the time of encoding is learned best (reviewed by Bower, 1992; Niedenthal, 1993).
- Material that is emotionally charged is learned better than material that is more neutral (reviewed by Banaji & Hardin, in press; Dutta & Kanungo, 1975).
- An individual's thoughts, recollections, free associations, fantasies, interpretations, and judgments are likely to be thematically congruent with their mood state. For example, individuals make more optimistic judgments about the future when happy and more pessimistic judgments when sad (reviewed by Forgas, 1991; Matt, Vazquez, & Campbell, 1992; Mayer, Gaschke, Braverman, & Evans, 1992).

Although the first of these effects has been difficult to demonstrate reliably (see Bower & Mayer, 1989), there has been reasonably strong support for

the other three. The last of these effects is especially relevant to understanding the remembered self. Ever since Postman and Brown (1952) first
demonstrated that emotions facilitate the recall of cognitive material congruent with the induced affect, this effect, termed *mood-congruent recall*
has been found rather reliably for both positive and negative emotional
states (e.g., Bower, Montiero, & Gilligan, 1978; Madigan & Bollenbach,
1982; Natale & Hantas, 1982; Snyder & White, 1982; Teasdale & Rezin,
1978; Teasdale & Taylor, 1981; Teasdale, Taylor, & Fogarty, 1980; Wright
& Mischel, 1982). Some studies of affect and memory have shown dis-
crepant results for positive versus negative affect. In these studies, positive
affect inductions promoted the recall of positively toned cognitions, while
negative affect inductions failed to lead to parallel effects (Clark & Waddell, 1983; Macht, Spear, & Levis, 1977; Mischel, Ebbesen, & Zeiss, 1976;
Teasdale & Fogarty, 1979). It appears that although mood-congruent recall
is a rather general phenomenon, it may be easier to find among nondepressed individuals for positive events (Matlin & Stang, 1978) and
among clinically depressed individuals for negative events (Matt et al.,
1992) that are experienced more recently in an individual's life (Salovey
& Singer, 1989).

Moreover, and especially pertinent to this volume, mood-congruent recall is unusually likely for thoughts regarding the self (reviewed by
Sedikides, 1992a). Kuiper and Derry (1982), for example, have demonstrated that participants experiencing depressed mood states are much more
liable to process and recall information with mood-congruent content when
it is relevant to themselves as compared to when it pertains to others or to
the environment. If we think of the self as composed of beliefs about one's
physical and mental qualities and capacities, images of one's behavior in
various social settings, one's short- and long-term goals, and a collection
of self-defining memories, it is clear that all of these aspects of the self are
emotionally charged and should thus be especially easily cued by arousing
experiences.

We conclude this section by noting that the theoretical underpinnings and
predictions of network theory have not gone unchallenged. For one, it is
difficult to reconcile the lack of support for the first of its four major predictions with the stronger support for the other three, as described above.
Second, evidence for mood-driven attention and encoding is more strongly
obtained for people experiencing anxiety than those who are depressed,
while mood-congruent recall is more likely found in depression than
anxiety—nuances not originally anticipated by network theory (Williams,
Watts, McLeod, & Matthews, 1988). Moreover, network theory assumes

symmetrical effects across pleasant moods for positive memories and unpleasant moods for negative memories. Yet, at least in some laboratories, it has been easier to obtain effects in the positive than negative domain (Isen, 1985). As we suggest elsewhere in this book, perhaps this asymmetry is because individuals try to terminate negative unpleasant moods by thinking about mood-incongruent events in their lives (Clark & Isen, 1982; Erber & Erber, 1992; Parrott & Sabini, 1990). This motivationally oriented hypothesis, however, is not captured in the strictly cognitive network theory.

The Judged Self

Let us take a more in-depth look at the specific ways in which emotions influence not just our recollections but also our judgments about the self. In *A Christmas Carol* by Charles Dickens, Ebeneezer Scrooge has a hideous dream in which ghosts of Christmas past, present, and future haunt him with horrible images of the consequences of his miserly ways. Upon awakening from this nightmare, Scrooge is relieved and joyful that these awful memories were only a dream. His mood is suddenly positive, and he begins to think about himself differently: that maybe lying deep within him is a generous, caring self. Consistent with these thoughts, Scrooge vows to spread good cheer throughout London and is particularly altruistic toward his long-time clerk, Bob Cratchet.

Dickens has provided us with a clear example (at least in part) of an emotion-induced change in the way in which the self (Scrooge's self) is evaluated. Moreover, Scrooge, feeling the positive emotions of relief and joy, then engages in a variety of prosocial behaviors. Dickens implies that Scrooge's change in mood also led to his thinking about himself quite differently and that his altruism was the behavioral manifestation of these emotion-induced changes in his self-concept.

So, what kinds of changes in judgments about the self can we expect to observe after emotions are aroused? Aspects of the self that might be particularly reactive to emotional experiences include: (a) self-esteem and other evaluative aspects of the self and (b) specific thoughts concerning one's ability to accomplish certain tasks or actions.

Self-Esteem.   An obvious set of cognitions about the self influenced by emotion are those that represent individuals' regard for themselves—that is, their self-evaluation or self-esteem. Mood ratings tend to correlate with self-esteem scales (Wessman & Ricks, 1966), and cognitive theories of depression suggest that lowered self-esteem is one of the causal factors in affective disorders (Beck, 1967).

A few studies have aroused emotions and then measured changes in self-evaluation. For instance, Underwood, Froming and Moore (1980) induced happiness and found that all participants subsequently felt more skillful, competent, proficient, and successful than after sadness was induced. Similarly, Mischel, Ebbesen, and Zeiss (1976) induced positive and negative moods through success versus failure feedback on an intelligence test and found that participants correctly remembered their personal liabilities less than their assets when they expected to succeed than when they expected to fail. Further, those participants who experienced success remembered significantly more assets than did those who experienced failure. In a similar study (Natale & Hantas, 1982), participants made to feel sad in a hypnotic mood induction procedure were less likely to recall positive life experiences, had weaker memory strength for positive information about themselves, and were biased toward recalling false negative information in self-descriptions. Participants who were induced to feel happiness were less likely to recall negative events involving themselves and more likely to recall positive events. Wright and Mischel (1982) found that induced positive affect led participants to form higher expectations for future performances, to recall more positive outcomes, and to make more favorable self-appraisals. Conversely, negative emotions led to lower expectations about future performance, recall of fewer positive outcomes, and less favorable self-appraisals. In our own research, some time after a laboratory mood induction, we asked participants to evaluate themselves on a brief, twelve item scale that asked them, as compared to their classmates, how they regarded themselves on a variety of dimensions that were important to members of this group (Salovey, 1986). Our participants viewed themselves more positively on all dimensions when happy than when feeling neutral or sad.

We also measured how emotions affect evaluative thoughts about the self in a less direct way. We expected that emotions should lead to the differential availability of specific dimensions (or branches) in the self-concept. One way in which the dimensions that characterize the self are identified is through a statistical procedure called multidimensional scaling (MDS). The MDS procedure can be used to create a map of personality traits that describe the self. The way these traits change as one reads them from, say, the left side of the map to the right side of the map or from the top of the map to the bottom constitutes two dimensions of the self. Of course, additional dimensions can be represented as well.

Multidimensional scaling studies of the self-concept (e.g., Conte & Plutchik, 1981) often yield two dimensions underlying various self-rating tasks: a social-evaluative dimension (my good versus bad traits) and an activity dimension (my active, extroverted traits versus quiet, introverted traits). However, we predicted that the availability of these dimensions to the self is not uniform during emotional experiences. Because individuals are expected to become more self-focused following the induction of a mood state, dimensions concerned with social evaluation should become less important relative to dimensions reflecting self-generated processes among individuals experiencing an emotion as compared with individuals in more neutral moods.

We asked participants to rate themselves on a variety of self-referent personality traits (Salovey, 1986, experiment 1). In this study, participants completed this task while experiencing either happy or neutral moods. As expected, the two-dimensional solution reflected a social-evaluative dimension with positive and negative endpoints, and an activity dimension with active/extroverted versus passive/introverted poles. Using a special kind of MDS analysis called Individual Differences Multidimensional Scaling (INDSCAL), we assessed the importance given to these dimensions by the participants experiencing happiness versus those in the neutral condition. Happiness seemed to cause participants not already self-focusing to shift their attention more internally and to become less attuned to the social-evaluative aspects of the self relative to the activity dimension. Of course, it is also possible that happy individuals are simply less likely to care about social evaluation, independent of any shift in attentional focus. In very recent work at Yale University, we have tried to replicate these effects of emotions on the dimensions of the self (DeSteno & Salovey, 1993). So far, once again, there is evidence that the induction of happy moods causes a decrease in attention to evaluative aspects of the self.

Thoughts About One's Abilities.   In addition to global evaluations of the self, the other self-reflective judgment that seems especially sensitive to emotions concerns beliefs about one's capabilities. The idea that thoughts of this kind account for an individual's behavior is one of the major theoretical underpinnings of social learning theory (Bandura, 1977a; 1986) and cognitive behavior therapy (Meichenbaum, 1977; Salovey & Singer, 1991). Clinical psychologists working from these perspectives focus on individuals' thoughts about themselves revealed during therapy, because these cognitions are believed to have a direct effect on performance in social situations. The most influential statement of this position is Bandura's self-efficacy theory (Bandura, 1977b). Bandura contends that an individual's expectations of personal efficacy in some domain determine whether certain behaviors are initiated and then sustained "in the face of obstacles and aversive experiences" (p. 191). Self-efficacy seems to be in part responsible for the selection of particular actions and for mobilization of effort and persistence at a task (Schwarzer, 1984).

It turns out that self-efficacy expectations change when emotions are aroused. Correlational work by Kanfer and Zeiss (1983) suggests that depressed individuals have lower self-efficacy expectancies than do nondepressed individuals in a variety of situations. In addition, induced mood appears to influence self-efficacy expectations regarding behavior in domains such as romance, athletics (Kavanagh & Bower, 1985), and helping other people (Salovey, 1986). For instance, we measured the effects of mood on these kinds of thoughts using a helping self-efficacy questionnaire, which presented participants with numerous helping situations and asked them to indicate how confident they were that they could offer help in each of them. As compared with a neutral mood control group, participants experiencing joy felt themselves much more capable of carrying out a variety of helping behaviors (see Salovey & Rosenhan, 1989, for a description of this study).

Similarly, Salovey and Birnbaum (1989) constructed a twenty-six item scale to measure beliefs about one's capacity to engage successfully in health-promoting behaviors among a group of college students suffering from bad colds or flu. Subjects completed the measure after experiencing happy, sad, or neutral mood inductions in the laboratory, and these judgments varied as a function of assigned mood. Sad students perceived themselves as considerably less able to carry out health-promoting behaviors (and they were also less likely to believe that these behaviors would relieve their illnesses).

Although the exact mechanisms by which emotions exert these effects on memory and judgment are still being debated, a brief trip to a clinic specializing in the treatment of affective disorders reveals the potency of the adhesive that binds emotions and memory. In the next chapter, we discuss another aspect of the remembered self that is, in part, bound up with emotion: the historical and psychological veracity of our self-defining and other autobiographical memories.

6

◆

The Misremembered Self

You have probably heard the Maurice Chevalier song from the movie *Gigi*, where former lovers Chevalier and Hermione Gingold recount for each other, decades later, the story of their last romantic date together (if you haven't heard it, see Ross & Holmberg, 1990, pp. 140–141). The scene is standard Hollywood fare, of course, but what's interesting about this account is that the two tell very different versions of the story, right down to the clothes they remember each other wearing. And, after each conflicting verse, the lovers stare into each other's eyes and sing "Yes, I remember it well." Personal memories that seem vivid and detailed may not be at all accurate, an idea captured by Donald Spence (1982) in his book *Narrative Truth and Historical Truth*. People may have vivid memories that, historically speaking, could not be possible, such as seeing Teddy Roosevelt on television or collecting pennies with the Lincoln Memorial on the reverse in the early 1950s.

In this chapter, we discuss the accuracy of autobiographical memory. In particular, we review three perspectives that try to account for distortions in such reminiscences. The first is the notion of repression, that unpleasant memories are banished from consciousness and not especially accessible to retrieval (Bonanno & Singer, 1990). The second perspective is that of positive illusions (Taylor & Brown, 1988), the idea that individuals construct a happier version of their past than is necessarily the case as a way of maintaining, in the words of Shelley Taylor (1989), the architect of the positive illusion perspective, a "healthy mind." These two points of view, repression and positive illusions, respectively, are what Gypsy Rose Lee sang about when she advised that one should "accentuate the positive and eliminate the negative."

The third framework is the implicit theories and personal histories perspective (Ross, 1989). This point of view emphasizes neither the forgetting of the bad nor the enhancement of the good. Rather, it argues that we construct personal histories from autobiographical memories that are consistent with our personal (implicit) theories about ourselves—in particular, how we have changed and in what ways we remain stable. Moreover, we tend to elicit information from others that confirms these theories about ourselves (Swann, 1987). These implicit theories can often lead to biases in what we remember about ourselves.

Repression

As a starting point, let us consider a modern definition of repression suggested by David Holmes (1990). He describes three characteristics of repression: (a) the selective forgetting of material that causes the individual pain, (b) that such forgetting is not under voluntary control, and (c) that repressed material is not lost but can be retrieved when its impact on the individual is less anxiety provoking. As Howard Shevrin has stated, repressed information is "gone but not forgotten" (1990, p. 103).

Sigmund Freud (1894/1962) first used the terms *repression* and *intentional forgetting* to refer to what he called the warding off from consciousness of memories and ongoing thoughts that created anxiety for the individual. Later, Freud (1926/1959) included repression as one example of a set of defense mechanisms each of which was tied to particular kinds of neurotic syndromes. Many of these famous defense mechanisms were thought to operate through the forgetting or distorting of painful memories; hence, repression, in psychoanalytic circles, began to be thought of as the "queen" of the defenses (see Erdelyi, 1985, or J. L. Singer, 1990b, for good histories of this construct).

A Cognitive Perspective

Despite considerable discussion in the psychoanalytic literature, including a long-lasting debate on what Freud really meant by repression (Is it different from suppression? Must forgetting be unconscious?), in scientific psychology repression has had a rather spotty history. The scientific literature from the first half of the century was perhaps best captured fifty years ago in David Rapaport's (1942) volume *Emotions and Memory*, in which he reviewed a plethora of studies—with a wide array of methodological shortcomings—showing that unpleasant events are not recalled as accurately (or even at all) relative to pleasant events. After considering the methodological limitations of this line of research, as well as that produced during the thirty years that followed, David Holmes (1974) concluded that there was no reliable evidence for the existence of repression.

Twenty years later, however, research on repression has come roaring back, in part due to theoretical insights and methodological procedures contributed from the field of cognitive psychology (e.g., Bower, 1990) and clever demonstrations from the experimental social psychologist's laboratory (e.g., Wegner, 1989). Bower (1990) provides a useful delineation of cognitive processes that may account for the forgetting of unpleasant memories. We outline these processes below.

Motivated Nonlearning. Bower (1990) notes that people can "consciously control the *initial registration* of an event—how much attention they give to it, how they categorize the event, and how they relate it to their other knowledge" (p. 219). In unpleasant situations, people may actively try to avoid encoding all of the awful and gory details of such events and avoid rehearsing in memory what is encoded. Just as we shield our eyes during gruesome scenes in horror movies, we may defend against the initial encoding of information about ourselves that we would rather not remember. Shelley Taylor describes a vivid example:

> An attractive woman in her mid-fifties is driving under the speed limit in the left lane. Behind her are a pair of angry boys in a pickup truck, honking the horn and gesturing for her to move over. As they finally succeed in passing her, they make uncomplimentary observations about her driving and then speed away. Throughout the event, she appears oblivious. Not once does she turn to look at the boys, or, as far as one can tell, even check her rear-view mirror to see what all the commotion is about. Has she noticed the event? Almost certainly. Will she remember the event later in the day? Probably not, at least not as well as someone would who had engaged in a shouting match with the boys (Taylor, 1989, pp. 145–146).

One of us once worked with a client who, in the course of discussing her family, mentioned that she could remember very little about her own wedding. She related that others had discussed the vocal and embarrassing fight that her parents, who had separated shortly before the wedding, had that day. But Sharon, the client, could recall virtually none of it. Several sessions later, Sharon remembered that she had left her wedding reception early, perhaps out of fear that her parents were about to blow up at each other. Her initial report of not remembering many of the details of her wedding, which seemed like a classic case of repression, was because she had absented herself from much of the party. She could not remember the reception because she had not encoded much of it in the first place. Sharon protected herself from encoding troublesome memories by physically leaving the scene of the action. We may also psychologically absent ourselves from encoding emotion-laden events by, for example, getting drunk, become distracted by unimportant details, or simply not attending to them. The absence of such memories may look like repression, but, in fact, there is no trace in our long-term store.

Motivated Overwriting of Memories. By overwriting, Bower (1990) is referring to the learning of different associations to the cues that normally would trigger the recall of depressing, humiliating, or otherwise unpleasant autobiographical events. So associations that are negative to a particular person or situation could be replaced by rehearsing new, more pleasant associations, effectively wiping out those that are repugnant. For instance, if one has undergone cognitive therapy successfully and has trained oneself to substitute automatically positive images and memories for distressing ones, it is likely that those distressing memories will not be as easy to retrieve.

Over time, for example, Sharon may reconstruct a memory of her wedding that is not historically true by telling stories in response to queries from friends and families about events that she suspects happened. In a sense, she can use the standard wedding script to fill in the gaps in her memory of her own wedding. Over time, these stories may become assimilated into her recall of the original event. After one of our own weddings, two relatives insisted that they had never spoken to one another at the wedding because they had a long history of ignoring each other at previous family functions. Years later, the family watched a videotape of wedding highlights and discovered, to everyone's amusement, that these two relatives had hugged and kissed each other at the reception.

Retrieval Failures. Bower believes that retrieval failures constitute the largest contributor to forgetting (Bower, 1990). The idea here is that, although the past events may reside intact in memory essentially forever, we often do not generate the cues that would make them accessible to us. Thus, that embarrassing children's birthday party during which we threw up ice cream and cake on the hosts' living room carpet may not readily come to mind as adults not because it has disappeared from long-term memory but rather because we rarely generate or receive a cue specific enough to call it to our attention. One of the major ways in which mnemonic devices work is by providing a structured set of retrieval cues that allow us to recall forgotten material easily.

In this sense, the computer metaphor for human memory is appropriate. When a file on a computer's hard drive is erased, the contents of the files are not physically removed from the hard drive. Rather, the labels or tags for the files are erased so that the contents of any one file can no longer be retrieved. Over time, the files may be overwritten by new material, but not necessarily. The file may remain on the disk indefinitely; it just cannot be accessed because its label—the retrieval cue—is gone. Like psychotherapy, some computer utility programs can be used to relabel a file and retrieve its forgotten contents.

Representative Lines of Research

Present-day research findings that are consistent with the idea of repression have been generated primarily through laboratory research on posthypnotic amnesia, self-deception, and subliminal perception.

Posthypnotic Amnesia. It was Freud who most enthusiastically suggested that posthypnotic amnesia, the tendency not to remember events that took place during a hypnotic trance after the trance is over, may provide the vehicle for understanding repression and the influence of repressed information on consciousness. Freud viewed posthypnotic amnesia as resulting from the repression of memories associated with the hypnotic experience, even though these memories were not necessarily unpleasant (Kihlstrom & Hoyt, 1990). These beliefs formed the basis of a method of studying repression by Luria (1932). Luria suggested to subjects during hypnosis that they had committed a ruthless and gruesome crime but also that they would not remember anything about it. After the trance was ended, the subject rarely remembered much about the hypnotic experience. However, in a word association test, subjects would tremble and fidget when words related to the criminal act were used as cues. The idea was that although subjects couldn't remember the suggested criminal act, its psychic impact still could be measured. Similar results have been obtained with milder hypnotic suggestions regarding anxiety (Levitt, 1967) and aggression (Reyher, 1967).

Self-Deception. Harold Sackeim at New York University tries to capture the notion of repression as essentially self-deception (Sackeim, 1983). He defines self-deception as the situation in which an individual holds two contradictory beliefs simultaneously but only one of these beliefs is subject to awareness. What determines which belief is subject to awareness and which one is not, in this view, constitutes a motivated act (Sackeim & Gur, 1979).

Consider the following example. One of us studies jealousy (e.g., Salovey, 1991). In interviewing research subjects, we always stumble upon individuals who insist, without any doubt, that they have never felt jealous. Jack insists that his wife of several years, Deborah, would never have an affair or cause him one moment of jealousy. Yet, at the same time, Jack always scans his telephone bill for unusual calls, rummages through Deborah's purse, and, occasionally, reads her mail, all the while insisting that he isn't the jealous sort. Sackeim (1983) would suggest that, although Jack claims he is not jealous, indirect evidence suggests that at the same time he holds a set of very suspicious beliefs about his wife. And, if he ever catches Deborah in a compromising act, he probably will claim that, in his heart, he always knew that she could not be trusted. Sackeim suggests that we often hold logically contradictory beliefs, but keep only one set in conscious awareness because this deception helps to avoid pain and, more importantly, to advance potential pleasure.

At a recent meeting of the International Society for Research on Emotions (ISRE), the philosopher Laurence Thomas suggested that self-deception might be involved in the process that he calls "doubling." Doubling is the state in which a person engages in behavior directly contradicted by deep-seated values and beliefs. Thomas points to the case of Nazi doctors at Auschwitz who engaged in horrible experiments that resulted in the deaths of thousands of people yet went home each night to their families or even practiced life-sustaining medicine in clinics outside the walls of the death camp. It seems hard to imagine such daily hypocrisy without invoking concepts like self-deception and even repression.

Tendencies toward self-deception appear to be fundamental and relatively unchangeable. Richard Lettieri (1983) recruited individuals to participate in a psychotherapy to increase self-awareness. These individuals first listened to a lecture about the importance of self-awareness and self-knowledge and then learned Gendlin's (1979) focusing procedure in which they practiced attending to their inner feelings and the personal meanings attached to them. On scales measuring self-deceptive tendencies, subjects did not differ before and after this treatment. So even a form of psychotherapy designed to help clients get in touch with deeply rooted feelings and memories does not seem to reduce tendencies toward self-deception.

Subliminal Perception.   The idea that repressed memories might be revealed through subliminal perception—the influence of information (usually unseen visual cues) on subsequent behavior without awareness of the original information itself—dates back to work at the turn of the century by Poetzl (1917) that was refined in midcentury by Fisher (1956). Poetzl and Fisher exposed subjects to fleeting (nearly subliminal) visual images for about one-hundredth of a second—for example, a bird in flight. Subjects generally could not identify the image immediately after seeing it. However, themes of birds or bird-like images were subsequently identified in their dreams and free associations. Sometimes, Poetzl reported, threatening images would be transformed into safer ones in subsequent dreams and other accounts.

In more modern work, Howard Shevrin (1988) presents individuals with subliminally exposed words that relate to the person's particular conflicts, anxieties, and problems. When subjects are exposed to these words, they show a response called an event-related potential (ERP) measured by electrodes attached to the scalp; neutral words do not cause the ERP response. Interestingly, when these same words are presented supraliminally—that is, for longer periods of time so that the individual can see them—recognition is slower than for the neutral words. Shevrin believes he has demonstrated a process that is a lot like repression: the unconscious mind seems exquisitely sensitive to these conflictual words, but the conscious mind is slow to recognize them. This may represent the difference between denial or "suppression", a conscious act, and repression, an unconscious one.

Positive Illusions

Without resorting to concepts like repression or subliminal perception, social psychologists have been documenting systematic ways in which individuals distort their past in the service of feeling better about themselves in the present. Two major lines of work in this regard are what Greenwald (1980) has termed *beneffectance* and Taylor (1989) *positive illusions*.

In 1980, Anthony Greenwald authored a landmark paper in which he argued that the ego is characterized by biases that are "strikingly analogous to totalitarian information-control strategies" (Greenwald, 1980, p. 603). Of particular relevance here, Greenwald argued that we tend to remember ourselves as more influential or responsible for events than others and also that we tend to take responsibility more for desirable than undesired outcomes, a revision of personal history that he called beneffectance. Greenwald likened this process to an Orwellian government that reconstructs past history in order to place its leaders in the most favorable light.

There are many ways in which these pervasive biases influence the remembered self. For example, we tend to believe that we control outcomes that are chance events (Langer, 1975). This behavior can be seen in the gambling casino, where individuals may play games like roulette, in which the outcomes are entirely random, but believe that they have developed some sort of system that allows them to earn money above the pre-established odds. Similarly, people often speak of a chance meeting with a future spouse or lover as predetermined rather than due to luck (but see Bandura, 1982). The past is often reconstructed as if the individual were the master of his or her fate. People are reluctant to admit to being in the right place at the right time, preferring instead to ascribe their successes to special insights, planning, or skill.

The tendency to take responsibility for outcomes that may be random, however, seems limited to positive events. Losses are blamed on the incompetencies of others, forces beyond control, or mere misfortune. As therapists, we often see clients make dramatic and positive changes in their lives, while at the same time some others plunge into deeper despair. At case conferences, we rarely blame ourselves for a client's intractability, deterioration, or, in the extreme case, suicide. Yet, we often point to key insights or techniques on our part as the cause for therapeutic success (cf. Meehl, 1973).

Similarly, we are likely to take responsibility for outcomes that in retrospect, seem more positive. During the Watergate scandal, a bumper sticker began to appear on cars all over the country saying, "Don't Blame Me, I Voted for McGovern." The 1972 election had produced a landslide victory for Nixon over McGovern, but, but two years later the bumper stickers were so numerous that it seemed the vote must not have been counted correctly.

In describing these biases in recollecting self-relevant information, Greenwald (1980) took the interesting position that they are necessarily harmful, even if relatively pervasive. "The ego's biases," he wrote, "will produce cognitive stagnation in a person who is capable of greater developmental achievement" (p. 614). Interestingly, Greenwald advances this position while at the same time citing evidence from others suggesting that individuals suffering from depression more accurately represent their role in producing positive outcomes (e.g., Alloy & Abramson, 1979).

Shelley Taylor (1989), on the other hand, argues that the kinds of self-serving memory biases described by Greenwald, what she calls *positive illusions*, promote mental and physically well-being. Five years ago, Shelley Taylor and Jonathon Brown (1988) wrote a highly influential article in *Psychological Bulletin* titled "Illusion and Well-Being" that has become one of the most cited papers of the last decade in psychology. Their thorough and scholarly tour through fifty years of literature catalogues the ways in which individuals distort the truth about themselves and then documents how such distortions serve to promote positive mental health rather than neurosis. Most theorists working in the psychoanalytic tradition on repression claim that this defense proves psychologically costly to the individual; although the person repressing memories of painful experiences might be spared the immediate pain generated by ruminating about them, psychoanalytic theorists believe that ultimately such repressed memories cause more severe harm through their unconscious influence on everyday behavior. Not so, according to Taylor and Brown, who, instead, view the accentuation of the positive and the elimination of the negative as the forces that conspire to keep us feeling good about ourselves.

Their article, which documents a number of positive illusions—unrealistically positive views of the self, the illusion of control discussed above, unrealistic optimism about the future—picks up where Greenwald's totalitarian ego leaves off and should be required reading for all mental health professionals. What is unique and more relevant for the issues with which we grapple here is the contention that such distortions in beliefs and memories concerning oneself are characteristic of the mentally healthy person. Taylor (1989) provides a touching series of accounts of individuals who managed to cope with tragedy—losses of loved ones, physical disabilities, breast cancer—by misremembering and distorting information about themselves and the world.

As we wrote this chapter, the northeaster of 1992 was ripping its way through the mid-Atlantic and New England states. Higher tides than had been recorded for over one hundred years combined with rain, sleet, snow, and strong winds to cause severe flooding along the shoreline. Thousands of beach-front homes were destroyed in New York, New Jersey, and Connecticut as old seawalls were battered by the waves. A report on the radio featured a family in Brooklyn whose home was washed out to sea. No one was injured because the family was not home at the time; they were at synagogue praying at the Sabbath morning service. Interviewed the next day on the radio, the father of this family said, "We prayed to God, and he spared us; had we not been at synagogue, we wouldn't have survived."

We remain agnostic about whether this man's interpretation of the unfortunate events in his family's life represent's illusion or reality. We do note, however, his choice in understanding the event. Because they were at synagogue rather than at home, the members of his family were spared personal harm, although they lost everything. Wouldn't just as parsimonious an explanation have been that God responded to his family's prayers by destroying their home? But, of course, this man chose not to understand the sequence of events in this way. His version allowed him to maintain faith, thankfulness, and purpose in the face of what is clearly a catastrophe. In a way, it is a positive illusion: faith spared his family.

Sometimes, it would seem, a more negative remembered self is created in order to promote longer-term psychological adjustment. Although neither of us treated her in psychotherapy, we know a thirty-year-old woman who has been happily married to a businessman for five years and is the mother of two small children. Though college educated, she has chosen to devote herself to full-time motherhood. By all accounts, this woman seems mentally stable, outgoing, an excellent parent to her two wonderful children, and a leader in her community. Yet, this woman firmly believes that her childhood was characterized by physical and mental abuse by virtually all of the members of her family. Although we cannot evaluate the veracity of her claims (and we in no way want to minimize either the frequency or mental health implications of child abuse) no one who knew this person as a child—family members, close friends of the family, teachers, peers, guidance counselors, family physicians and the like—believes that her childhood was in any way remarkable. We are all aware of cases in which a conspiracy of silence surrounds the abuse of a child, but let us also consider the hypothesis in this case that these memories of abuse, although very real to this individual, are memories of events that never happened.

It seems that this individual's motivation to raise her children, pursue her interests, and be active in the community is fueled by the view of herself as a survivor, as someone who, against all odds, succeeded in overcoming an abusive childhood. To challenge this memory would be to rob this individual of her identity. In a way, this sense of surviving against the odds is a positive illusion, even if its origins are quite negative. Now many therapists might argue that confronting the veracity of these childhood memories is crucial, ultimately, for a conflict-free adulthood and successful parenting. But it is hard to argue with the apparently successful way in which this woman lives her daily life. Might the process of identifying these childhood memories as a misremembered self do more harm than good? In a sense, we have provided an example that is precisely the opposite of repression. Here we have the vivid memory of negative events that may not have transpired in the service of promoting a positive working self-image.

The Construction and Maintenance of Personal Histories

So far in this chapter, we have discussed distortions of the remembered self that could be said to be "in the service of the ego." Whether through repression or the creation of positive illusions, these failures and fabrications of memory generally serve to bolster how one views oneself—that is, they are *self-enhancing*. Another tradition in modern psychological research on memory and the self suggests that the creation or distortion of memories is not necessarily motivated by self-esteem bolstering. Rather, in this view, individuals misremember the events of their lives in order to be seen and to see themselves as consistent. The idea here is that we have rather well-articulated senses of who we are in the present, and then we distort memory in order to create a sense that we have always been that way. Moreover, we seek opportunities for interactions with others that will underscore and perpetuate this sense of self. This idea is probably best captured in work on implicit theories and memories by Michael Ross at the University of Waterloo and on self-verification processes by William Swann at the University of Texas.

The Implicit Theory Perspective

Perhaps we can take a broader view of the self that moves beyond the repression of negative memories or the creation of positive illusions and that suggests, instead, that much of our personal history is created after the fact. An intriguing view has been articulated by Ross and Conway (1986), who suggest that our present implicit theories about ourselves are used to reconstruct our memories of the past. For example, many people believe that personality is consistent over time (this is an implicit theory) and, as a result, are more likely to remember events from the past that demonstrate how similar their present self is to their past self.

As Ross (1989) notes, the recall of one's personal story involves an active, reconstructive process in which one uses present knowledge to piece together a story about the past. Ross describes the following example. How does an individual recall his or her attitude toward capital punishment five years ago? Ross suggests that the individuals would begin by noting their present attitude, which then serves as a benchmark around which memories of the past are constructed. Individuals assume that they are stable over time, and if they are presently against capital punishment, they always were so. They then marshall stories as evidence consistent with this belief. Thus, past instances exemplifying attitudes against capital punishment are remembered and contradicting instances are conveniently forgotten. The implicit theory that our present attitudes are the same as our past ones helps us to organize a set of memories into a coherent story about ourselves that may or may not be accurate. Overall, this implicit theory creates a pervasive bias such that people believe they are more consistent in their beliefs, traits, and attitudes over time than they actually are.

Ross (1989) notes that the implicit theory that our personal qualities are stable over time is especially strong when these qualities are sources of positive self-esteem. He quotes Nietzsche (1886/1966, p. 80): "'I have done that,' says my memory. 'I cannot have done that,' says my pride, and remains inexorable. Eventually—memory yields." People seem more likely, for instance, to construct stories demonstrating that they have always been smart than that they have always been clumsy. According to Ross, individuals develop theories of change or stability that reinforce their desired images of themselves, although consistency is often more important than self-bolstering. A similar proposal has been made by investigators working on processes that have been labeled *self-verification*.

Self-Verification

Another potentially distorting influence on the way in which we construct memories about ourselves is the strong desire to have other people see us as we see ourselves, a motive termed *self-verification* by William Swann (1983, 1985). We seem to be motivated to act in ways that elicit reactions from others that confirm our self-concepts. Hence, we are likely to remember ourselves acting in consistent ways and to create stories about ourselves that verify longstanding views of ourselves. Moreover, we seek out situations, friends, lovers, and so on that allow us to interact in ways that increase the likelihood that other people will see us as we see ourselves (Secord & Backman, 1965). The bottom line, in this view, is that we desire self-confirmatory feedback in order to maintain a stable self-view.

This pervasive mind set creates all kinds of distortions in the cognitive processes that are the focus of this book. First, as Swann (1987, p. 1041) observed, "to the extent that people are motivated to acquire self-confirmatory feedback, they should be especially attentive to it." Individuals embrace statements from others that confirm their self-concept and, by contrast, quickly dismiss others' contrary opinions.

Perhaps the prototype of the difficult psychotherapy client is the individual for whom this self-verification process works too well. Such a person is incapable of entertaining feedback that in any way contradicts the self-concept. The problem is especially obvious when the self-concept is off base. For instance, we have an acquaintance who was a successful playwright in high school and college. Sally wrote scripts that the drama club would produce, and in college she was regarded as a budding talent when a play she authored was recognized by a national writers' organization. However, as Sally moved into young adulthood, her life was complicated by family turmoil, the death of her mother after a long and debilitating illness, and her own bout with depression. Now, some fifteen years later, Sally has held a series of nontheater jobs requiring original writing but usually in the service of someone else's goals—copy editing, newspaper reporting, grant writing, and the like. During this time, she has not been able to generate much original work.

In her middle thirties Sally clings to the notion that she is a promising and fairly famous playwright and that if she could make the right connections, she would be on her way to Broadway and a Tony. She spends considerable time on the telephone tracking down well-known playwrights for advice and encouragement. Occasionally, after a series of telephone calls from Sally, a playwright will send her a rather generic letter of encouragement such as:

Dear Sally,

Play writing is a difficult profession that requires incredible tenacity. I am impressed with your desire to do well and wish you luck with your writing.

Yours sincerely,

Many times, Sally has invited us to lunch to show us these kinds of letters and to announce to us that she now knows she is on her way to fame and fortune. No matter what kind of reality check we try to provide, Sally always counters with something like "but Neil Simon says he was impressed with me" and backs up the claim with a highlighted passage from a letter like the preceding one. Any positive adjective is granted unbelievable attention by Sally. She cannot see these letters as attempts to be polite and encouraging but to terminate the "relationship." Rather, they confirm for her what she already knows about herself.

Even more relevant to the remembered self is the way in which these self-views channel the encoding and retrieval of information into and from memory. If we perceive ourselves as lovable, we are more likely to remember, days later, a series of positive things someone has said about us and to forget negative statements. If we perceive ourselves as unlikable, we will have the opposite experience (see Swann & Read, 1981b, for a report of exactly this experiment). Sally is able to recall every instance in which a famous playwright made a positive comment to her, no matter how innocuous the compliment. More important, we can assume that Sally's persistent telephone calls and letters to relatively busy people occasionally produces indignation or even anger. Yet, Sally, has never told us a story (can she remember such an incident?) that ended this way. As far as Sally is concerned, she is a promising playwright, and her interactions with the world have only confirmed this self-concept for her.

We tell Sally's tale because it is a good example of self-verification processes at work, not because we want to imply that such processes characterize only disturbed individuals. Most of the research on self-verification has involved as participants perfectly normal individuals conscripted from introductory psychology classrooms. These processes seem to characterize both the healthy and the troubled mind. More importantly, self-verification is true not just for our positive qualities but for negative attributes as well (e.g., Swann & Predmore, 1985). We reject feedback from others that disconfirms negative views of ourselves and disparage the source of such feedback (Of course my mother liked my banjo playing. I'm not any good, but she's my mother"). And, later, if we elicit positive feedback despite a negative sense of self, we are likely not to remember the experience (Swann & Read, 1981a).

Ronnie Janoff-Bulman (1992) has recently analyzed the psychology of survivors of traumatic experiences, in part from the standpoint of these tendencies toward the verification of existing beliefs about oneself. In particular, she relates self-verification to resistance in clinical work. Given that a major purpose of psychotherapy is to alter individuals' conceptions of themselves, why should we surprised when client's only remember those few comments we made that confirm their dysfunctional self and resist all attempts to provide positive feedback? Janoff-Bulman (1992, p. 40) observes that "resistance actually reflects our powerful tendency to maintain rather than change the fundamental beliefs that have enabled us to make sense of ourselves and our world. . . . Clients may reject or devalue therapists and their advice; they may stop coming to therapy sessions or may come late; they may not do their homework assignments; they may fill sessions with superficial, irrelevant information; they may engage in denial or rationalization, or intellectualization. In all cases, the client is indicating his or her resistance to change . . . preexisting theories of reality." We have more to say about the remembered self in the context of psychotherapy in the next chapter.

Reconciling Repression, Positive Illusions, and Personal Histories

How can we reconcile the repression and positive illusion perspectives, with their emphasis on accentuating the positive and eliminating the negative in what we remember about ourselves, with the implicit theory and self-verification perspectives, which suggest that we recall information about ourselves that confirms our existing beliefs for better or for worse, on the other? Swann (1987) suggests several reasons why the findings from both of these literatures accurately reflect reality, even though self-verification may be more important than repression and positive illusions (collectively referred to as self-enhancement).

First, for most of us, our self-concepts are relatively positive. As a result, distortions in memory like repression or positive illusions look the same as distortions produced by self-verification processes. Either way, we tend to not encode negative information and to recall selectively positive information. As Swann (1987) notes, only individuals with chronically negative self-views should remember selectively negative information about themselves.

More importantly, Swann (1987) suggests that emotional reactions to feedback generally result from self-enhancement tendencies, but cognitive reactions are better predicted by self-verification theory. So, although we tend to greet positive feedback with joy and negative feedback with sorrow or anger, we consider either kind of feedback accurate so long as it is consistent with the way we view ourselves. Depressed individuals and others with low self-esteem are caught in a bind. They are more likely to seek out or try to remember negative information about themselves because they consider it more accurate. Yet, it leaves them feeling depressed. Perhaps such processes account, in part, for the chronicity of depressive disorders (see also Moretti & Shaw, 1989).

Conclusions

In this chapter, we have reviewed accounts of why individuals may not remember accurately the events of their lives—why the remembered self may sometimes be fictional. Of course, as we discussed earlier, our goal is not necessarily accuracy in exposing the remembered self. We are more concerned with the memories individuals retrieve in order to define their identity whether or not they are historically accurate. We are content to assume that many of these memories are not accurate, although we doubt that the individual is knowingly fabricating them. What is most intriguing to us about the self is that identity may be as determined by events we believe happened to us as ones that did. Our illusions, fantasies, and manufactured memories are as much a part of our identity as our mental representations of objective past and present events. We are what we imagine ourselves to be, and we strive to motivate others to cooperate in this construction of the self.

7

◆

The Remembered Self in Psychotherapy

In the popular imagination, psychotherapy begins with an older European man settling into his leather chair and saying, "Tell me about your childhood." Although psychotherapy has exploded into literally hundreds of different formats and techniques that bear only a slight resemblance to this psychoanalytic caricature, this stereotype does contain an element common to all therapies. Whether behavioral, humanistic, cognitive, or psychodynamic, therapists at some point ask clients to recall important memories from their lives. Often, these first communications in therapy—memories of parents, of childhood pleasures and fears, of early interactions with peers, of important milestones, injuries, or deaths—shape much of the therapist's initial hypotheses about clients' style and the quality of their interpersonal relationships (Spence, 1982, p. 93–94). At the same time, as clients sift through and select memories to tell the therapist, they may experience a range of affective responses to the chosen and rejected recollections. Both the easy pleasure of a familiar canned memory, told with relish at family gatherings, and the disorienting terror of a memory spontaneously recalled and spoken aloud for the first time are possibilities when the therapist requests clients to describe events from their lives.

Psychotherapy, then, is a direct route, and an increasingly common road, to the expansive country of the remembered self. Although writers or artists rely naturally upon introspection to create a life story or dramatis personae, and see their own lives in the larger terms of fiction, spiritual struggle, or even myth played out for an audience beyond themselves, psychotherapy now offers millions of individuals the unique opportunity of sharing the narratives of their lives with a relative stranger, who listens with solemn interest and heightened attention. Although a fundamental premise of this book is that we are all storytellers, weaving our own versions of our life story as we pass through the stages of identity formation, we rarely articulate this story to ourselves or others. It lives within us, composed of hundreds of self-defining memories that hang together in patterns that may be only barely detected by our consciousness. In rare moments in our lives, during a long intimate conversation with someone from whom we seek understanding or validation (ironically, this could be someone with whom we are quite close or simply a "stranger on a train"), as part of a testimonial to a self-help group such as Alcoholics Anonymous, or after an excruciatingly painful defeat or loss, we might step back and demand such narrative unity from our memory. What each of these moments has in common with entry into and sustained work in psychotherapy is a commitment to articulate one's knowledge of oneself, to ask and attempt to answer the question, "Who am I?" To begin this process, one turns to the territory of the remembered self—narrative memories, important goals, and affective responses that link the past and future to the experience of here and now.

To understand how the remembered self emerges and plays a powerful role in the process of psychotherapy, it is necessary to look at how psychotherapists have thought about the role of memory in psychotherapy. Despite narrative memory's omnipresence in therapy, the dominant psychotherapeutic movement of most of this century, psychoanalysis, has considered it more a veil than a virtue. This position has had tremendous influence: it served as the basis for Freud's ultimate rejection of the veridicality of claims of childhood seduction, and it has militated against more literal interpretations of narrative memories reported in psychotherapy. If we are to argue for the importance of self-defining memories in psychotherapy and their value as an interpretative tool, it is necessary to build a position counter to the psychoanalytic case for screen memories. In doing so, we must discuss in depth the Freudian, Adlerian, and ego psychology perspectives touched upon in chapter 2. In addition, we present a contemporary theory of narrative memory in psychotherapy that highlights the importance of narrative memories' content and themes: Arnold Bruhn's cognitive-perceptual theory. Finally, employing a case study, we demonstrate how our own perspective on the remembered self, based in the work of Adler, Tomkins, Bruhn, and McAdams can be applied to narrative memories generated in psychotherapy.

Earlier Perspectives on Memory and Psychotherapy

In the last two decades, Bruhn (1984, 1985, 1990a, 1990b; Bruhn & Last, 1982) has been the most active and prolific scholar regarding the recall of memories (particularly early memories) in psychotherapy. In making this statement, it is important to distinguish that Bruhn is interested, as are we, in what is recalled by the client as opposed to what is forgotten or repressed. One hundred years after Freud's first papers, the majority of clinical researchers still prefer to pursue the elusive warded off content of memory, as opposed to attempting to build models of memory and personality that would accord importance to what the individual does recall and pronounce significant.

In excellent reviews, Bruhn (1984, 1990a; Bruhn & Last, 1982) has clearly presented the three dominant views of memory's role in psychotherapy for the greater part of this century: the psychoanalytic, Adlerian, and ego psychology perspectives. First, it is important to note that each of these approaches has emphasized early—and, at times, the earliest—memory from individuals' lives. The reason for this heightened focus on early memory is clarified when we discuss the theories. However, on occasion, each perspective's theory of early memory has been recruited by its adherents to explain all memories produced in psychotherapy.

Freud and Screen Memories

As Bruhn details (see also Langs, Rothenberg, Fishman, & Reiser, 1960; Mosak, 1958; Spence, 1982), the study of memory and psychotherapy began with Freud's paper on *screen memories* (Freud, 1899/1973). Freud subsequently expanded his theory of childhood memories in chapter 4 of *The Psychopathology of Everyday Life* (Freud 1901/1973; see also 1914/1973, 1920/1973, 1938). He also applied his theory through a psychohistorical analysis of Goethe and Leonardo da Vinci (Freud, 1917/73, 1910/73). In exploring the roots of repression and displacement, Freud reasoned that our failure to remember most of our experiences of early childhood may be caused by a repressive response to the passionate emotions that accompanied our first sexual desires and conflicts during the oedipal stage. However, he wondered why clients on occasion had been able to recall a few vivid, incomplete, memories from childhood that were paradoxically rather trivial. Through self-analysis (thinly disguised as a case from his practice), Freud emerged with the proposition that the trivial memory is actually a screen, hiding symbolically in its bland elements clues to repressed material of a powerful sexual and affective nature.

Freud traced the apparent vividness and intensity of the screen memory to its underlying repressed content, much in the same way we are first captivated by the far-off lights of a distant ship or train without realizing the enormity and powerful structure behind the signal illumination. Freud also suggests that, just as the lights of the ship seem to change in intensity and color as the ship grows near, the images of the screen memory, after the re-pressed memory content emerges, may be revealed to be distorted recol-lections in which some of the events recalled did not take place at all.

Regarding the inherent importance of the content of the screen memory, Freud defined "the concept of a 'screen memory' as one which owes its value as a memory not to its own content but to the relation existing be-tween the content and some other, that has been suppressed." (Freud 1899/1973, p. 320)

In this declaration, he laid out an epistemological stance for the psycho-analytic movement regarding how certain types of early memories (i.e., vivid incomplete memories of rather trivial content) should be handled in psychotherapy. By the method of free association to the manifest content of the memory, certain latent material relevant to sexual conflicts experi-enced before, after, or at the time of the memory can be retrieved. This is the "Sherlock Holmes" tradition of psychoanalysis, as Spence (1990) calls it, and it is most familiar to us as a method of dream interpretation. The manifest content of the memory represents a "symptom substitution" that serves as a compromise between repression and the motive to recall an im-portant experience in one's life (Freud, 1899/1973, p. 307). Thus, the sur-face content of early memories can often serve a "concealing" function as Langs et al. (1960, p. 523) point out.

Subsequent psychoanalytic thinkers followed this perspective on screen memories for most of this century (Fenichel, 1927/1953; Greenacre, 1949; Kennedy, 1971; Kris, 1956a, 1956b;), though as Bruhn and Last (1982, p. 120) explain, later positions, such as those advanced by Kris and Kennedy, argued that the screen memory is connected to repeated experiences from a whole phase of development rather than to a few specific repressed mem-ories. Spence, a contemporary psychoanalytic thinker, has offered a more critical view of the screen memory position:

> Freud was never able to provide a clear rule that would allow us to separate the "real" memory—the central, veridical core—from the subsequent distortions. (For example, when is a particular memory de-tail no longer vivid?) Thus we can never be sure where to stop in our attempts to deconstruct the screen. (Spence, 1982, p. 89)

Spence goes on to note that because the ending point of memory retrieval is not clear, the therapist's power of suggestion can play an influential role, mostly through the client's unconscious desire to satisfy the therapist by supplying the right kind of data. Freud (1938) anticipated this slippery slope argument and wrote that interpretations or "constructions" offered by the therapist require time in order to determine their correctness. One should be on the lookout for associations and parapraxis that confirm the therapist's construction; the client's immediate assent or denial will not be the best judge of its accuracy. Freud suggests that "In the course of future developments everything will become clear" (Freud, 1938, p.385). Yet we imagine that Spence would ask in return, "How much in the future? How much of a role will the therapist's influence play in this clarity?"

Spence (1982, p. 123) suggests that there is an inherent pull within the therapy for narrative coherence, a good fit to one's life story, and that both patient and therapist are susceptible to relying upon an elegant, but inaccurate, interpretation that brings premature closure to understanding. In the meantime, what Spence calls the "pure memory" (p. 61) may continue to be left unspoken, alive in the mental world, but lacking accurate language for expression because of the overdetermined narrative constraints that therapy has imposed upon the client.

It should be clear that while Spence has voiced an important note of caution in the interpretation of screen memories, he has not rejected the idea of the defensive function of certain repetitive memories (Spence, 1988). Spence offers an example from Nabokov's autobiography, *Speak Memory*, in which the novelist describes the parallel between a visit he made to an elderly, helpless, and obese childhood governess and, immediately after he left her, his viewing of an awkward swan struggling to enter a moored boat. Years later, when he learned of the governess's death, the image of the swan was the first memory to come to mind. Spence suggests that the swan memory protects Nabokov both from the immediate pain in the present related to her death (by changing consciousness to the past) and from the recollected pain of his earlier visit in which he witnessed her advancing helplessness.

As this example displays, the screen memory (and notice it is no longer restricted to early childhood memories) still remains a viable construct for a psychoanalytic thinker like Spence, though it is evaluated with greater caution and more sensitivity to the context in which it is recruited (see Kihlstrom & Harackiewicz, 1982, for a nonpsychoanalytic empirical study of early memories and screen memories). Yet the more powerful enduring legacy of Freud's remarkable insights in that first screen memory paper has been the century-long empirical study of repression's influence on memory, or what we discussed in Chapter 6 as the "misremembered self" (see Dutta & Kanungo, 1975; Rapaport, 1942; and J. L. Singer, 1990a, for thorough reviews of this literature). We turn now from this concern with concealing memories to an approach that emphasizes the revealing quality of memory.

Adler and the Manifest Content of Memories

> Out of the incalculable number of impressions which meet an individ-
> ual, he chooses to remember only those which he feels, however
> darkly, to have a bearing on his situation. Thus his memories represent
> his "Story of My Life"; a story he repeats to himself to warn him or
> comfort him, to keep him concentrated on his goal, to prepare him, by
> means of past experiences, to meet the future with an already tested
> style of action. (Adler, 1931, pp. 73–74)

With these words, Alfred Adler staked out a slightly different terrain of
the remembered self. If memories represent the story of one's life, then the
manifest content of the memories must be taken very seriously. The narrative memory and its retelling within one's ongoing stream of consciousness helps to define the self and focus one's behavior toward desired goals.
(As the discussion of memories and goals in chapter 3 has already indicated,
the Adlerian position is sympathetic to our perspective on the remembered
self.) What matters, then, is not what has been forgotten—repressed—but
what is being remembered—revealed.

Ansbacher (1973) reviews the history of Adler's interest in early
memory. His first paper on the subject (Adler, 1913, cited in Ansbacher,
1973), in a striking parallel to Freud, is a disguised account of a set of his
own early memories. Adler describes a physician who traces his choice of
profession to several early experiences in which death was prominently featured. He became a doctor to overcome his fear of death and to affirm life
by helping to heal the sick. As this example indicates, Adler worked with
the manifest content of the memories to find a common theme that was relevant to the current lifestyle or attitude of the client; there was no attempt
to use free association to find derivatives of the surface elements of the
memory.

By the time of the last edition of *The Neurotic Constitution*, Adler (1927)
had come to feel that the earliest childhood memory was of the greatest
projective value. He was influenced by the work of his student, Paul
Schrecker, who published the first paper to emphasize the importance of
the earliest recollection (Schrecker, 1913/1973). Schrecker wrote, "What
is reported as a first childhood recollection serves the function of supporting the life plan, be it directly or by detours" (p. 155) and Adler added later
on, "The first memory will show the individual's fundamental view of life;
his first satisfactory crystallization of his attitude" (cited in Ansbacher,
1947, p. 201).

Adler concurred with Freud in the belief that this earliest memory might not at all be an accurate rendering of a lived experience. Both felt, as Freud put it, "falsifications of memory are tendentious" (Freud, 1899/1973, p. 322), but they parted company on the mechanism of selectivity in directing the memory's content. For Adler, selectivity in memory was not caused by repression but by the attempt of individuals to find elements of memory that would be consistent with their current perceptual and attitudinal framework (Bruhn & Last, 1982; Mosak, 1958). Finally, as Bruhn and Last conclude, the Freudian and Adlerian perspectives take different views of causality. For Freud, the repressed memory determined the screen memory's content and the individual's subsequent motives and behaviors. For Adler, the individual's current goals and behaviors determined the nature of what was recalled.

For most of this century, there has been a small, steady flow of empirical papers and case studies based upon Adler's theory of early memories. Olson (1979), has pulled many of the more important clinical papers together in his edited volume and provides an annotated bibliography. Bruhn (1984, 1990a, 1990b) also offers comprehensive reviews of this literature. Most of this work has been concerned with the use of early memories as a projective technique (for example, Mosak, 1958); they have obvious appeal in that they are easy to administer and are much more time efficient than a Rorschach or TAT protocol (Bruhn, 1984).

There are also some obvious liabilities to the use of early memories as a projective device. Verbal intelligence would certainly influence the richness of description and amount of detail, and level of education might affect the individual's tendency to embellish the memory with symbol, metaphor, or novelistic touches. A real life event of particular salience (an earthquake, assassination, or birth of a sibling) might make such an impression that it comes to mind immediately, but is not a central issue for the individual's personality. In other words, not all memory is driven by personal or affective influences; some recollected events may be in a sense more purely cognitive or mechanical. Perhaps the largest drawback to early memories as a formal projective test is the lack of clear criteria for how to interpret an early memory protocol. Most Adlerians have eschewed scoring procedures and relied instead upon inferential extraction of major themes and repetitive patterns. An obvious problem with this method is that often the same clinicians or investigators draw inferences from the memories and from the therapy material; their familiarity with their clients cannot help but bias their understanding and interpretation of the early memories selected for analysis.

The Integrative Position of the Ego Psychologists

The third traditional perspective on memory and psychotherapy, the ego psychology approach, can be understood as a compromise position that concerns itself with both the manifest and latent content of the memories. In the late 1940s and 1950s, ego psychology's ascendence led to a redirection of interest away from drive theory and toward the defensive operations individuals use to protect themselves from anxiety over instinctual conflict. Projective techniques (Rapaport, Gill, & Schafer, 1945–1946) began to be seen as methods for determining the client's characteristic defenses and interpersonal patterns. Two researchers, who have since gained considerable prominence, Robert Langs and Martin Mayman, developed separate scoring systems for early memories that were based in an ego psychological perspective (Langs, 1965a, 1965b, 1967; Langs & Reiser, 1960; Langs et al., 1960; Mayman, 1968; Mayman & Faris, 1960). Langs's method contained many questions about roles of the self, other, and the environment as conveyed in early memories. It also tallied a variety of manifest details from the memory (number of people in memory, setting, number of words used to describe it, etc.). Reliability for this system was established by comparing the ratings of three judges, who had scored the early memories independently (see Langs et al., 1960). Although Langs successfully applied his method to distinguish diagnostic categories of clients on the basis of their early memories in both predictive and postdictive studies (Langs, 1965a, 1965b, 1967), there have been no subsequent published reports regarding this scoring system by Langs or other researchers.

Mayman describes his approach in the following way:

> Like the manifest content of dreams and other conscious thought processes, early memories provide a potentially rich source of data from which to infer defensive and adaptive choices made by the ego as it seeks to come to terms with powerful internal and external demands. Early memories may be analyzed as if they were fantasied representations of self and others, rather than as factual accounts of a few scattered events in a person's life. Clinicians stand to learn much about an informant's character structure and psychopathology if they treat his early memories not as historical truths (or half-truths) but as thematic representations or prototypical dilemmas, life strategies, and role paradigms around which he defines his relationship to himself and to his personal world. (Mayman, 1968, p. 314)

Mayman (1968; Mayman & Faris, 1960), as part of the Psychotherapy Research Project of The Menninger Foundation, applied his scoring system to the identification of *relationship paradigms* from early memories. His scoring system drew upon the narratives of early memories to identify needs, conflicts, defenses, compromise formations, and interpersonal patterns that emerge at the different psychosexual stages of development.

Solely a descriptive method, the scoring system was designed primarily for the purposes of clinical assessment rather than research. At the beginning and end of therapy, clients would provide early memories in response to a structured interview that presented different memory cues (i.e., earliest, second earliest, memory about mother, memory about father, etc.). There are no published reports of quantitative investigations of this scoring system's validity or reliability.

More recently, Ryan (a student of Mayman's) and Bell (1984), working in the same tradition, applied an object relations scoring system to the early memories produced by hospitalized psychiatric clients over the course of treatment and at a six-month follow-up. Memories were scored for the quality of object relations in four progressive categories with five levels within each category. The categories move from simplistic portrayals of others as destructive, arbitrary, or abandoning to much more complex representations involving ambivalent motives, empathy, and personal detail. Ryan (1970) used this scoring system with early memories to predict psychotherapists' diagnoses of neurotic clients' level of disturbance and their quality of alliance with their therapist in their initial therapy hour. So far, this system has not been adopted by other investigators.

As Bruhn (1984) summarizes, ego psychologists saw early memories not only as avenues to repressed conflicts but to the manner or means of this repression. Through analysis of an individual's set of early memories, one could identify characteristic defenses recruited by the ego to ward off unconscious conflict. The ego psychology perspective accepted the Adlerian view that early memories were primarily reconstructive and revealed important aspects of the current personality. At the same time, it preserved the essence of the Freudian position by portraying the early memory as a defensive product of a libidinal conflict. For the ego psychologist, early memories were both concealing and revealing. Unfortunately, because of the complexity of its scoring methods, ego psychology's approach to early memories has yet to have a major impact on mainstream personality and clinical psychology.

Bruhn's Cognitive-Perceptual Theory

Having reviewed the three traditional perspectives, we turn to Bruhn's cognitive-perceptual theory, which proposes the use of autobiographical memories as a major projective technique in psychotherapy (Bruhn, 1985, 1990a, 1990b; Bruhn & Last, 1982). We first discuss some of Bruhn's early empirical work and then turn our attention to his cognitive-perceptual perspective. It is interesting to note that Bruhn studied under Schiffman, who in turn was once Silvan Tomkins's student (see chapter 2 for a discussion of Tomkins's influence on our approach to the remembered self).

In his initial work (Bruhn & Schiffman, 1982b), Bruhn developed an early memory scoring system tailored toward the prediction of internal and external locus of control in a sample of college students. All of these students had filled out the Rotter Internal External Locus of Control Scale and provided their earliest childhood memory in a written paragraph. Using a portion of their sample, the authors identified coding categories for early memories that would discriminate the early memories of students with an internal locus from students with an external locus of control. Applied to the remaining 215 students in the sample, the coding system developed from the pilot study correctly identified the internal or external locus of control in eighty-three percent of the subjects. Bruhn and Schiffman (1982a) stress that success in this kind of prediction study requires the careful tailoring of the early memory scoring system to the relevant dimensions of the variable one hopes to predict. An atheoretical or nonspecific early memory scoring system or a scoring system taken from another assessment instrument, such as the TAT, would be unlikely to be sensitive in discriminating personality styles or diagnostic categories.

In a second line of investigation, Last and Bruhn (1983, 1985) successfully employed children's earliest memories to predict both the type and degree of psychopathology in a diverse sample of eight- to twelve-year-old boys drawn from nonclinical and clinical populations. Each child's earliest memory was written down by the experimenter and scored with the Comprehensive Early Memory Scoring System (CEMSS), an original measure developed by Last and Bruhn for this project. It consists of nine major categories: characters, settings, sensory-motor aspect, relation to reality, object relations, thematic content, affect, damage aspect, and memory age. Across the categories, there are forty-eight separate variables. Two judges scored each memory independently on these variables and achieved ninety-three percent agreement before discussion.

Last and Bruhn (1985) demonstrated that certain items from the CEMSS (perception of self as active or passive, presence of mother or father in the memory, perception of the environment as hostile or benign, setting of the memory at home or away from home) could significantly predict both clinicians' judgments of a child's degree of psychopathology and the child's profile on the Child Behavior Check List (CBCL; Achenbach, 1978). In their discussion, Last and Bruhn (1985) suggested a structure/content distinction in early memory interpretation analogous to the Rorschach form/content differentiation. Structural variables such as perception of the self or relation to reality might be more linked to the degree of psychopathology, but content variables (characters, theme, setting) might better predict the child's diagnostic type. As yet, these authors have not reported any attempts to apply the CEMSS to memories generated in the course of psychotherapy.

In an effort to explain why early memories might be correlated with personality structure or diagnostic type, Bruhn proposed his *cognitive-perceptual theory*. Cognitive-perceptual theory is a theory of personality that places autobiographical memory at its center. An individual's memories are "fantasies about the past that reflect present concerns" (Bruhn 1990b, p. 42). For his theory of memory, Bruhn returned to the famous work of Bartlett (1932) and borrowed the principles of *utility* and *adaptation*. Individuals remember what is useful to them and what helps them adapt to their external demands (Bruhn, 1990b, p. 13). If the circumstances of an individual change, the content and selection of memories will subtly change to conform to the demands of these new experiences. This dynamic process of memory reconstruction is governed by a principle of *attraction*. In the course of development, individuals form *attitudes* (in an Adlerian sense) about the nature of the world, other people, and themselves (e.g., the world is unjust, other people are smarter than me, I have the potential to change the world). Autobiographical memories coalesce around or are attracted (in a magnetic sense) to these attitudes or frames of reference in the personality. There then emerges a *perception-memory-perception feedback loop* in which one's current attitude shapes new perceptions to fit with existing memories until a rich complex of selected memories adhere to this attitude in memory. Only an experience of sufficient novelty alters this frame of reference through which past and present experiences are filtered. Bruhn also emphasizes the process of *justification*, in which the individual unconsciously shapes recollections to fit with their prevailing attitudes (see the discussion of the totalitarian ego in the previous chapter and in Greenwald, 1980).

A second prominent selective force in determining memory recall is *mood.* Although Bruhn does not review the experimental literature regarding mood and memory (see Blaney, 1986; J. A. Singer & Salovey, 1988), he subscribes to the widely held proposition that memory encoding and recall tend to be congruent with one's current mood, so that information that shares the same affective quality as one's present mood is learned and recollected better. Other principles that organize memory are shared content, time period, people, or place. According to Bruhn, memories that are stored in multiple categories are more likely to be significant and affectively intense for the individual.

A major premise of cognitive-perceptual theory is that humans are governed by psychological needs, as opposed to biological drives in a psychoanalytic sense. Rather than reducing each individual's memories to sexual or aggressive derivatives, cognitive-perceptual theory seeks to identify the idiographic pattern of needs each individual possesses. Accordingly, the content of autobiographical memory can be divided into two types: "negative affect memories that reflect the frustration of major needs" and "positive affect memories that depict the satisfaction of major needs" (Bruhn, 1990b, p. 58). This characterization of memory as reflecting the attainment or nonattainment of important needs has been empirically demonstrated by J. A. Singer (1990a) and Moffitt and J. A. Singer (1993), as detailed in chapter 3. Of particular importance in this regard are negative affect memories, which, Bruhn proposes, are often about unresolved issues or unfinished business. These memories goad us toward either the resolution or the abandonment of the unresolved concern. Positive memories orient us toward situations that have brought us pleasure in the past and they also enable us to rebound from setbacks and depressed moods. We can see in these postulates what Bruhn means by the adaptive and utility principles of memory.

In applying his cognitive-perceptual perspective to an early memory from a client, Bruhn focuses on the following aspects of the memory:

1. The major issue or task present in the manifest content.
2. The individual's needs and interests.
3. The individual's perception of self and others.
4. The individual's perception of the environment.
5. The individual's initial expectations.
6. Affect—the various emotions present and their intensity.
7. The interplay of the major issue and the affects.

Besides emphasizing these qualities of the memory, Bruhn attempts to identify any unresolved conflicts in the memory. Bruhn explores a set of early memories for all of the characteristics listed above and then emerges with an overall formulation, or what he calls a *precis* (Bruhn, 1990b, p. 72), of the major need expressed, the dominant self-other-environment perceptions, and the recurrent pattern of affects for the individual in question. This analysis ultimately resembles the summary statement one might read about a Rorschach or TAT protocol. Using this method, he has presented both clinical (Bruhn, 1985) and historical case studies (see his studies of Eisenhower's and Golda Meir's early memories in Bruhn & Bellow, 1984, 1986) to support his ideas. An important aspect of his therapeutic approach is to collect a sequence of memories from which overlapping themes and interpersonal patterns may be extracted.

We have discussed Bruhn's work in detail because it offers an important clinical-personality perspective on memories generated in psychotherapy that is congruent with our view of the remembered self and our analysis of self-defining memories. As with any new theory, there are still many questions to be answered by the cognitive-perceptual perspective. First and perhaps foremost, we look forward to further integration by Bruhn of his clinical-personality perspective with contemporary cognitive psychology. Although the work of Bartlett (1932) still seems seminal some sixty years after its publication, it would be fascinating to see how cognitive-perceptual theory would blend with, contradict, or embellish the cognitive models of Anderson and Milson (1989), Bower (1981), Tulving (1972), or Schank (1990).

Another likely development in the theory would be an analysis of how attitudes crystallize in personality and in what manner they are stored in memory. We also would like to learn more about the relationship between the forgotten and the remembered. Bruhn has suggested that the number of traumatic repressed memories that individuals possess has been highly overestimated because of the original psychoanalytic focus on severely disturbed client populations. In his own experience with a private outpatient population, such traumatic memories appear only rarely. This question seems crucial in trying to map the remembered self and one that requires empirical investigation, however complex the task may be.

The Remembered Self in Psychotherapy

Cognitive-perceptual theory is a bridge from psychoanalytic theory to contemporary theories of memory's role in personality theory. In the section that follows, we talk about our initial efforts to apply our own perspective on the remembered self to memories generated in psychotherapy. Our approach emphasizes the identification of self-defining memories and an attempt to locate these memories in the greater narrative of an individual's life story. In doing so, we continue to draw upon components of Bruhn's cognitive-perceptual theory, Tomkins's script theory, and McAdams's life story theory of identity. Yet, by integrating ideas from each perspective, we inevitably diverge from them as well. Although there is no contradiction between Bruhn's use of Bartlett's perspective on memory and Tomkins's script theory, we feel Tomkins's cognitive-affective approach is more congruent with current models of social cognition and information processing (J. L. Singer & Salovey, 1991). Yet, we place much more emphasis than Tomkins's theory does on clients' ability to recognize and discuss with some self-awareness (assisted, of course, by their therapists) the crucial self-defining memories that have played pivotal roles in their lives.

In defining these crucial self-defining memories, the therapist looks for the key features articulated in chapter 2: affective intensity, vividness, repetition, linkage to similar memories, and the presence of enduring or unresolved concerns. In addition, substantiation of Tomkins's script theory principles is sought by detecting across a series of memories recounted in a psychotherapy an overarching narrative sequence. More specifically, if this narrative sequence conveys the same unresolved conflict for the individual that has persisted through different periods of his or her life, one can identify a nuclear script abstracted from these self-defining memories. Once the nuclear script is identified, demonstration of its influence upon the client's interpersonal relationships and actual behaviors occurs through analysis of the relationship between the therapist and the client and the history of the clients' interactions outside of treatment. This evidence for the nuclear script is registered by the therapist and either silently informs the therapeutic interventions or is discussed explicitly with the client. In the latter case, imagery from the nuclear self-defining memory or memories can become a shared vocabulary or metaphor upon which the client or therapist may draw from time to time. This common language can highlight the re-emergence of the memory's theme at junctures in the psychotherapy or the client's life.

In contrast to this application of narrative memory material in psychotherapy, Bruhn's clinical theory and published clinical reports have tended to emphasize personality assessment more than intervention strategies. In this regard, Bruhn advocates a more formal assessment procedure (Bruhn, 1990a, b), while we have relied on identification of self-defining memories as an inherent ingredient of taking a life history in the initial evaluation sessions of the psychotherapy. To some extent, our perspective on self-defining memories is more narrowly focused on application of the themes gained from these memories to interpretation of interpersonal interactions within and outside the therapy. Bruhn's use of early memories is more congruent with the projective technique tradition, which uses the material supplied by the client to produce a rich and comprehensive psychodynamic formulation.

Finally, by way of comparison to Bruhn or Tomkins, we attempt to locate the self-defining memories and their scripted themes in the larger developmental context of the individual's life. Drawing upon McAdams's life story model of identity discussed in chapter 3, we trace the interplay of the client's thematic lines of intimacy and power—how their memories reflect upon the issues of love and work in their lives. We also examine the narrative complexity with which the these thematic lines are woven in their life. Are the memories they tell filled with complexity, ambiguity, and nuance, or do they simplify, polarize, and disambiguate each encounter into the same old story?

We look, as well, at the ideological setting that serves as the background for their recollections. What is their belief system about the world, their values and expectations regarding justice, tolerance, and reciprocity from others? Following next in the life story model, the nuclear episodes that typify the life story are clearly at the heart of all three theories, but we emphasize more strongly than any of these theories the location of these nuclear episodes within explicit narrative memories that individuals frequently summon from the ongoing stream of consciousness. These self-defining memories are pictorial supplements to the schematic outlines of the self proposed by the theorists we have discussed, such as Higgins and Markus. The therapist learns of them not by clever inference, but because clients desperately need these memories to know themselves and to be known by others.

McAdams's identification of imagoes in the life story converges with object relation concepts when applied to memories in psychotherapy. The psychotherapist begins to see the prototypical characterizations that the client employs for himself or herself, for parental figures, for friends, enemies, or lovers. These imagoes will vary in levels of intimacy and power as well as in the complexity and subtlety of their internal representation by the client. Although we value McAdams's myth-inspired typology, as described briefly in chapter 2, we have yet to apply such a fine-grained analysis to the prototypical characters identified in a set of self-defining memories.

Finally, we are sensitive in our analysis of clients' self-defining memories to the plot or perceived outcome of their life stories. Clients may believe their memories are the stories, that there is no possibility of new worlds to conquer or create. They may feel stagnated and locked in their past; they live out the present and anticipate the future as only frustrating repetitions of failures or losses. Alternatively, they may see their memories as ripe with indications of what the future promises or as assurances that what was does not have to be again. As psychotherapists, we are acutely aware of what clients' self-defining memories tell us about their expectations for therapy and for the endings of their stories.

Our sensitivity to plot in a client's life story is also a reflection of our overall concern with what point the client has reached in the life cycle. As indicated in chapter 3, self-defining memories first take hold of the imagination as one enters adolescence. The opportunity to reconstruct or re-envision a self-defining memory may be much greater in that period than in middle age and older age. On the other hand, a client's capacity to understand a self-defining memory as more than a memory, to critique it as a metaphor, ideally increases with age, as maturity allows us to detach from ourselves and question our first perceptions and emotional responses to events. Insight gained from psychotherapy combined with wisdom gained from lived and felt experiences hold out the promise that we literally can see our memories change and thus gain relief from some of the suffering certain repetitive ones have engendered.

In previous work (J. A. Singer & J. L. Singer, 1992), Tomkins's script theory was applied to a series of memories produced by a client in psychotherapy. In the following case study, we illustrate how identification of clients' self-defining memories can help them articulate their life stories and gain greater control over their courses.

A Case Study of the Remembered Self in Psychotherapy

In our initial sessions with clients, we usually elicit a series of self-defining memories that help to tell the narrative of the individual's life history. In contrast to what Freud might have predicted, we find that these initial memories are often some of the most revealing and meaningful material the client produces in the psychotherapy. With deference to Spence's warning that the therapist may use early revelations to shape the course of subsequent therapy, we would submit the following reasons for the intrinsic value of the initial memories reported in psychotherapy.

Clients are determined to convey who they are in as telegraphic a means as possible. To accomplish this, they will try to select the memories they consider critical to their self-definition. These memories are the well-rehearsed stories they have told to themselves or others in an effort to get at the truth of their identity. Despite their familiar quality, they are vivid and deeply felt in the retelling. In their role as representative experiences in the individuals' lives, these memories are often linked to similar incidents of commensurate sadness, shame, anger, or disappointment in their lives. Finally, these memories are unfinished, unprecipitated in some important way that will become the work of therapy to identify and resolve. Borrowing from McAdams, the struggle to integrate these memories into a coherent story of the self may give unity and purpose to the client's psychotherapy.

One might ask: if these initial memories in psychotherapy are so available and important, why does the therapy take so long and why do therapists probe for so much more additional information? We suggest the following analogy. Many artists, particularly writers and musicians, experience a great breakthrough with their first works. To the public or even critic, it seems like the artist has burst on the scene with a new narrative voice or musical sound, a fresh and original style. The second work finally appears after a long wait and raised expectations. Not infrequently, it is universally considered a disappointment that lacks the creativity or fire of the first effort. Such regression toward the mean, which is statistically inevitable, is hastened because the audience has forgotten that the artist had put a whole life of preparation into that first work. It had been practiced and honed for years with a minimum of popular or critical expectation. The second work cannot repeat the first, yet if the first drew upon the major substance of one's life to that point, from what material is the second to be crafted? Additionally, freedom from self-consciousness and expectation (others' and one's own) has become impossible. The second work often ends up more constructed and less spontaneous, more artistic and less revealing or vulnerable.

This creative process, we believe, is highly relevant to psychotherapy, especially for clients who are attending their initial sessions of psychotherapy. They have built up a storehouse of memories that help to give their life meaning. In beginning therapy, they have their pre-determined set of memories that they can present without much hesitation to the therapist. In subsequent sessions, as the relationship with the therapist enters into more complex interpersonal territory (e.g., transference and resistance), their disclosure of past experiences is more likely to be filtered through their feelings about the therapist's scrutiny and their judgments about what the therapist wants to hear. What was spontaneously revealed in the throes of the first sessions' pain and necessity becomes more self-conscious and perhaps even calculated as the client confronts the escalating demands of therapy to take action and make changes.

Obviously, this position is somewhat contrary to a classical psychoanalytic formulation. A psychoanalytic therapist might argue that a client's initial memories are the defensive screens one brings to the therapy. Over time, and once resistances have been confronted, these memories will be deciphered to reveal hidden experiences that previously had been inaccessible to the consciousness of the client. Our experience is that the movement from concealing to revealing memories is truer for more severely disturbed clients, while individuals operating in a neurotic or normal range often unload powerful revelations early and then quickly retreat into an intellectualized and defensive mode for some time after these early leaps into therapy. The more disturbed client begins in a climate of defensiveness and extreme distrust and only allows a relationship that approaches intimacy to emerge over time. The more normal clients begin with good will and an inclination to trust, but move toward doubt as the possibility of change in their lives and movement into the terrain of the unknown loom closer. Ultimately, just as maturing artists move on to more complex and deeply satisfying works than their first or second accomplishments, such clients will eventually produce material that complements and enriches their initial memories. Yet, even then, we still hold that these newer revelations will not refute the initial memories, only reveal more layers of meaning than were originally apparent or implied.

In identifying memories offered in initial sessions as particularly self-defining, we are not proposing that any memory described in the first few sessions of a therapy is immediately to be taken as such. An initial memory must still meet the criteria of self-defining. The client must convey emotion in the retelling and describe it with compelling vividness. Subsequently, they should return to this memory at important points in therapy. They should also see the memory as linked to other memories of similar thematic import. Finally, the memory should capture a major issue or conflict that has been a focus of work or struggle in the therapy. After an initial session, we form hypotheses about possible self-defining memories; only subsequent revelations by the client will confirm our suspicions. (Here, of course, enters Spence's necessary concern that, by subtly guiding the client in the therapy, we confirm our own suspicions.)

In the following case history, we show how initial self-defining memories played a valuable role in understanding the client. We also argue that these memories coalesced into a nuclear script for the client, a recurring pattern of "good things turning bad" or "bad going to worse." Further, as Tomkins suggests, the client was motivated to repair this disintegrative tendency of her nuclear script, but, at the point therapy was interrupted, her efforts had only begun to curtail repetitions of the scene she hoped to mend. We do not offer this case analysis as a formal method of assessment. Rather, it is a demonstration of how the manifest content of self-defining memories, if organized thematically, can be a powerful interpretive tool in psychotherapy.

The client, Helen (whose name and identifying traits have been changed here), was a single woman in her early twenties living in an extremely wealthy suburb of San Francisco. She was seen in outpatient therapy twice a week over a period of three years. She had recently graduated from college and was living at home with her parents. She felt paralyzed by a conflict between her desire to please her parents by entering a conventional career and an equally strong desire to become an actress. In the meantime, she worked as a retail store clerk. Her inertia in her work was matched by a conflict of equal magnitude in her romantic life (love). She was involved with two men at the same time, one of them an established, prosperous lawyer in the city and the other a fellow employee at the store where she worked. She described the lawyer as honest and responsible, but boring. They did not discuss feelings with each other and, though they would often sleep next to each other, did not engage in sexual activity. She painted a very different picture of the other man; he was "wild," extremely emotional, and sensitive to her feelings. They had a highly charged relationship with many romantic encounters and much sexual activity. Both men were no longer merely suggesting marriage to her, but had come to expect it.

The client described her father as a very impressive man who had recently retired from an executive position in a major bank. Similar to the lawyer, he was unexpressive of emotion and rather controlled and formal in his behavior, although he had lived a more raucous life before he married and in the first years of his marriage. He had worked relentlessly throughout Helen's childhood, and she had often felt deprived of his company or affection. She characterized her mother as highly religious and conventional, concerned with social appearances, and manipulative in a passive-aggressive manner. Her mother also tended to cry easily and to handle stress by compulsive cleaning and straightening of the house.

In the third session, the client recounted the following three memories

Memory 1

I was about three years old. My father had come home drunk and my mom was screaming at him. I was in bed in the children's wing. Sud-

denly, he burst into my room naked and crawled in next to me. My
mother shouted at him and made him leave. I was terrified. I remember sitting in the bed, stunned and crying.

Memory 2

My father drove up to my two sisters and me in his Porsche. He said,
"This time Helen gets to go for a treat with me." I got into the car and
drove off alone with him to the candy store.

Memory 3

My grandmother was lying in bed near death from a stroke. My
mother stood over my older sister and me, forcing us to repeat the
rosary over and over again. My sister was crying and I was afraid, but
my mother didn't stop or let us go.

In a later session, six months into the therapy, she also recalled another
memory.

Memory 4

My mother had told me how when she was a little girl, her mother
would make wishes by blowing away an eyelash that had fallen on her
cheek. I got into the habit of pulling out my eyelashes and making
wishes when I was upset. My mother caught me one time and got very
mad. She made me promise that *for her* I wouldn't do it any more. But
I still couldn't help myself when I got upset.

The client described the first memory with controlled anger and eventual tears. The memory was clear and imagistic in its depiction of the surprise, fear, and ultimate confusion she experienced as a little girl the night
of the intrusion. Across the subsequent memories, the initial emotions and
narrative sequence from the first memory were repeated and extended. In
the first memory, Helen finds herself in bed with her father (whom she repeatedly discussed in therapy in idolizing terms), but there is nothing pleasurable or satisfying about this experience. Her father is drunk and runs
away, humiliated; her mother is in an angry fury. Helen is left alone in her
bed, filled with terror at the behavior of her parents.

In memory 2, we see the image of the father as seducer again, but this
time the memory remains positive because the seduction takes the form of
a fancy car and a treat as opposed to more explicit sexual content. In memories 3 and 4, we see a deepening of the theme that the mother's pain takes
precedence over her children's. Just as her mother left her crying and

confused in memory 1, she ignores the children's fear while praying in memory 3 and, in memory 4, asks Helen to stop pulling out her eyelashes for her rather than for Helen herself.

Of these memories, the first certainly constitutes a nuclear scene that has been magnified by the other three (as well by several other related memories not recounted here). The magnification process (analog magnification of the negative affective scene), we suggest, has yielded the following nuclear script. Satisfaction of sexual fantasies takes place with the influence of alcohol and gives only the briefest triumph. This satisfaction is followed by an extreme sense of shame and humiliation, which results in total rejection and isolation. The connection is made that to achieve one's desire or to have one's wishes granted (by receiving attention from the father or pulling out the eyelashes) is synonymous with bringing pain to oneself and to one's mother. The only safe outlets for fulfillment of fantasy are material comfort and oral gratification.

Having identified a nuclear script from these thematically connected memories, the therapist attempted to examine ways in which this nuclear script might play itself out in the therapy. In early months of the therapy, Helen often came late to sessions. In exploring the reasons behind her lateness, she revealed that she felt guilty having someone like the therapist be so good to her and that she had to punish herself by depriving herself of a portion of each session. When she would come in several minutes late, she would wear the expression of a contrite little girl and asked timidly if the therapist was angry with her.

At other points in the therapy, she complained about the therapist's refusal to discuss his personal life or to accept extravagant gifts from her (expensive bottles of wine and a check for ten times the agreed-upon fee). After such refusals to allow the seduction script to be repeated, she would experience tremendous sadness and then turn anger upon herself. She would describe her sense of shame that she was letting herself "go naked" before the therapist while he let her know so little of himself.

Helen also used the transference to play out the portion of her nuclear script related to her mother's self-absorption and failure to empathize. She would have stretches in the therapy where she would speak about her determination to be a "good client" and to help the therapist feel like a "real success." She would quickly turn these resolutions upside down through a socially inappropriate episode, such as getting drunk and picking up a man or fighting violently with one of her boyfriends, which would lead her again to overwhelming feelings of self-hatred and self-destructiveness.

The instantiation of the nuclear script in her interaction with the therapist was most powerfully realized in the second year of the therapy, when the following incident occurred. Helen, quite uncharacteristically, arrived a few minutes early for her session and found the therapist chatting with a female colleague in the waiting area. In the session that followed, Helen repeatedly made inquiries about the woman she had seen and became intrigued with the idea that she might have been the therapist's lover. In effect, the therapist's carelessness had allowed her to recreate within the therapy a variation on her own nuclear scene. In exploration of the meanings of this incident for Helen, she pointed out her desire to blend into the shadows ("to become nothing") when she saw the therapist engaged in conversation with the other woman. She then added that if she had come late, the incident would not have happened. This last thought is notable in that it reflects her sense that when she finally had allowed herself to have the pleasure of a full session, she was again punished: to give into desire inevitably leads to tragic and humiliating consequences.

In the next session after her discovery of the therapist with "another woman," she arrived with the gift of an expensive handmade sweater. In discussing her reasons for the gift, she revealed her feelings of guilt over taking up the therapist's time and taking him away from his conversation with the other woman. She claimed that it hurt her that she had hurt him. The therapist asked her if there might be some anger mixed in with her guilt and hurt; it would be understandable for her to be angry at the therapist for showing interest in someone else so close to her own session's time. Helen denied that she felt angry. She protested and said it would be wrong to be angry at someone you cared for when they were doing something that made them happy. She was only angry at herself for intruding on the therapist's time.

In this sequence, we see the powerful repetition of the nuclear script. In this case, the client gives into her fantasy of pleasure and allows herself to come to the session on time. Her expected gratification results in a sense of betrayal and acute humiliation; she feels herself alone and in the shadows once again. Rather than allow herself a legitimate rage at the players who betray and humiliate her, she turns the anger and condemnation upon herself. In the next session, feeling denigrated as a person, she attempts a material seduction (similar to the sports car and candy) by offering the sweater, but is again rebuffed when the gift is not accepted. Finally, she renounces her desire to have the therapist all to herself and ends up feeling self-hatred. Her initial desire fuses with feelings of self-destruction, as when she pulls out her eyelashes and uses them for wishes simultaneously.

Without going into an extensive discussion, it should be clear from the client's history that this nuclear script played a role in her interpersonal relations outside the therapy. Very much idolizing her father, she chose a boyfriend who matched her father in many important respects. Yet she could not allow herself to give into this gratification completely because of the traumatic consequences of such previous gratification. Unable to form a sexual relationship with this fatherly boyfriend, she allowed her sexuality to be expressed in drunken nights with the man from her store. However, even in this relationship, she received punishment for her pleasure; this second man treated her cruelly, beat her on occasion, and often lied to her. She felt that both men were demeaning and condescending to her, but that she deserved this for being unlovable and a "slut," as her mother once called her during an argument. As one more repetition, she repeatedly gave extremely expensive presents to both men and received equally extravagant gifts in return from them.

Over the course of therapy, Helen and the therapist were able to return numerous times to the self-defining memories that provided the raw material for her nuclear script. Helen could eventually say to the therapist, this is one of those times where I feel like pulling on my eyelashes—a common language between them for a moment where gratification was leading her to desire punishment. She also returned to the original memory of her father's intrusion into her room and allowed herself for the first time more open anger at her father. In returning to the memory, she subsequently recalled a second memory from that same period. In this memory, she overheard her father secretly making a phone call to a girlfriend. She began to see her own affair in the context of her father's behavior. In discussing these memories, and in determining their manifestations in current behavior, she began to embody Freud's dictum of remembering rather than repeating. Yet, in contrast to Freud's formulation of the repetition compulsion, Helen's progress was gained not from inaccessible memories brought to light, but from careful attention to the meanings and themes of memories that were in her awareness from the very start of therapy.

Slowly, Helen was able to come on time to sessions without feeling guilty about giving this pleasure to herself. She was able to feel a safer boundary around her feelings about her father and was able to become sexually active with her lawyer boyfriend. She reduced her drinking and eventually ended contact with the second boyfriend. She also found a position in a large Silicon Valley computer firm and worked her way up in the marketing department.

The therapy ended when the therapist relocated, but it was clear that certain portions of the script, specifically those involving her mother's empathetic failures and the subjugation of Helen's feelings to her mother's, needed continued work. Overall, though, her memories reported in psychotherapy provided a rich and dynamic source for understanding her interactions with the therapist, as well as a powerful context for learning more adaptive ways of handling events in her life.

Helen's case takes on a greater depth when her self-defining memories and their nuclear script are located within the larger context of her life story. Using McAdams's framework, we can explore the following components of her identity. Helen displayed a strong ambivalence about intimacy. The imagery of her memories was filled with unsatisfying pictures of human intimacy. Either she was caught in the other's needs (her father's violation of her, her mother's narcissism, the therapist's other woman) or she was left alone, filled with self-loathing and frustrated. Finished with college and in her middle twenties, Helen was entering the intimacy stage of the life cycle with severe misgivings and confusion about how to be intimate with another person.

Her confusion about intimacy may have been due in part to the conflation of power themes with those of intimacy. Helen conceptualized her parents' relationship in rather unabashedly aggressive terms. Her father was a strong, self-contained businessman (she once described him as a "powerful beautiful fish, eating everything in sight"), while her mother was weepy, ineffectual, and only powerful in her bitterness. Helen admired her father's independence, mastery, and strength; his success, and to a certain extent, his cruel indifference, formed a good measure of her ego ideal. When she sought intimacy, she located a man who repeated many of her father's admired traits: success in the business world, self-discipline and self-possession. Yet finding a man like her father, who satisfied her respect for power, also paradoxically thrust her into the symbolic role of her mother, the dependent complement to the head of the household. Although not at all a feminist, she still drew her self-image from identification with her father and found this traditional feminine role unacceptable. This same ambivalence was played out simultaneously in the work arena, where she vacillated between a more artistic and a more business-oriented career. As she struggled with these conflicts, her only fulfillment of her power and intimacy needs occurred when she drank and had sex with a man who violated all of the conventional norms of her parents. Her clear confusion of intimacy and power themes, as well as ambivalence about her own gender identification, suggested that she had not satisfactorily achieved an identity status and that she hovered between the active searching of a moratorium status and the escapism of identity diffusion.

The narrative structure of her self-defining memories also indicates her proneness to simplify and reduce characters to villains or heroes. It is hard to imagine the father who sweeps her off to the candy store as the same man who invades her room. There is similarly little room for nuance in the portrayals of her mother's sadistic behavior. Rather than filling the narratives of her life story with ambiguity and structural twists and turns, her memories repeat a same simple theme of seduction, exploitation, isolation, and self-loathing. Her imagoes are the protagonists and antagonists of these passion plays: the seducer, the passive-aggressive martyr, the confused and lonely child.

Helen's memories have an ideological setting that betrays little trust in human tenderness or reciprocity. Deceit is a currency she has learned from an early age; exploitation is the expected response from intimate others; and alcohol lubricates each sexual relationship. It is no wonder that the plot or generativity script of her life story offers such a bleak and self-destructive ending. The image of a child without eyelashes, unable to blink away her tears, punishing herself when she wishes for a better future, is a grotesque commentary on her story's potential final chapters. It is a powerful argument for psychotherapy that effective intervention can rewrite such endings or at least raise the prospect of more satisfying ones.

The Remembered Self in a Social-Cognitive Framework

What marks our approach to the remembered self in psychotherapy, as well as the cognitive-perceptual and script theory approaches, is the shared conviction that the manifest content of the memories has inherent value for understanding clients in psychotherapy. As Langs et al. (1960) remarked, to make use of the manifest content does not mean that inference or dynamic interpretation are ruled out, but the process of extensive free association for a "content behind the content is not pursued" (p. 525). What are the implications of this perspective for psychoanalysis? If analysis of the manifest content of a series of self-defining memories could lead to an insightful understanding of the goals, beliefs, and relationship patterns of the client, the monolithic prominence of the unconscious content detected by the psychoanalyst would be challenged. A reconceptualization of how to understand memory in psychotherapy inevitably leads to a questioning of psychoanalytic theory and its dual emphasis on conflict and the unconscious.

One returns to the familiar observation that Freud developed a theory of personality through the scrutiny of an abnormal population. Yet one practical consequence of psychotherapy's greater public acceptance in the second half of this century was its inclusion as an employee health benefit, with a resulting explosive increase in access for individuals who seek counseling. It is quite possible that the relatively well functioning client who seeks counseling around a failing marriage, career change, or loss of a spouse may have a great deal of access to their most important goals. It follows that the therapist may find that the memories reported by these individuals express richly and effectively important themes of the therapy without recourse to a deciphering process. The screen memory of early childhood and the reliance upon symbolic communication may reflect the more neurotic tendencies of the individual rather than basic properties of human functioning. Even Helen, who represents a more severely troubled client and who was not initially conscious of all the potential implications of the memories she reported, was able to return to these memories as touchstones in the course of her therapy. She observed with the therapist how their themes and affective patterns were being played out in both the therapy and her life outside the therapy. With sufficient safety and trust experienced in the therapeutic relationship, Helen raised the possibility of revising the predictable ending to the nuclear script embodied by these memories. As she made progress in this regard, the memories began to change in their affective meaning.

Ultimately, Tomkins's, Bruhn's, and our own approaches to memories in psychotherapy challenge the epistemological hold of psychoanalytic thinking. When Freud (1901/1973) wrote, "It may very well be that the forgetting of childhood can supply us with the key to understanding of those amnesias which lie, according to our more recent discoveries, at the basis of the formation of all neurotic symptoms" (p. 46), he ties the banner of screen memory to the wagon of a conflict-reduction model of personality. The assumption of the Freudian position is that beneath the screen memory, dream, or parapraxis, there invariably will be an identifiable and familiar finite set of sexual or aggressive conflicts (e.g., Oedipal urges, castration anxiety, homosexual fantasies, sadomasochistic wishes, etc.). From our perspective—and from Bruhn's, Tomkins's, and Adler's—what will be detected would be individualized patterns of interpersonal relationships involving longstanding goals or beliefs. Although Helen's nuclear script could be interpreted in terms of the more traditional Oedipal triangle, the nuclear script of another client described by J. A. Singer and J. L. Singer (1992) centered on themes of inferiority, public humiliation, and social isolation. The reduction is not to instinctual conflicts, but to narrative patterns that reflect the individual's unique understanding of what will come of his or her intentions and how it feels to attain them or see them thwarted. The common metapsychology of these perspectives draws upon a social-cognitive framework in which human beings are motivated to organize and reduce the complexity of external and internal information into economical and time-saving schematic patterns (J. L. Singer & Salovey, 1991) that provide meaning and direction to their lives.

This vision of the human being as an information processor is inherently more present and future oriented than a model of human nature that depicts the individual as motivated by drive reduction and shaped by early responses to psychosexual conflicts. Viewed through a Freudian lens, the individual looks backward in an effort to confront biologically imposed psychic struggles that place him or her within a human tradition of the clash between nature and culture. From a social-cognitive viewpoint, the individual draws upon history (personal memory) to abet efforts at constructing an identity and interpersonal world that fulfills an imagined ideal of self and communal fulfillment (McAdams's blend of intimacy and power). Under a Freudian interpretation, the individual digs up and sorts fragments of the past to make sense of where he or she has been. In doing so, the individual betrays a belief that knowledge of oneself will only come from knowledge of one's relationship to the past. Under a social-cognitive interpretation, the individual applies the lens of understanding to the way the remembered experience relates to and comments upon the current sequence of events. It does not matter how the narrative schema or script of a memory came into being (in fact the continually reconstructive nature of memory would make this kind of unearthing of original influence exceedingly difficult), but how its influence persists in or is revised by the present. The job of therapy is to challenge one's application of narrative patterns to one's life—to free oneself from the self-defeating script of memory rather than to locate the manner in which the events of the memory first enshackled the self.

It may be no coincidence that the Adlerian perspective on memory, which is closest to the cognitive-perceptual and our own perspective, was fashioned by a man who was a lifelong socialist and social reformer. Adler saw the possibility of the malleability of human nature—a socialist vision of a new order and a new man. The remembered self as a guide to the individual's present and future holds open a utopian possibility: what we were and are is always, in theory, subject to what we can become. The Freudian view is eminently more a perspective of realism; we battle ceaselessly with a past that pulls us again and again into the ageless sexual and aggressive conflicts that are our species' lot. Although the social-cognitive theorist may admit that the prospect of an individual achieving his or her goals and reaching a harmonious union of self-concern and other-concern is decid-edly difficult and exceedingly rare, the critical factor may be the tilt of the head toward the road ahead or the road behind. In Freud, we have the last great theory of the old world, grounded in nineteenth-century philosophy and science. For all their limitations, the social-cognitive theories we have described are decidedly new world perspectives, embracing a more flexi-ble view of both the self and the future. Although in recent times, we have felt increased doubt and disquiet about the future, we remain sympathetic to a view on memory that looks both backward and forward. For clients like Helen, memories need not be an imprisoning maze that leads one repet-itively to the same blocked passages. Rather, they can provide, through careful analysis, an uncoiling ribbon that leads one, in time, to a way out of the past.

A Final Note on Misremembering and the Therapist

We hope that this chapter has underscored the value of exploring memo-ries in psychotherapy. At the same time, we feel we must end on a cau-tionary note. A collaborative therapeutic relationship is a likely precursor to successful work with memories. However, it is important for therapists to be mindful of the possibility that they may elicit memories from their clients that confirm their own hypotheses about the client. Perhaps without being aware of it, therapists may shape the narratives generated by clients to conform to pre-existing theories or clinical hunches.

In the literature on clinical judgment (reviewed in Salovey & Turk, 1991; Turk & Salovey, 1988), the pervasive tendency to seek information that confirms pre-existing expectations and to ignore disconfirming informa-tion has been labeled *behavioral confirmation* and is captured by the phrase "seek and ye shall find" (Snyder, 1981). Mark Snyder describes behavioral confirmation as the process by which an individual's preconceived beliefs and expectations guide interaction in such a way that these initial beliefs, even when false, come to be confirmed by the other person's behavior. For instance, we often ask questions that are not objective, but rather reflect expected outcomes. If we think someone is an extrovert, we might solicit a memory about the last time the person went to a party (cf. Snyder & Swann, 1978). These kind of questions elicit a biased set of information or, worse, cause the person to behave in a way that confirms the initial expec-tation (e.g., although really introverted, the person describes a story about going to a party and interacting with others because that's what the thera-pist requested).

Frequent reports in the literature state that, over time in therapy, clients' behaviors come to match the theoretical frameworks of their therapists (Frank, 1974; Scheff, 1966). Clients even come to report dream material that is consistent with the therapist's orientation, reporting Freudian symbols to psychoanalysts, Jungian symbols to Jungian therapists, and so on (Whitman, Kramer, & Baldrige, 1963). The responsible therapist must guard against the tendency to influence clients to report specific sorts of memories because they think these will be pleasing to the therapist.

8

◆

Conscious Thought, Narrative Memory, and the Science of Psychology

I will not make poems with reference to parts,
But I will make poems, songs, thoughts, with reference to
ensemble,
And I will not sing with reference to a day, but with
reference to all days,
And I will not make a poem nor the least part of a poem but
has reference to the soul,
Because having look'd at the objects of the universe, I find
there is no one nor any particle of one but
has reference to the soul.

—From *Starting From Paumanok,* Whitman (1892/1958, p. 45.)

In the preceding chapters, we have described diverse ways that memory and emotion intersect in personality. In this final chapter, we would like to write "with reference to ensemble." We would like to show how the various parts of the remembered and misremembered self we have introduced are bound by common theoretical and methodological concerns. As we attempt to draw these linkages, we are mindful of the dangers of proposing still another overly ambitious and ultimately unsatisfying model of personality. Rather, we hope to highlight what we see as some crucial convergences without making claims that these favorite topics of ours are the sum total of personality.

First and foremost, we believe that greater attention to narrative memory signals a new train of thought in mainstream psychology. Borrowing the fuel of both constructionist and feminist thinking, this train has already

189

left the station and is gathering steam. One contribution of this book may be to demonstrate how thoroughly nontraditional methods and arguments are penetrating the laboratories of relatively conventional clinical, social, and personality psychologists. In the spirit of this contribution, this chapter presents perspectives on conscious thought and narrative memory that encourage an opening up of established views, both in mainstream personality and social psychology and in psychoanalytic circles.

The Importance of Conscious Experience in Personality

Throughout the chapters of this book, it is clear that we have taken seriously what people say about themselves. We have listened to their narratives of memories both in our roles as researchers and as psychotherapists. Does this mean we accept these words at face value, as the direct and full expression of the inner workings of our subjects and clients? As chapter 6 makes clear, the answer is a resounding "Not at all." The unconscious is alive and well, as a recent special section of the *American Psychologist* (Kihlstrom, Barnhardt, & Tataryn, 1992; Loftus & Klinger, 1992) would attest. What we do believe is that much of people's behavior is enacted in the interests of the conscious goals, hopes, and fantasies that accompany their waking thoughts and daydreams. Although all of us are prey to misremembering, through positive illusions, post hoc justifications, externalizations, and denials, we could barely function on a daily basis if we did not pursue and attain many of our stated ends. In fact, one clear demarcation between so-called normality and mental illness is the tendency of mentally ill individuals to engage in self-defeating and self-destructive behavior. Severely depressed individuals wish for happiness and perpetually find new evidence for gloom. Obsessive-compulsive individuals seek a sense of security and safety, but repeatedly question the very steps they have initiated to reassure themselves. The core of neurosis from a psychodynamic standpoint is the repetition compulsion in which individuals inevitably return to maladaptive patterns of behavior based upon early childhood experiences.

When still in college, one of us visited a friend who had been admitted to a psychiatric hospital after a severe manic episode. The friend spoke in a conspiratorial whisper about how much she hated the ward and the nurses. She vehemently denied there was anything wrong with her and was enraged that she had been locked up. When asked what she could do to get out, she replied that she was no longer considered a danger to herself or others and could sign out at any time. She quickly changed the subject, only to return within minutes to the injustices she suffered as a "prisoner" of the unit. The contradiction between her overt statements and her behavior highlights how mental health relies upon a rough parallel between stated intentions and subsequent actions.

In chapters 2 and 7, we described how major traditions in clinical and personality psychology—psychoanalysis and behaviorism—have chosen not to make this congruence of conscious intention and action central to their scientific enterprise. Given that psychoanalysis has traditionally extrapolated theories of the person from work with a clinical, and often severely disturbed, population, it is hardly surprising that its focus has not been on effective and purposeful functioning. In addition, psychoanalysis, in companionship with other scientific disciplines, suffers from the seductive attraction of studying the counterintuitive, of uncovering meanings that are less obvious and perhaps even the opposite of what the layperson might have anticipated. Finally, as Masson (1984) suggests, Freud may have felt that the presentation of certain conscious intentions and behaviors was too appalling and unpalatable for the climate of his times (e.g., the alarming incidence of incest described by his clientele). He found refuge in a theory that placed sin in the unconscious, the "bedroom of the mind," instead of in the chambers of his patients' homes. By dismissing the veridicality of these incest memories, Freud left a legacy of suspicion, encouraging subsequent generations of scientists and practitioners to distrust the stated memories recalled by individuals whom we study in the laboratory or treat in the therapy office. Yet detecting how memories camouflage underlying wishes, as we have attempted to demonstrate, is only one part of the puzzle of personality; the explicit content of these same or other memories may be linked meaningfully to individuals' important conscious goals.

To some extent this argument is about levels of explanation. The proponents of studying conscious experience discussed in this volume—Robert Emmons, Hazel Markus, David Little, Eric Klinger, and Jerome L. Singer, among others—argue that there is value in studying personality at what Buss and Cantor call a "middle-level unit" of analysis (Buss & Cantor, 1989, p. 1). This middle level of personal strivings, possible selves, personal projects, current concerns, or active fantasies and daydreams offers some of the self-descriptive aspects of traits, while at the same time drawing upon the more directional aspects of motives. Yet the question may always be raised: Should we go to the next level of reductive explanation? For example, if an individual's personal strivings are listed and used to account for changes in well-being or other aspects of emotion and behavior, one can always ask, "How did this individual arrive at this particular set of strivings?" The assumption behind this question is that there are underlying motives that account for the major goals individuals are typically trying to achieve. If we go a step further and say that strivings may be linked to underlying motive dispositions (as suggested in chapter 3), we may then ask from whence originate motives for agency and communion.

The psychoanalyst might argue these concepts are simply fancied-up terms for the bottom-line drives of aggression and sex. Each reduction does not seem wrong, but may, at times, take us away from the questions we seek to answer. If a personality or clinical psychologist wants to learn more about how individuals experience their own consciousness, how it feels to be them, and how the values of their particular culture are reflected in their own beliefs and choices, the descent to the most basic instinctual level may lose much of this nuance and social context. Although one may reach a certain scientific purity by delving to first principles, one may forsake the person as a phenomenon in his or her own right. Pitching one's investigation at the level of conscious memories, goals, affective responses, and narrative patterns decidedly preserves aspects of the whole person that are disregarded by reductive approaches. If the study of motives may give us an overall understanding of what makes a person tick, of who that person is in a deep psychological sense, the study of self-defining memories and personal strivings may tell us more about what that person is likely to feel or do in a given situation (Emmons, 1989; Emmons & McAdams, 1991). Depending on the questions asked and the purpose of the investigation, one or the other of these perspectives may be more appropriate.

When psychoanalytically oriented scientists and practitioners dismiss all aspects of conscious behavior in favor of hidden agendas, they may end up conducting the proverbial search for the needle in the haystack. As one searches for the glinting silver truth, one tosses handfuls of hay to each side. If the hay is conscious experience, only sifted through for what is hidden beneath, then a fundamental and impractical oversight may be occurring. Why not bundle this bountiful crop and bring it into market? One could buy a box of needles and then some. The flaw in this analogy obtains only if we believe the particular missing needle (an unconscious thought or wish) holds a privileged position in our mind. This has been the conceit of psychoanalytic practitioners throughout this century; the unspoken, by the nature of its hidden quality, demands more attention in our explanatory accounts of motivation than self-reported desires. This may be so, but we have not yet brought the hay of conscious goals and wishes to market yet and have not seen what these commodities could purchase for us. Given this uncertainty, it may seem premature or even superstitious to believe that only by finding the one needle we understand the person best. We might learn much more about normal and well-functioning personality by studying the convergences rather than the disjunctions among memory, affect, and goals.

It is a testament to the privileged position that the unconscious holds in contemporary thinking that we cannot promote the importance of conscious thought without wondering what we are really trying to hide. Freud once characterized the birth of psychoanalysis as the final dislodging of humankind's divine pretensions. First, Copernicus removed us from the center of the universe. Darwin then demonstrated that our dominance over the animal kingdom was another grand illusion. Finally, in Freud's view, psychoanalysis had subverted forever our belief in the mastery of mind over instincts and emotions. Whether we are fundamentally driven by unconscious motivations is still a debatable proposition, but there can be no doubt that contemporary thinkers have lost confidence in our ability to know what we know. In this postmodern age in which we daily experience the unanticipated fallout of our supposedly rational technology, self-scrutiny and doubt are our daily ration. As the poet, W. H. Auden, wrote about Freud:

> to us he is no longer a person
> now but a whole climate of opinion
> under whom we conduct our different lives.

> —from *"In Memory of Sigmund Freud," Auden (1975, p. 166)*

Yet how does one escape from a paralysis of intention? If every assertion holds within it a doubled image, an opposite or unknown impulse, how do we summon up the faith of our convictions? How do we act? In the same poem, Auden imagined that the analyzed individual upon completion of self-exploration would be:

> able to approach the Future as a friend
> without a wardrobe of excuses, without
> a set mask of rectitude or an
> embarrassing over-familiar gesture.

> —*Auden (1975, p.165)*

This was the promise of psychoanalysis, that we would leave aside the dogma of the obsessive and the empty enthusiasm of the hysteric. We would approach the world with the maturity of an individual who assumes complexity and disappointment are one's due. We would not be prone to simple truths and broad proclamations,

> if he [Freud] succeeded, why, the Generalised Life
> would become impossible, the monolith
> of State be broken and prevented
> the co-operation of avengers.
>
> —Auden (1975, p. 165)

We would be free of the certainty of "avengers" who knew their right was the only right. But in dismissing certainty, we might become ensconced on the couch of speculation, lost in interminable analysis. What about those moments, rare though they may be, when we have cut through the confusion of our many warring impulses and reached some existential understanding of ourselves, when we have momentarily grasped the ring of who we are and will become? Could there be a psychology that seeks these moments, these epiphanies of self-understanding? Could it be possible that certain self-defining memories capture exactly this self-knowledge, and rather than dismissing them as smoke screens for something lurid far beneath, we might embrace them as examples of human insight and courage in the face of the daily uncertainty that we know all too well? We might do so with the clear awareness that self-deception and repression compete forcefully and often victoriously against human impulses toward clarity and self-understanding. At a more mundane level, we might also acknowledge that certain self-defining memories are conflict-free and ego-oriented; they simply express an individual's pure enjoyment or frustration about an experience of mastery or failure, respectively (see White, 1959).

What this book proposes is a renewed respect for conscious thought and self-knowledge in the formation of personality, while at the same time recognizing the continuing influence of the unconscious. If memories are linked to current desired goals and appear to reinforce those goals, we may have defined a valid relationship among intention, emotion, and behavior without recourse to the unconscious. The correct test of this relationship is to see if it is explanatory of future behaviors and emotional responses to similar situations or memories. If the relationship between memory and goal portrays a view of reality (e.g., success brings me happiness and a sense of respect) that does not come to pass (e.g., each success leaves me more guilt-ridden and miserable), then the specters of distortion and self-deception must be summoned and inspected. Often overshadowed by psychoanalytic theory, personality psychology of this century has too often allowed these specters to dominate our thinking. An old adage taught to first-year medical students is "When you hear hoofbeats, don't think unicorns." Dynamically oriented personality psychology has too often started with a pursuit of unicorns to the neglect of the dray horses of daily life. In addition to these mundane convergences of intention, affect, and memory that may define the constancy and continuity of personality over a lifetime, psychologists until recently have neglected the study of memories in which individuals confront ambiguity, extreme anxiety, and psychic pain and emerge with new clarity and understanding of themselves. One participant in our self-defining memories study wrote about the following memory:

> I remember in high school how I had reached a low point in my senior year. A girl I liked had just dumped me, and I was starting to wonder if there was anything special or valuable about me. My friends were all on sports teams or presidents of this or that club. I felt like an also-ran, a real loser. I was walking home one day when my mother pulled up in our car. She said a story I had submitted to a contest had won third prize in the whole nation. I couldn't believe it. She asked if I wanted a ride home and I said I'd rather walk. I walked along on the greatest high and felt like here was my opening, a way I could be me! Writing had been something I played with before, but ever since that day, since that very walk home, I've made it a central part of my life.

This memory is certainly an example of what Maslow (1968) would call a *peak experience*, a moment of self-actualization in which the subject felt an ecstatic joy and an insight into what his purpose on earth might be. Csikszentmihalyi (1990) has also characterized moments in individuals' lives in which consciousness reaches a harmony with the task at hand and the person enters a flow state. This sense of *optimal experience* consists of a deep concentration and a heightened awareness of the enjoyable activity, while time and wider space seem to slip away. Csikszentmihalyi (1990) has tracked this experience in a wide variety of individuals, including painters, rock climbers, surgeons, athletes, and even academicians.

Privette (1983) has compared the shared and separate domains of peak experiences, flow, and *peak performances*. Peak performances (Privette & Landsman, 1983) are moments of athletic, academic, occupational, or artistic triumph in which individuals transcend their personal bests and reach a new level of skill and accomplishment. Each of these three positive experiences may be compared along dimensions of structure, self-awareness, and activity-passivity. For example, a flow state is a highly structured focus on an absorbing activity, while a peak experience may offer an expansive vision of self or world that is felt as boundless and liberating. Similarly, peak performance may lead to a heightened sense of self and one's own efficacy and power, but certain flow states or peak experiences may lessen one's awareness of self. One may lose oneself in the task at hand during flow, or one may feel a transcendent connection to all of humanity or the universe during a peak experience. Finally, peak performances and flow experiences are more active and engaged moments involving intentional behavior; peak experiences, in contrast, may emerge when one enters a more passive and receptive mode (see McAdams, 1990b, pp. 499–503 for a helpful discussion of these distinctions).

What these researchers have offered us is the possibility of a personality psychology that recognizes the strength of the human spirit alongside our capacity for self-deception and instinctual pursuits. In a recent landmark book, Judith Herman (1992) confronts the very taboo subject that launched psychoanalysis, incestual abuse, but she offers a richer understanding of what it means to recover from this trauma than any previously offered by psychoanalysis. Similar to the individual caught up in a peak experience, the victim recovered from trauma experiences a reuniting with others in a common purpose; the profound exile from relatedness finally ends. In reaching some clarity and meaning through the examination of painful memories related to their trauma, survivors come to realize that:

> to some degree, everyone is a prisoner of the past. . . . Commonality with other people carries with it all the meanings of the word *common* It means belonging to a society, having a public role, being part of that which is universal. It means having a feeling of familiarity, of being known, of communion. It means taking part in . . . the everyday. It also carries with it a feeling of smallness, of insignificance, a sense that one's own troubles are 'as a drop of rain in the sea.' The survivor who has achieved commonality with others can rest from her labors. Her recovery is accomplished; all that remains before her is her life. (Herman, 1992, p. 236)

Psychodynamic therapists have traditionally emphasized the first half of the equation of trauma, the effect of repression and defense. Yet here we see an eloquent formulation of the second half—the heightened life brought about by recovery. If our psychology of personality is to be comprehensive, we need to understand what happens to the individuals who leave the therapist's office, successfully treated, and begin their lives.

Yet, acknowledging our capacity for self-knowledge also means recognizing the difficulty of achieving it. These moments of clarity and recovery are obviously hard won. Self-defining memories can easily become the artificial rendering of an experience that postcards or prepared slides offer to the tourist. We are reminded of a recent episode of the television program, "Sixty Minutes," that focused on a reporter's first tour of Beirut, Lebanon, since heavy bombing and fighting had subsided. He described how citizens still held onto their prebombing image of the grand plaza of the city. Despite its blackened and shelled-out appearance, with shattered storefronts and collapsed buildings, the local merchants insisted on selling postcards of the plaza as it looked before the damage.

The Study of Self-Defining Memory

A life of self-analysis and contemplation requires that we continually sift through the pictures of ourselves offered by narrative memory. If we succumb to nostalgia, then memory as a means of reaching clarity about who we are will fail us. We believe the real memories—memories that let us inside ourselves honestly—do exist, but we must work and challenge ourselves to maintain them. Of what labors does this work consist? We hope the preceding chapters have pointed to some important questions to ask about the collection of self-defining memories we call our own. For example, one might raise the following concerns. Why does this memory still evoke strong emotion in me after all the years since the incident occurred? Does this memory reflect upon a goal or ongoing concern in my current life? If it does, what commentary does this memory offer about my prospects for the attainment of this goal or the resolution of this concern? Does the way I recall this memory, the amount of specificity with which I narrate it within my mind, hold any significance for me? Is the vagueness of a particular memory possibly in the service of a desire not to recall painful or uncomfortable details? Is the generality of this memory indication that it stands for a body of similar recollections and that it has taken on their collective personal and emotional significance? By telling someone this memory, would I be conveying a significant aspect of myself to this other person? What are the possible aspects of distortion and self-deception at play in this memory; how certain am I about the veridicality of this memory? How might I be using this memory to inflate or deflate my self-image? Am I letting this memory replace the need for new action and challenge—am I living in the past instead of the present and future?

Many of these questions about memory are not at all part of the traditional lines of inquiry practiced by psychotherapists. Only Adler and, among better-known contemporary therapists, Martin Mayman and Arnold Bruhn have made these kinds of questions a central part of psychotherapy. Inherent in many of these queries is a respect for the individual's capacity

for self-exploration and honesty. Collaboration between client and therapist sharpens the focus on important meanings and feelings evoked by the
client's unique collection of self-defining memories. Of course, as chapters 6 and 7 caution, there is always the risk that either therapist or client
will unconsciously shape the memory narratives to conform to the presup-
positions or theoretical bias of the clinician. Therapists who choose to work
explicitly with clients' memories as a major topic of therapy may need to
keep this danger and precautions against it foremost in their minds (see
again chapter 7).

How does the research psychologist obtain meaningful answers to the
same questions about memory we have just discussed? Chapters 3 and 4
presented first efforts in this regard by both the authors and other researchers. The collection of self-defining memories, personal strivings, and
ratings of affective responses to these memories and strivings seems an important first step. Content analysis of the memory organization and the thematic concerns of the memories also makes inroads into gleaning the
significance of particular memories for individuals (see Bruhn, 1990a, b;
Smith, 1992). In proposing these methods, we are reminded of McClelland's distinction between *operant* and *respondent* measures used in personality research (Emmons & McAdams, 1991; McClelland, 1985).
Operant measures emphasize a freedom of response; there are few constraints on the format, content, or length of a subject's response. Projective
tests, such as the Draw-a-Person, TAT, or Rorschach, allow for the spontaneous protocols that characterize operant measures. Respondent measures
tend to structure responses by offering a series of questions to be answered
with a rating scale, true/false, or multiple choice format. The typical personality scale (e.g., 16PF, NEO-PI, CPI) would fit the criterion of a respondent measure.

McClelland has proposed that operant measures capture a different dimension of personality than respondent measures. Because of their more
flexible and free-floating nature, operant measures are able to induce subjects to reveal deeper and more dispositional motives of personality. These
motives (e.g., to be intimate with others, to be powerful, etc.) color our
daily choices and guide our goal-directed activities over the long haul of
our lives. Emmons and McAdams (1991) give a clear description of the
different aspect of personality revealed by respondent measures:

> By contrast, respondent measures are more likely to tap consciously
> articulated and cognitively elaborated values. Such values are less
> likely to predict daily, operant behavioral trends but may be useful in

predicting immediate responses to highly structured situations (respondents) that provide incentives that closely match the value.(p. 648)

This distinction raises the question for the researcher about where personal strivings and self-defining memories fit into this framework. When we ask subjects to list their strivings and memories, are we tapping into these deep motives accessed by operant measures or are we reaching more immediate situational concerns? The Emmons and McAdams (1991) study correlated themes of intimacy, affiliation, achievement, and power in personal strivings with similar themes in an operant measure (TAT) and a respondent measure (Jackson PRF). Personal strivings correlated moderately with both measures, suggesting that personal strivings tap into both implicit and explicit motives.

In recent work, we have correlated the thematic content of self-defining memories (e.g., intimacy and power) with personal strivings and respondent measures (SCL-90 and the Weinberger Adjustment Inventory). Self-defining memories show moderate relationships to both personal strivings and to these respondent measures (Moffitt, Zittel, & Singer, 1993). We have a study under way that is examining the relationship between TAT responses, self-defining memories, and dream protocols (Evans, 1993), and while conclusions regarding these relationships would be premature, McAdams (1982) did demonstrate significant relationships between social motives scored from TAT stories and autobiographical memories of peak experiences. The emerging picture from these past and in-progress studies raises the possibility that self-defining memories occupy a similar middle ground to personal strivings, between the extreme fantasy-oriented operant procedures of the TAT and Rorschach and the more structured respondent tasks requested by self-report personality inventories. Accordingly, repetitive affective memories that play a role in personal self-definition would inform the researcher both about the overarching disposition of individuals and more proximally about what their short-term preferences and situational choices may be.

We have seen, however, in chapter 4 that self-defining memories are sensitive to instructional sets. Researchers must be careful to examine how the manner in which they ask for autobiographical memories will influence the content, affectivity, and narrative style of the memories they receive in return. We have yet to examine whether the race, gender, or ethnicity of the experimenter or the physical setting and sociocultural environment of the experiment influences the kinds of self-defining memories generated. We also have not examined possible variations in self-defining memories depending upon the age or social background of the respondents. By tracking each of these nuances in our approach to the recruitment of self-defining memories, we eventually will be able to determine the susceptibility of self-defining memories to social desirability and immediate context.

Perhaps the most interesting and ultimately most revealing test of self-defining memories as a useful measure in personality research will be to examine both subtle changes and steadfast consistencies in the same memory over a period of decades in an individual's life. Longitudinal research would allow us in the most ideal circumstances to learn of an important experience in an individual's life as it is happening or shortly after it has occurred. We could then trace how this experience becomes a part of personal history, evolving over six months, a year, five years, a decade, and so on. Tracking the editing and re-editing of this memory over time would allow us to examine the influence of Tomkins's *script* processes, such as the linking of this memory with similar affective sequences and the revival of this memory in new situations that evoke its themes or conflicts. By periodically sampling the individual's personal strivings, we could determine more effectively whether ebbs and flows in affective responses to particular self-defining memories were contingent in part upon the current status of strivings in a personal striving hierarchy.

For example, at one point in one of the authors' lives, a memory of peer rejection would bring acute embarrassment and pain to the surface. Now, perhaps due to greater wisdom, misanthropic defenses, or more self-confidence, these memories have generally ceased to have an acute emotional impact. Yet in new surroundings that require extensive socializing and the formation of new peer alignments (e.g., a new community or work place), these memories may return momentarily with some of their earlier affective intensity. Longitudinal scrutiny over an individual's life could capture with great precision both situational and developmental factors that lead to the reciprocal activation of feelings about both particular personal strivings and self-defining memories. Finally, longitudinal study of the person would allow us to observe how a life story emerges through the narrative memories that remain over the decades. Just as the poet, Walt Whitman, whose words began this chapter, shaped and reshaped his great masterpiece, *Leaves of Grass*, throughout his life, adding, deleting, and reordering the poems with each new edition of the work, so do we all add, delete, and alter our collection of self-defining memories until we reach a final edition brought on only by our own death. And who is to say that, in some crucial sense, the life that we remember is not the life we lived?

All of these research proposals to examine instructional sets, sociocultural influences, and developmental factors indicate the challenging and nearly overwhelming task one undertakes in attempting to portray the whole person. The personological expedition that Henry Murray began over fifty years ago has yet to find that one fabled trade route that would revolutionize all commerce in the field of personality. Still, with the emergence of a younger generation of personality psychologists versed in the thinking of Murray and Tomkins, as well as the contributions of cognitive science, psychophysiology, and the best of contemporary psychoanalysis, we are indeed in a new age of exploration. Fundamental to this new era is a lack of oppressive ideology and a willingness to learn from diverse theories and from diverse disciplines outside psychology.

We see ourselves as part of this integrative trend. By no means advocates of traditional psychoanalytic theory, we are also not rebel angels who repudiate the notion of the unconscious and hidden motive. We offer a mixed vision of the person, one that blends both conscious and unconscious processes and that puts particular value on the prospect of individuals' capacity to achieve meaningful insight into themselves through the medium of memory. If a scheme of personality that has room for both conflict-free and conflict-based aspects of motivation seems muddled, we would submit that sometimes a muddle is the closest approximation of reality one can advance. As recent proponents of *chaos theory* have suggested (Gleick, 1987), what appears patternless or random may simply have an order or sequence that is calculated by a different temporal unit or geometric model. As we grow more ambitious in our attempts to submit the world to science, we are increasingly forced to give up some of the convenience of our linear models in the interest of capturing complexity. We believe the daunting prospect of understanding human personality is a task fraught with such complexity.

Research presented in this book (our own and others') suggests that the study of narrative memory is one beginning step toward capturing the complex interactions of affect, cognition, and motivation in personality. Yet to read and appreciate narrative memories is not enough for social scientists; psychologists, if they are to separate their activity from the realm of drama or journalism, must apply scientific analysis and psychological theory to these narratives. Our goal, as chapters 2 through 6 attempt to demonstrate, is to show how a respect for the richness of narrative may be integrated with the application of scientific methods of experimentation and measurement. In the next section of this chapter, we argue for breaking down distinctions between a qualitative psychology that relies heavily on the presentation and interpretation of narratives and a quantitative psychology that favors rating scales, response latencies, and physiological measurement. In keeping with the general theme of the book, we propose a more integrated and, we believe, balanced model of scientific research.

The Importance of Narrative in Scientific Psychology

For most of this century, there has been a war in American psychology, sometimes declared, sometimes not, between two modes of inquiry into human behavior and personality. Although this struggle has been waged between academics and almost entirely in print and conversation, it has, at times, had the vehemence of a religious or nationalistic struggle. This conflict is about differing versions of the truth and how that truth is to be pursued, or whether or not it makes sense to pursue it at all. The two camps have had a variety of names: scientists versus humanists, positivists versus phenomenologists, empiricists versus psychotherapists, left-brain thinkers versus right-brain thinkers, true scientists versus pseudo-scientists, proponents of a male psychology versus those of a female psychology, and so on. The debate between these two camps obviously predates psychology and has its roots in philosophical debates about the essence of knowledge and the rules of evidence to apply to knowing a phenomenon. In its particular manifestation in our current times, the dichotomy may be characterized by what Jerome Bruner (1986) calls "two modes of thought":

> One mode, the paradigmatic or logico-scientific one, attempts to fulfill the ideal of a formal, mathematical system of description and explanation. It employs categorization or conceptualization and the operations by which categories are established, instantiated, idealized, and related one to the other to form a system. (p. 12)

The other mode of thought is the "narrative mode":

> The imaginative application of the narrative mode leads instead to good stories, gripping drama, believable (though not necessarily "true") historical accounts. It deals in human or human-like intention and action and the vicissitudes and consequences that mark their course. It strives to put its timeless miracles into the particular of experience, and to locate the experience in time and place. . . . The paradigmatic mode, by contrast, seeks to transcend the particular by higher and higher reaching for abstraction, and in the end disclaims in principle any explanatory value at where the particular is concerned. (p. 13)

Looking first at the paradigmatic or positivist position, psychology has experienced an accelerating trend toward technological and quantitative sophistication (Reis & Stiller, 1992) in its quest for scientific rigor and precision. The goal of this quantification, in the image of the physical and biological sciences, is to reduce human behavior and personality to fundamental laws and principles (paradigms) that would allow for prediction and controlled change. In the study of personality, the famous warriors on this quantitative side are trait theorists, personality psychologists in the social learning tradition, and, more recently, researchers who advocate an evolutionary biological approach to personality (e.g., Buss, 1986; Buss & Craik, 1983; Gangestad, 1989; Kenrick, 1989). These three groups may disagree about the relative contributions of traits, situations, and biology to the explanation of behavior, but none of them is likely to dispute the supremacy of quantitative analysis to adjudicate their disagreement. These trait theorists, social learning theorists, and, more recently, evolutionary biology theorists occupy the majority of territory alloted to personality psychologists by American departments of psychology, as well as the majority of space in the premier U.S. and British personality psychology journals. Together, they represent the American psychological mainstream and its response to the question of how personality should be studied.

Their methodological doctrine, their "Invictus," as it were, goes something like this:

> Personality, as an object of scientific scrutiny, must be studied according to the same principles that a chemical compound or a sound wave would be. We begin with theories that specify hypothetical relationships among variables. We then operationalize and quantify these variables. We then submit these variables to controlled empirical confrontation, always entertaining alternative explanations to account for the results of our empirical tests. Statistical analyses and logical arguments allow us to determine if our original hypothesized relationships still offer the best account of the observed relationships in the data.

Who then are the opponents of the empirical, data-driven scientists? Who are the Luddites, forsaking the objectivity of quantitative analysis for the interpretive world of narratives, case studies, and introspection? On the losing side of this war for virtually the entire century (though they have recently begun a new guerrilla offensive), the opponents of positivist psychology have traditionally suffered from a diaspora or exile from the dominions of power. They are hardly a unified band and share less of a common philosophy than their hardier mainstream opponents. They consist of psychoanalysts, humanistic psychologists, phenomenologists, constructivists grounded in hermeneutic analysis, and some feminists, who also draw upon a mixture of psychoanalytic, Marxist, and deconstructionist critiques.

The strongest and most longstanding opposition force, psychoanalysis, faced periods in this century in which it almost usurped the ruling authority of American empiricism. This near usurpation occurred when psychoanalytic ideas were assimilated into the bastions of empirical orthodoxy. Hull's learning theory (1941) or Miller and Dollard's (1941) drive reduction theory in the 1930s through the 1950s raised the possibility that a theory, built from clinical observation in addition to objective experimentation, would guide the future of personality research. This guidance, of course, could proceed only if these theoretical proposals could be translated into proper operationalized variables and tested rigorously. Research by Sheffield, Wulff, and Becker (1951), and Bandura (1965), among others, as well as the disappointments of the New Look movement in perception, eventually revealed the unholy alliance of psychoanalytic ideas and mainstream American psychology. By the mid-1960s, American psychology had begun a new intente cordiale with the information-processing paradigm, and the slow banishment of psychoanalysis from the corridors of power had begun. The subsequent movement of American psychiatry toward a fierce commitment to pharmacological treatment has served to marginalize psychoanalysis even further.

Two stories from contemporary psychology and psychiatry experienced by one of us (J. A. S.) illustrate the depth of psychoanalysis's exile. When I interviewed for a faculty position at a highly esteemed clinical psychology program, it became clear that a changing of the guard was in motion. In the morning, I met with senior faculty of impeccable psychoanalytic credentials, peers and students of brilliant analytic figures like David Rapaport and George Klein. Later in the day, I spoke with younger senior faculty who emphasized the importance of publishing in the most rigorous and empirically oriented journals that favored work of a social-cognitive nature. I also met with the clinical students of the program, who described the warring tension they felt between wanting to follow in the footsteps of their psychoanalytic mentors and realizing that the future of their department and the field was pulling them in another direction. Finally, I met with a dean of the university who explained to me the importance of "high impact" researchers who could garner grant monies and publications and help move the university into the very highest echelon of major academic institutions. I remember looking upon black and white portraits of analytically oriented thinkers hanging in rows on the wall of a seminar room shortly before my scheduled talk and thinking that this world had moved into the past.

The second story demonstrates how much more brutally the battlelines have been drawn in American psychiatry. During my clinical psychology internship, a new chairman of psychiatry arrived with the charge to remake the department by emphasizing basic biological and neuroscience research. The chair studied cellular activity in slime molds and saw little room for psychological, let alone psychoanalytic, research in a pharmacologically oriented psychiatry department. Early retirements, departures, and transfers ensued. A psychodynamically oriented adolescent unit closed down. For me, the most poignant moment occurred when an entire floor of offices used by psychoanalytically oriented faculty was redesigned to make laboratory space for the slime mold tanks. The space was completely gutted, with debris tossed out the window into a serpentine construction chute. I remember working in the children's unit below and looking out the window as planks of wood and strips of floor slid from the chute into the dumpster. For a moment, I imagined a tweed-coated man with monocle and goatee, still poised in a listening attitude, pad in hand, riding his leather-bound chair out the chute and into the ruins below.

These stories point to an emerging consensus (despite some protestations, see Edelson, 1984) in the mainstream psychological community that psychoanalysis is not a science and cannot sit at the same table with the true behavioral sciences. Despite Freud's efforts to tie his metapsychological theories to the prevailing natural science theories of his time, it is accurate to state that psychoanalysis as a theory and as a method is distinctly different from American empirical psychology. Some contemporary psychoanalysts see Freud's linking of psychoanalysis to natural science as a fundamental misunderstanding of his own discovery (Schafer, 1983).

Yet, despite this admission, one must marvel at the staying power of the narrative mode of thought as originally studied by psychoanalysts. Just as the graying generals of postwar American experimental psychology have finally won their long-contested battle against their similarly long-in-the-tooth psychoanalytic contemporaries, a new band of guerilla fighters has emerged. Drawing upon the French school of psychoanalysis and literary criticism, a new breed of psychologists has embraced a hermeneutic and constructivist perspective that challenges directly the premises of objectivist American psychology (Chodorow, 1978; Cushman, 1990; Gergen, 1985; Gergen & Gergen, 1988; Gilligan, 1982; Hermans, Kempen, & van

Loon, 1992; Howard, 1991; Riger, 1992). These forces no longer seek the reconciliation of empirical psychology and psychoanalysis that character-ized the middle decades of this century. In fact, their opposing ideology centers on the purported weaknesses and perceived damage created by the privileged position assigned to quantification.

Although there is a diversity of thought represented in this loose coali-tion of deconstructionists, contextualists, feminists, and phenomenologists, they, like their empiricist counterparts, share some common assumptions. First and foremost, they believe that American psychology has neglected the study of meaning for the sake of structure and function. Drawing upon the physical and biological sciences, dating all the way back to Wundt, em-pirical psychology has approached the study of human beings as another material problem. Physical scientists do not seek empirical answers to the question, "Why is there light?" They seek to explain the physical proper-ties of light and the conditions in which light is amplified or reduced. The explanation or study of meaning may suffer if it is attempted through a medium best suited for the description and quantification of material ob-jects. Donald Polkinghorne (1988) writes:

> For example, when narrative meaning is translated into categories
> derived from a description of objects in the material realm, crucial
> dimensions of the narrative experience are lost, including the
> temporality that it contains. In addition, translation across realms of
> existence requires reduction of complexity and loss of information,
> as for example, when narrative's intricacy is reduced to only those
> structures or operations that are recognized in the organic or material
> realms. (p. 10)

The translation of narrative information (for example, a short story or a self-defining memory) into the linear relationships studied by empiricists may sacrifice a defining characteristic of narrative in this view. As Bruner (1986) explains, the key to a captivating narrative is not its one-dimensional reality, but its ability to be written by its readers or listeners as they incor-porate its text. As we read a story or recall an autobiographical memory, we are constructing its meaning and its emotional value for us; this mean-ing and emotional effect may differ with each return to this narrative. A methodology that stops time and samples elements of this narrative will fail to grasp the multiplicity of this phenomenon.

A related difficulty the constructionists address is the problem of con-text. The paradigmatic or positivist method seeks to reach essential laws, to decontextualize an object of study in order to demonstrate its unity with other phenomena bound by similar laws. Yet the removal of context is always an arbitrary choice. An experimenter may acknowledge the influence of gender differences upon an observed relationship, but may not choose to analyze by age or ethnic identity. The experimenter may overlook the effect of the gender of the experimenter or the social demands placed upon college students when confronted with an experiment that threatens to reveal their inner secrets. Controlling for these so-called extraneous factors may miss the point. Removing these other influences may make for a cleaner experiment, but it sacrifices a more complex knowledge of the multiple contributors to a particular phenomenal experience. In our discussion of memory narrative organization in chapter 4, we demonstrated how three different types of instructions to subjects led to differing proportions of summary and single-event memory narratives. As we described, Reiser's and Barsalou's models of memory were both built upon results that had been heavily influenced by the type of instructions provided. If these effects of context are not given careful attention, then we might begin to treat a particular finding about memory as a general proposition, ignoring how sensitive this result was to its contextual housing. At a more fundamental level, Kenneth Gergen (1985) has questioned whether the most carefully controlled experiment, which acknowledged multiple mediating variables and influences, would be enough:

> It is first asked whether the folk models of mind within a culture necessarily determine or constrain the conclusions reached within the profession. How can the psychologist step outside cultural understandings and continue to "make sense"? (p. 268)

These proponents of the study of the narrative mode of thought ask: How much are our so-called scientific conclusions influenced by a failure to acknowledge the alternate political and social meanings raised by the phenomenon we are studying? Scarr (1985) offers the example of how social scientists in the 1950s and 1960s reacted to the explosion of single-parent homes resulting from increased divorce rates and general social dislocation. Broken homes, according to social scientists, led to father-hungry boys who suffered problems in masculine identity and were less likely to develop traditional masculine, quantitative skills. Now, in contrast, Scarr says, scientific assumptions about domestic influences have changed in response to the women's movement and the necessity of two-parent incomes. Far from worrying about boys' threatened sense of manhood, researchers advocate developing the androgyny of boys, who are encouraged to share the domestic chores of cooking and cleaning that were once the sole purview of their mothers and sisters.

Sampson (1978) has suggested that, beyond the influence of these

transitory political and cultural movements on our momentary understanding of the truth, an overarching "value orientation" has characterized
the entire enterprise of paradigmatic and empiricist thinking. Sampson
(1978) writes:

> The critical element in [paradigmatic thinking] is its concern with a
> world of abstract, general, and universal facts and thus its ahistorical
> and acontextual approach. (p. 1333)

Sampson cites the example of Rosenthal's (1966) identification of experimenter effects and points out that, according to the paradigmatic perspective, these influences are only understood as flaws in the experimental
method rather than recognized as a significant part of the contextual interaction between experimenter and subject. He links this emphasis on the abstract and ahistorical perspective in science to the cultural values of a
"male-dominant, Protestant-ethic oriented, middle-class, liberal, and cap-
italistic society" (Sampson, 1978, p. 1335). Citing the work of Merton
(1957), Sampson proposes that both English Protestantism of the seven-
teenth century and fledgling science were liberation movements that sought
to separate themselves from the tyranny of religious and feudal autocracy
during the Middle Ages. By championing universal laws, they freed themselves from both previous religious history and the accepted social hierarchies of that history. Yet, at the same time, if individuals were not bound
by the established social orders of the previous centuries, they would require some other order to organize them or social chaos would ensue. Science offered the possibility of revealing a divine plan that guided all the
world according to a set of immutable and supremely logical laws. The discovery of ahistorical and abstract truths was a vindication of God's eternal
order. A corollary of this conviction was that the material reality, including one's own material well-being, revealed the work of God in the world.
Such a value placed on instrumental and utilitarian aspects of one's life fit
well with a science of mechanics rather than meaning.

There is much more to this coupling of social values and scientific enterprise, but the point is clearly made. Advocates of the narrative mode of
thought see the promotion of the paradigmatic mode of thought by American psychology as primarily a product of sociopolitical and economic
forces as opposed to a statement about its superior access to knowledge of
human personality.

We have heard much of what the proponents of constructivist and
phenomenological perspectives find wrong with the established order. The
paradigmatic mode of thought neglects the pursuit of a multiplicity of

meaning. It decontextualizes and limits the possibility of extracting meaning from the particular in a given historical moment. It can fail to recognize sufficiently the influence of culture, politics, and values on the formulation of its theories and the conclusions it draws about the so-called objective world. It has championed an ahistorical individual who answers only to a material reality that reflects the immutable plan of the universe.

What, then, is the alternative to this dominant paradigm? This loosely allied band of psychoanalysts, phenomenologists, and feminist thinkers ask us to return to narratives located in what Bruner would call the *particular*, meaning both real time and surrounding context. Researchers need to interpret texts in light of the meanings they have acquired from their role in social, political, and economic interchanges. It is necessary to begin with the acknowledgement of how subjective and transitory one's understanding or interpretation of the data may be. Our formulae and technology cannot prevent our own unique interpretations of the hard facts they provide. Peer review cannot step outside an era's group think or acceptance of a Kuhnian paradigm. The challenge of this hermeneutic perspective is to identify the stories we tell ourselves and others and then to explore the functions the stories serve for the individual and for the larger culture.

In chapter 3, we discussed self-defining memories generated by college students. Overwhelmingly, these stories concerned themes of either relationships or academic or athletic accomplishment. In reading the two-hundreth memory about scoring the winning goal, final basket, tie-breaking run, or perfect ten, one begins to realize that this study revealed as much about the subjects' social class and culture as it did about the enduring basis of personality. Subjects, in telling the stories of their own lives, reflect the concerns and myths of the greater culture with an alarming lack of divergence. Where are memories of religious community, of powerful friendship, of silent reflection or contemplation? Where are memories of an active pursuit of social justice or civil rights? Where are joyful memories of family outings? Where are memories of willing responsibility toward the elderly and appreciation of the knowledge they might have to share? What a phenomenological perspective makes clear through narrative analysis is that there are risks to any decontextualized claim about the nature of personality. Based on the memories we have collected, it would be attractive to conclude that two basic motives (love and work) are the bedrock to all personality research. Yet we must understand that in a social system that emphasizes small economic units that are easily transferable and interchangeable, placing one's priorities on work and one's most immediate intimate relationships is strongly dictated. So as long as we go to work and come home to a spouse, we are living a vision that the normative culture embraces. Yet, that vision has clearly been constructed for us by the prevailing ideology and its culture carriers—parents, teachers, clergy, politicians, and so on. The narrative life histories we create, the self-defining memories we collect, coalesce into the story of our age, of the salient values and aspirations of the era in which we live. In acknowledging this blending of the individual into a larger cultural gestalt, we are also conceding that the remembered self of this book's title is itself a construction of both the individual and the methods we employ to examine that individual.

Baumeister (1986, 1987) has detailed how psychology's current concept of the self is only one of several understandings of the self that Western thought has entertained. Dating from the late medieval period, he lists seven historical stages in the definition of the self, culminating in our current preoccupation with the uniqueness of self and the need for self-exploration. Our current problems with self-definition and personal meaning would have been practically incomprehensible to the majority of individuals living in some of the earlier historical periods he describes. Other researchers (Hermans et al., 1992; Markus & Kitayama, 1991), critical of contemporary research, have highlighted the cultural limitations of investigations that begin with the premise of the autonomous individual. Certain methods of investigation, such as reliance upon introspective reports of thoughts or feelings or scales of self-esteem or personal attitudes, may be both alien and inappropriate for non-Western populations.

The phenomenological perspective requires a recognition that decontextualized data sacrifice a depth of meaning, which researchers, as agents of social and political influence, can ill afford to ignore. One of the powerful promises of narrative as a major source of information in the social sciences is that it resists decontextualization. Unlike quantitative data, which are explicitly designed to be abstract, context-free, anonymous, and objective, narratives contain within them the implicit assumption of conversation: someone is telling and someone else is listening. Rather than removing the communicator and creating the impersonal fact, narrative demands an awareness of who the speaker is and what his or her agenda might be. This demand of connectedness between speaker and audience is a fundamentally different view of how science is to handle its approach to knowledge. It asks the investigator to know the world, while still embedded within it; it does so because it does not entertain the possibility that one can escape the world, that one can be disconnected from the other.

Contrast this perspective with a view that science and its laws are separable from the social context in which that science is conducted. This perspective leads to the creation of technologies, whose ecological and moral implications are only examined after harm has been uncovered. The application of science and technology without attention to context means the loss of conversation, the failure to see the other. This depersonalization of research leads to the free use of findings for any moral end. Scientists, who have seen their ideas or technology put to nefarious ends (eugenics, nuclear weapons, overconsumption of natural resources), often take a philosophical stance that their role in society is to uncover truths and contribute to objective knowledge; it is the role of politicians and citizens to determine how that knowledge should be used. What is lost in this argument is that the negative uses of scientific knowledge are not arbitrary, but may be directly linked to scientists' choice to absolve themselves from moral responsibility for their own creations. As much as we romanticize the image of ourselves as absent-minded professors lost in the laboratory, oblivious to the time, the day, or season, we cannot absolve ourselves from our part in the cultural conversation. There is a loss of moral responsibility when the separation of the self from others is championed over an acknowledgement of our mutual "entanglement." (We borrow this last word and much of this argument from a recently completed doctoral dissertation by Gary Greenberg (1992), in which he cogently critiques the nihilist tendencies of philosophical, scientific, and therapeutic positions that advance strong boundaries between self and other.) Interestingly, contemporary science's return to the study of ethics, necessitated by legal and moral confrontations about abortion, fertilization, the right to die, animal to human transplants, and so on, may mean that all of us who perform research, whether or not we want to, will have to take up the communal conversation we have often evaded.

In this discussion of the proponents of narrative, we have highlighted first their critique of an exclusive reliance on quantitative methods and then their advocacy of context, multiple interpretations of meaning, and recognition of the dialogue between writer and reader, speaker and listener. Yet, we are reticent to dispense with quantitative methods in the face of the criticisms from the phenomenonological camp. There is a name for the brand of democratic socialism practiced in Sweden that has allowed the country to navigate a successful path between collectivization on the one hand and outright capitalism on the other: *the middle way.* We also believe in a middle way regarding this ongoing struggle between positivists and phenomenologists. Sometimes choosing a middle way pleases no one; each side sees the shortcomings and compromises that have allowed you to slip toward the opposing side of the argument. We feel this risk is acceptable if psychology is to build an inclusive rather than a divisive science. In the final section of this chapter, we present new research from our laboratory that illustrates in a small and unremarkable way how quantitative and narrative data can meld together to provide a vision of a phenomenon that would be weaker in the absence of one or the other method.

Using Narrative and Quantitative Techniques to Examine Racial Identity and Prejudice

After participating in a faculty and staff workshop on racism, we became curious about how attitudes of prejudice or racial and ethnic misunderstanding take root in personality. Given our interest in emotional memory, we decided to ask subjects to recall their earliest memories of when they became aware there were different racial or ethnic groups in the world. If they could not recover a memory of this event, we asked them to list their earliest memory of an episode of prejudice or racism. We also asked subjects demographic information, including gender, age, religion, type of high school attended (private, public, parochial), degree of integration present in their high school, and parents' approximate income level. We distributed the survey to the entire campus community in order to achieve a more diverse cross section of exposures and attitudes to racial and ethnic difference. We ended up with over 240 responses, roughly fifteen percent of the community, and the responses reflected a good mixture of undergraduate students, graduate students, faculty, and staff (Singer, Zittel, Tyson, & Kirmmse, 1993).

What is important for our current discussion is to compare the two types of information provided by quantitative and narrative methods. Not surprisingly, our demographic profile described an upper middle class, white sample that had been raised in segregated neighborhoods and attended segregated schools. For example, eighty-eight percent of the respondents had attended a mostly or completely white high school. The implications of these segregated circumstances become clear when we look at the following breakdowns of their earliest memories about the recognition of racial and ethnic differences in the world. Over the entire sample, only nineteen percent of the respondents could recall a memory about the recognition of racial differences that did not reflect themes of segregation, prejudice, or both. Over fifty percent of the respondents' first exposure to a person of color was through an incident of prejudice or racial misunderstanding. Only nine percent of the respondents characterized their first encounter with someone of another race or ethnicity as a positive experience. Regarding the recognition of difference, parents were three times more likely to present negative role models (rejecting of difference) than positive role models (accepting of differences). These and other statistics indicate that the vast majority of this sample began their lives experiencing racial difference as either a problem or something separate from the familiar world of family, friends, and neighborhood.

The data confirm what many of us already accept as a fairly accurate stereotype: the community of a typical northeastern private liberal arts college is based in a segregated society despite the best efforts of affirmative action and multiculturalism. What more could a careful reading of the respondents' narrative memories provide? What is contained in their words that would give additional information beyond the numerical reality of their segregation? The answer is that the memories convey in exquisite detail and emotion the experiential reality of learning about racial and ethnic difference from a basis of segregation. The memories contain the emotion, indelible imagery, and parental voices that coalesce to form the irrational attitudes and beliefs that become difficult to shake in later life. Here is an example of one such memory:

> I was about six or seven and the elderly couple who lived next door had two inner-city black children living with them over the summer. The children, a boy and a girl—fraternal twins—were about my age. I played a lot with them that summer, swimming in the pond, fishing. I don't recall feeling any particular way about their color. They were black—it was just like some people have brown hair, some blond. It wasn't a big deal.
>
> I liked the twins very much and one day invited the boy, Dennis, over for lunch. My parents were very polite to him—served him lunch. I thought everything was fine. After he left, my dad told my mother to spank me (he never spanked—just mom) for "having a nigger in the house." I remember that as the worst spanking I ever had—with a belt.
>
> It never occurred to me before then that there was something wrong with being close to a black person—I didn't see them (Dennis and Denise, the twins) as negatively different. Although I thought he (my dad) was wrong, I was very careful about playing with the twins after that. And, frankly, I have never had a friendship with a person of color since then.

If social scientists and policy makers are to address the problem of segregation, it is not enough to reduce the number of white students attending segregated schools. What this memory makes clear is that researchers and educators are going to have to address the emotion and visceral imagery that accompanies segregation. Our study presents the numerical reality of segregation, but unless we also attend to narratives such as this one and to the emotional meanings they contain, much of the message of the data may be missed. Reading narrative after narrative from these memories, we emerged with a clearer picture than we have ever had before of how segregation creates a negative reality of racial and ethnic difference. Respondents repeatedly told stories of meeting their first person of color away from home, on a trip, visiting relatives, or going to the city for the first time. Respondents described how there was the "one kid in my school" or "the one family in town." They wrote about special programs that bussed children of color to their schools during the year or to their neighborhoods for a brief two weeks of fresh air. Finally, and particularly painfully, they wrote of their exposure to people of color through subordinate roles in their own homes—as domestics, gardeners, or refuse collectors. One memory captures the dynamics and complexity of this aspect of segregation in a way that no numerical depiction could:

> Rather than a distinct memory, I recall an evolving awareness that our maid, whom I loved as a mother and who was black, was discriminated against. My first clue came about age seven when I just discovered foreign language. I asked her to say a word in French, and I was shocked when she could not. Slowly, I realized that she could not read or write. In adolescence, I realized with a shock of horror that she had always refused our entreaties to come play with us on the beach because no black people were allowed on the beach. Somewhere around that time, I understood the full implications of her race, her status as our maid, the circumscribed nature of her life.
>
> To this day, I admire the courage and grace with which she lived her life. My sisters and I were the only white people in a church of two-hundred at her funeral. There we felt the love and support of a community which I'm sure sustained her and others through many tough times. We also felt that most people there did not welcome us. I was glad to experience a small dosage of the hostility she endured in most areas of her life.

Within this one narrative, we see the ignorance, unintended arrogance, embarrassment, guilt, and shame experienced by a white privileged person raised in a segregated society. We even see how well-intentioned affection (the child urging her maid to play on a beach) can inflict injury upon the excluded other. Each of these attitudes and emotions, unless confronted and worked through by the individual, can serve to impede progress toward the removal of racism and segregation. We suggest that, for social science to make a contribution to the improvement of our current racially polarized society, it will need to address the complexity of cognitive and emotional reactions found in this memory. Quantitative methods that simply code the memories for certain themes and aggregate the results will lose these dynamic forces that have helped to forge each individual's value system and attitudes in response to racial difference. It is also not enough to treat these memories as anecdotes that add a nice humanistic touch to the end of a journal article. The experiential reality depicted in the memory narrative conveys the phenomenon of segregation, and it is in this real world that we live and work and make our decisions about what we will do about race. The memories engage readers in a conversation that invites a response; they implicitly ask readers to compare their own memories to the one described. On this basis, a dialogue that is particular and historical is begun. We believe that this narrative mode affects the reader in a way that is different and crucially complementary to the reportage of numerical results. If the reader is to be moved to further inquiry about the research topic and even to positive action, narrative and quantitative methods combined offer the most potent recipe to initiate this process.

Final Thoughts

This book, as all books of social science, is a work in progress. We have described our studies of memory and emotion stretching back through the last dozen years, and we have also discussed experiments that are only now being fully analyzed. We have described ideas that form the bedrock of our views on the person, and we have proposed more recent constructs that require further revision and elaboration. Our overriding goal has been to build bridges among related fields in psychology by demonstrating the exciting convergences in personality, social, and clinical theories. In one important sense, we did not tell the truth in the introduction to this book when we depicted ourselves as not tied to a particular ideological camp. We belong to the camp, if there is one, of younger psychologists who oppose the specialization and fractionation of psychology. We do not believe that truth can be found if each subdiscipline of psychology tends its own garden. Human beings are inherently social, thinking, feeling, and behaving entities. To know what makes one person different from another necessitates the asking of complex questions about their gendered, racial, cultural, economic, psychological, and biological realities. The beginning of the process of acquiring this multilayered information is, in our opinion, to respect the ability of people to tell researchers about themselves. We advocate a return of science to conversation, but conversation with a difference and with all the benefits of the technological and methodological advances we have achieved in this century.

We place narrative memory at the center of this conversation. As we discuss in chapters 2 and 3, there is no culture on this planet, from tribal societies to postindustrial cities, that does not tell stories and revere the past through rituals and myths. A common feature of totalitarian or dictatorial regimes is the suppression of history and the censorship of storytellers. In our own society, with its exaggerated emphasis on the self, each person becomes the repository of a personal myth, a life story that conveys the culture and rituals of the remembered self. By engaging individuals in conversation about their self-defining memories, we gain access to the repetitive themes and emotional concerns that shape and sustain the personality. Yet, as this final chapter suggests, each of these remembered selves belongs to a particular historical moment; this moment contains the dominant values, social motives, and myths of the society in which we live. Our self-defining memories, unique in detail and cast of characters, are less distinctive in theme than we might wish. By learning about our subjects' life stories, we learn as much about ourselves and by extension, our society.

Placing narrative memory at the center of personality asks us to expand our understanding of what a person is. Perhaps we are all like the storyteller of Mario Vargas Llosa's novel, *The Storyteller*, described in chapter 3. By recollecting our private worlds of wish and dread, we at the same time become the culture carriers, the preservers of our common heritage as a community. The stories we tell—of athletic triumph, first love, public embarrassment, lost love, spiritual awakening, parental strife, existential emptiness, familial loyalty—these most personal intimacies of memory, bind us together as one people at the very same time they reveal the indices of our individuality.

Our ability to listen to others' stories is the complement to our skill in weaving our own tales. In listening to others, we complete the circle of conversation, of what it means to be part of a social contract. Many thousands of studies have examined the effectiveness of various techniques in psychotherapy. We are convinced that the greatest initial healing effect of psychotherapy is the sense that we have found a listener, and in that discovery, we feel accepted again into the active commerce of human life. Yet the most successful psychotherapy does not stop with recognition of the client's importance as a teller of stories. Eventually, the client, through the experience of a genuine and empathetic relationship, learns to be a more effective listener as well. Any successful therapy we have conducted leaves us with the feeling that our own words have been understood and weighed carefully by the client. A true sign of the client's emerging health is his or her capacity to acknowledge the other, to see and listen better.

Psychology, as a science of people, needs to incorporate in its methods and its theoretical emphasis the connectedness of people as exemplified by narratives, which by their nature are idiosyncratic and shared simultaneously. A science too focused on the units of conversation rather than its flow loses this vital sense of storyteller and listener, of individual human life as simply a vehicle for connecting human lives. On the other hand, if we only record stories and admire them, we fail to see their patterns and repetitive meanings. If we allow stories only to entrance and hypnotize us, we miss the regularity and unity contained within them. We will lose our opportunity as scientists to predict and control patterns in the interest of human welfare.

The methods we advocate in this book reach out to this tentative balance; they look for ways of joining the conversation and gauging it at the same time, of respecting our inevitable connection to the other, our inextricable link to conversation, but acknowledging that we cannot allow the seductive passion of voices to overcome other means of knowing that do not rely on speech—the methods of mathematics and technology.

Long ago, as a child, one of us would end a day of play on the block by sitting and talking on the sloped driveway of a friend's house. The kids from the neighborhood would gather in the twilight, the final light of day limning the outlines of our sweaters and pants. We would sit in a rough circle, knowing it was only borrowed time until our parents would lift our names into the air and pull us inside with their voices; the square glow of their opened doors created intermittent flashes along the line of homes. What is striking, even to this day, is how we talked with each other. We talked about past events of the street that was our common field, racetrack, and playground. No more than nine or ten years old, we told stories of each other from previous falls or summers; we recalled rivalries with other blocks, ruthless skateboard drag races, afternoon matinees to which a few of us had gone together. For the most part, each child (there were always a few too taciturn or too young to dare to speak) gave forth a story, validating his or her membership in the circle, at the same time adding to the common memory. Contained in these stories were the identifying characteristics of the children who belonged to the circle, the uncanny speed of one, the insane daredevil quality of another, the generosity of a third. Who taught us, at that young age, to weave a community among ourselves through memory and story? How did we learn to define ourselves and our distinctiveness at the same time we were merging with a group?

Before we wax too nostalgic, we might add that the circles children form can be brutal in the rigid roles they assign and in the exclusivity that they practice. But in the acceptance of a common memory, in the acknowledgement of both the remembered self and selves, it becomes exceedingly difficult to deny the other, to commit cruelty without seeing its consequences for one's victims. Memory and the narration of memory cannot heal the world of evil, but they make silence about evil impossible. As long as we make our story known, as long as we strive to bring to consciousness what we know about ourselves, we give ourselves and others the opportunity to accord value—good or bad—to our lives. The self engaged in remembering says to itself and the world around: I was this, I am this, and soon, perhaps, I will be this.

The voices of our homes, our parents—our first past—always call to us; the circle of our social world pulls us in another direction, slowly effacing, as shadows blur our forms, the boundaries between ourselves and others who are part of the society we have entered. Years after we have left the circle of our childhood friends, we further define ourselves through efforts at adult life, whether in the work or domestic arena or in the economic and political. The one sustaining unity from the lighted door of our parents' home to the circle on the friend's driveway to the office and the home we have chosen for ourselves is memory. This memory is both ours and others'; it is both self-defining and defined by society. It is who you or I are individually and it is who we are together.

As the other children slipped away, contracting the circle to the older few, this writer always found a way, sometimes at the risk of punishment from exasperated parents, to be the last to leave. Even then, perhaps, I understood the privilege of listening to the telling of memories. Now, as psychologists, we both carry on the theme revealed by this self-defining memory. We listen to individuals narrate their memories and believe that from this listening, we will gain a better knowledge of each person and of people in general. And in this process, of telling and listening, both teller and listener reaffirm a common bond, a humanity inherent in conversation. Our listening gives us both a respect for the experience of history and a tempered but persistent hope for the attainment of goals as yet unrealized.

References

Abelson, R. P. (1981). Psychological status of the script concept. *American Psychologist, 36,* 715–729.

Abelson, R. P. (1983). Whatever became of consistency theory? *Personality and Social Psychology Bulletin, 9,* 37–54.

Achenbach, T. M. (1978). The child behavior profile: I. Boys aged 6 through 11. *Journal of Consulting and Clinical Psychology, 46,* 478–488.

Adler, A. (1927). *Understanding human nature.* New York: Greenberg.

Adler, A. (1930). *The neurotic constitution.* New York: Dodd, Mead.

Adler, A. (1931). *What life should mean to you.* New York: Grosset & Dunlap.

Algom, D., & Singer, J. L. (1984–1985). Interpersonal influences on task-irrelevant thought and imagery in a signal detection experiment. *Imagination, Cognition, and Personality, 4,* 69–83.

Alloy, L. B., & Abramson, L.Y. (1979). Judgment of contingency in depressed and nondepressed students: Sadder but wiser? *Journal of Experimental Psychology: General, 108,* 441–485.

Allport, G. (1937). *Personality: A psychological interpretation.* New York: Henry Holt.

Allport, G. (1961). *Pattern and growth in personality.* New York: Henry Holt

Anderson, J. R. (1983). *The architecture of cognition.* Cambridge, MA: Harvard University Press.

Anderson, J. R., & Bower, G. H. (1973). *Human associative memory.* Hillsdale, NJ: Erlbaum.

Anderson, J. R., & Milson, R. (1989). Human memory: An adaptive perspective. *Psychological Review,* 96, 703–719.

Ansbacher, H. L. (1947). Adler's place today in the psychology of memory. Journal of Personality, 3, 197–207.

Ansbacher, H. L. (1973). Adler's interpretation of early recollections: Historical account. *Journal of Individual Psychology, 29,* 135–145.

Antrobus, J. S., Coleman, R., & Singer, J .L. (1967). Signal detection performance by subjects differing in predisposition to daydreaming. *Journal of Consulting Psychology, 31,* 487–491.

Antrobus, J. S., Singer, J. L., & Greenberg, S. (1966). Studies in the stream of consciousness: Experimental enhancement and suppression of spontaneous cognitive processes. *Perceptual and Motor Skills, 23,* 399–417.

Atkinson, J. W. (1983). *Personality, motivation, and action.* Praeger: New York.

Auden, W. H. (1975). *Collected shorter poems, 1927–1957.* New York: Vintage.

219

Bain, A. (1868). *The senses and the intellect.* London: Longman.

Bakah, D. (1966). *The duality of human existence: Isolation and communism in western man.* Boston: Beacon Press.

Banaji, M. R., & Hardin, C. (in press). Affect and memory in retrospective reports. In N. Schwarz & S. Sudman (Eds.), *Autobiographical memory and the validity of retrospective reports.* New York: Springer-Verlag.

Bandura, A. (1965). Influence of models' reinforcement contingencies on the acquisition of imitative responses. *Journal of Personality and Social Psychology, 1,* 589–595.

Bandura, A. (1977a). *Social learning theory.* Englewood Cliffs, NJ: Prentice-Hall.

Bandura, A. (1977b). Self-efficacy: Toward a unifying theory of behavioral change. *Psychological Review, 84,* 191–215.

Bandura, A. (1982). The psychology of chance encounters and life paths. *American Psychologist, 37,* 747–755.

Bandura, A. (1986). *Social foundations of thought and action: A social cognitive theory.* Englewood Cliffs, NJ: Prentice-Hall.

Bandura, A., & Cervone, D. (1983). Self-evaluative and self-efficacy mechanisms governing the motivational effects of goal systems. *Journal of Personality and Social Psychology, 45,* 1017–1028.

Barret, D. M. (1938). Memory in relation to hedonic tone. *Archives of Psychology, 131,* 1–61.

Barsalou, L. W. (1988). The content and organization of autobiographical memories. In U. Neisser & E. Winograd (Eds.), *Remembering reconsidered: Ecological and traditional approaches to the study of memory* (pp. 193-243). Cambridge, Eng.: Cambridge University Press.

Bartlett, F. C. (1932). *Remembering: A study in experimental and social psychology.* New York: Cambridge University Press.

Baumeister, R. F. (1986). *Identity.* New York: Oxford University Press.

Baumeister, R. F. (1987). How the self became a problem: A psychological review of historical research. *American Psychologist, 52,* 163–176.

Baumeister, R. (1989). *Masochism and the self.* Hillsdale, NJ: Erlbaum.

Baumeister, R. (1992). *Breaking hearts: The psychology of unrequited love.* New York: Guilford Press.

Baumgardner, A. H., & Arkin, R. M. (1988). Affective state mediates causal attributions for success and failure. *Motivation and Emotion, 12,* 99–111.

Beck, A. T. (1967). *Depression: Clinical, experimental, and theoretical aspects.* New York: Harper & Row.

Beck, A. T. (1991). Cognitive therapy: A 30-year retrospective. *American Psychologist, 46,* 368–375.

Beckett, S. (1987). Memory, habit, time. In H. Bloom (Ed.), *Marcel Proust's remembrance of things past* (pp. 19–35). New York: Chelsea House Publishers.

Black, J. B. (1984). Understanding and remembering stories. In J.R. Anderson & S.M. Kosslyn (Eds.), *Tutorials in learning and memory* (pp. 235–255). San Francisco: Freeman.

Blaney, P. H. (1986). Affect and memory: A review. *Psychological Bulletin, 99,* 229–246.

Blatt, S. J. (1990). Interpersonal relatedness and self-definition: Two personality configurations and their implications for psychopathology and psychotherapy. In J. L. Singer (Ed.), *Repression and dissociation* (pp. 299–335). Chicago: University of Chicago Press.

Blesh, R. (1971). *Keaton.* New York: Collier Books.

Bonanno, G., & Singer, J. L. (1990). Repressive personality style: Theoretical and method-ological implications for health psychology. In J. L. Singer (Ed.), *Repression and dis-sociation* (pp. 435-470). Chicago: University of Chicago Press.

Bower, G. (1981). Mood and memory. *American Psychologist, 36,* 129–148.

Bower, G. H. (1990). Awareness, the unconscious, and repression: An experimental psy-chologist's perspective. In J. L. Singer (Ed.), *Repression and dissociation: Implica-tions for personality theory, psychopathology, and health.* (pp. 209–241). Chicago: University of Chicago Press.

Bower, G. H. (1992). How might emotions affect learning? In S. Christianson (Ed.), *The handbook of emotion and memory: Research and theory* (pp. 3–31). Hillsdale, NJ: Erl-baum.

Bower, G. H., & Cohen, P. R. (1982). Emotional influences in memory and thinking: Data and theory. In M. S. Clark & S. T. Fiske (Eds.), *Affect and cognition* (pp. 291–331). Hillsdale, NJ: Erlbaum.

Bower, G. H. & Gilligan, S. G. (1979). Remembering information related to one's self. *Jour-nal of Research in Personality, 13,* 420–461.

Bower, G. H., & Mayer, J. D. (1989). In search of mood-dependent retrieval. *Journal of So-cial Behavior and Personality, 4,* 133–168.

Bower, G. H., Montiero, K. P., & Gilligan, S. G. (1978). Emotional mood as a context for learning and recall. *Journal of Verbal Learning and Verbal Behavior, 17,* 573–585.

Brewer, W. F. (1983). The structure of human memory. In G. H. Bower (Ed.), *The psy-chology of learning and motivation: Advances in research and theory* (Vol. 17, pp. 1–38). New York: Academic Press.

Brewer, W. F. (1986). What is autobiographical memory? In D. Rubin (Ed.), *Autobio-graphical memory* (pp. 25–49). New York: Cambridge University Press.

Broadbent, D. (1958). Perception and communication. London: Pergamon Press.

Brown, J. (1984). Effects of induced mood on causal attributions for success and failure. *Motivation and Emotion, 8,* 343–353.

Bruhn, A. R. (1984). The use of early memories as a projective technique. In P. McReynolds & C. J. Chelume (Eds.), *Advances in psychological assessment* (Vol. 6, pp. 109–150). San Francisco: Jossey-Bass.

Bruhn, A. R. (1985). Using early memories as a projective technique: The cognitive per-ceptual method. *Journal of Personality Assessment, 49,* 587–595.

Bruhn, A. R. (1990a). Cognitive-perceptual theory and the projective use of autobiograph-ical memory. *Journal of Personality Assessment, 55,* 95–114.

Bruhn, A. R. (1990b). *Earliest childhood memories, volume 1: Theory and application to clinical practice.* New York: Praeger.

Bruhn, A. R., & Bellow, S. (1984). Warrior, general, and president: Dwight David Eisen-hower and his earliest memories. *Journal of Personality Assessment, 48,* 371–377.

Bruhn, A. R., & Bellow, S. (1986). The cognitive-perceptual approach to the interpretation of early memories: The earliest memories of Golda Meir. In C. D. Speilberger, & J. N. Butcher (Eds.), *Advances in personality assessment* (vol. 6, pp. 69–87). Hillsdale, NJ: Erlbaum.

Bruhn, A. R., & Davidow, S. (1983). Earliest memories and the dynamics of delinquency. *Journal of Personality Assessment, 47,* 597–603.

Bruhn, A. R., & Last, J. (1982). Early memories: Four theoretical perspectives. *Journal of Personality Assessment, 46,* 119–127.

Bruhn, A. R., & Schiffman, H. (1982a). Invalid assumptions and methodological difficulties in early memory research. *Journal of Personality Assessment, 46,* 265–267.

Bruhn, A. R., & Schiffman, H. (1982b). Prediction of locus of control stance from the earliest childhood memory. *Journal of Personality Assessment, 46,* 380–390.

Bruner, J. S. (1960). *The process of education.* Cambridge, MA: Harvard University Press.

Bruner, J. S. (1986). *Actual minds, possible worlds.* Cambridge, MA: Harvard University Press.

Bruner, J. S., & Klein, G. S. (1960). The functions of perceiving: New Look retrospect. In B. Kaplan & S. Wapner (Eds.), *Perspectives in psychological theory* (pp. 61–77). New York: International Universities Press.

Bruner, J. S., & Postman, L. (1947). Emotional selectivity in perception and reaction. *Journal of Personality, 16,* 69–77.

Bruner, J. S., & Postman, L. (1949). Perception, cognition, and behavior. *Journal of Personality, 18,* 14–31.

Buck, R. (1985). Prime theory: An integrated view of motivation and emotion. *Psychological Review, 92,* 389–413.

Buss, A. (1980). *Self-consciousness and social anxiety.* San Francisco: W. H. Freeman.

Buss, D. M. (1986). Can social science be anchored in evolutionary biology? Four problems and a strategic solution. *Revue European des Sciences Sociales, 24,* 41–50.

Buss, D. M., & Cantor, N. (1989). *Personality psychology: Recent trends and emerging directions.* New York: Springer-Verlag.

Buss, D. M., & Craik, K. H. (1983). The act frequency approach to personality. *Psychological Review, 90,* 105–126.

Cantor, N., & Kihlstrom, J. F. (1985). Social intelligence: The cognitive basis of personality. In P. Shaver (Ed.), *Review of personality and social psychology* (vol. 6). Beverly Hills, CA: Sage.

Cantor, N., & Kihlstrom, J. F. (1987). *Personality and social intelligence.* Englewood Cliffs, NJ: Prentice-Hall.

Cantor, N., & Kihlstrom, J .F. (1989). Social intelligence and cognitive assessments of personality. In R. S. Wyer, Jr., & T. K. Srull (Eds.), *Advances in social cognition,* (vol. 2). Hillsdale, NJ: Erlbaum.

Cantor, N., & Langston, C. A. (1989). Ups and downs of life tasks in a life transition. In L. A. Pervin (Ed.), *Goal concepts in personality and social psychology* (pp. 127–167). Hillsdale, NJ: Erlbaum.

Cantor, N., Norem, J. K., Niedenthal, P. M., Langston, C. A., & Brower, A. M. (1987). Life tasks, self-concept ideals, and cognitive strategies in a life transition. *Journal of Personality and Social Psychology, 53,* 1178–1191.

Carlson, J. G., & Hatfield, E. (1992). *Psychology of emotion.* Fort Worth, TX: Harcourt Brace Jovanovich.

Carlson, R. (1981). Studies in script theory: I. Adult analogs of a childhood nuclear scene. *Journal of Personality and Social Psychology, 40,* 501–510.

Carlson, R. (1982). Studies in script theory: II. Altruistic nuclear scripts. *Perceptual and Motor Skills, 55,* 595–610.

Carlson, L., & Carlson, R. (1984). Affect and psychological magnification: Derivations from Tomkins' script theory. *Journal of Personality, 52,* 36–45.

Carver, C. S., & Scheier, M. F. (1981). *Attention and self-regulation: A control-theory approach to human behavior.* New York: Springer-Verlag.

Carver, C. S., & Scheier, M. F. (1982). Control theory: A useful conceptual framework in personality-social, clinical, and health psychology. *Psychological Bulletin, 92,* 111–135.

Carver, C. S., & Scheier, M. F. (1990). Origins and functions of positive and negative affect: A control-process view. *Psychological Review, 97,* pp. 19–35.

Chodorow, N. (1978). *The reproduction of mothering: Psychoanalysis and the sociology of gender.* Berkeley: University of California Press.

Clark, M. S., & Isen, A. M. (1982). Toward understanding the relationship between feeling states and social behavior. In A. Hastorf & A.M. Isen (Eds.), *Cognitive social psychology* (pp. 73–108). New York: Elsevier North–Holland.

Clark, M. S., & Waddell, B. A. (1983). Effects of moods on thoughts about helping, attraction, and information acquisition. *Social Psychology Quarterly, 46,* 31–35.

Cohler, B. (1987). Resilience and the study of lives. In E. J. Anthony and B. Cohler (Eds.), *The invulnerable child* (pp. 363–424). New York: Guilford Press.

Collins, A. M., & Loftus, E. F. (1975). A spreading-activation theory of semantic processing. *Psychological Review, 82,* 407–428.

Conrad, J. (1900/1981). *Lord Jim.* New York: New American Library.

Conte, H. R., & Plutchik, R. (1981). A circumplex model for interpersonal personality traits. *Journal of Personality and Social Psychology, 40,* 701–711.

Conway, M. A. (1991). In defense of everyday memory. *American Psychologist, 46,* 19–26.

Conway, M. A., & Giannopoulus, C. (1991). *Dysphoria and decision making: Restricted information use for judgments of multiattribute targets.* Unpublished manuscript, Department of Psychology, Concordia University, Montreal, Canada.

Cooper, R. (1988). *The last to go: A family chronicle.* San Diego, CA: Harcourt Brace Jovanovich.

Crovitz, H. F., & Schiffman, H. (1974). Frequency of episodic memories as a function of their age. *Bulletin of Psychonomic Society, 4,* 517–518.

Csikszentmihalyi, M. (1975). *Beyond boredom and anxiety.* San Francisco: Jossey-Bass.

Csikszentmihalyi, M. (1990). *Flow: The psychology of optimal experience.* New York: Harper & Row.

Cunningham, M. R. (1988). What do you do when you're happy or blue? Mood, expectancies, and behavioral interest. *Motivation and Emotion, 12,* 309–331.

Cushman, P. (1990). Why the self is empty: Toward a historically situated psychology. *American Psychologist, 45,* 599–611.

Cushman, P. (1991). Political uses of the self in Daniel Stern's infant. *American Psychologist, 46,* 206–219.

Davis, P. J. (1990). Repression and the inaccessibility of emotional memories. In J. L. Singer (Ed.), *Repression and dissociation* (pp. 387–403). Chicago: University of Chicago Press.

Demorest, A. P., & Alexander, I. E. (1992. Affective scripts as organizers of personal experience. *Journal of Personality, 60,* 645–663.

DeRivera, J. (1978). A structural theory of the emotions. *Psychological Issues, 10,* whole no. 40.

DeSteno, D. A., & Salovey, P. (1993). *Mood and self-concept structure.* Unpublished manuscript, Yale University.

Dollard, J., & Miller, N. E. (1950). *Personality and psychotherapy.* New York: McGraw-Hill.

Dutta, S., & Kanungo, R. (1975). *Affect and memory: A reformulation.* New York: Pergamon.

Dyer, M. G. (1983). The role of affect in narratives. *Cognitive Science, 7,* 211–242.

Ebbinghaus, H. (1885/1964). *Memory.* New York: Dover.

Edelson, M. (1984). *Hypothesis and evidence in psychoanalysis.* Chicago: University of Chicago Press.

Edwards, A. L. (1959). *Edwards personal preference schedule manual.* New York: Psychological Corporation.

Ekman, P., Freisen, W. V., & Ellsworth, P. C. (1972). *Emotion in the human face.* New York: Pergamon Press.

Elkind, D. (1981). *The hurried child: Growing up too fast too soon.* Reading, MA: Addison-Wesley.

Ellis, H. C. (1990). Depressive deficits in memory: Processing initiative and resource allocation. *Journal of Experimental Psychology: General, 119,* 60–62.

Ellis, H. C., & Ashbrook, P.W. (1988). Resource allocation model of the effects of depressed mood states on memory. In K. Fiedler & J. Forgas (Eds.), *Affect, cognition, and social behavior.* Toronto: Hogrefe.

Ellis, H. C., & Ashbrook, P. W. (1989). The "state" of mood and memory research: A selective review. *Journal of Social Behavior and Personality, 4,* 1–21.

Ellis, H. C., Thomas, R. L., & Rodriguez, I. A. (1984). Emotional mood states and memory: Elaborative encoding, semantic processing, and cognitive effort. *Journal of Experimental Psychology: Learning, Memory, and Cognition, 10,* 470–482.

Elsbree, L. (1982). *The rituals of life: Patterns in narratives.* Port Washington, NY: Kennidat Press.

Emmons, R. A. (1986). Personal strivings: An approach to personality and subjective well-being. *Journal of Personality and Social Psychology, 51,* 1058–1068.

Emmons, R. A. (1989). The personal striving approach to personality. In L. A. Pervin (Ed.), *Goal concepts in personality and social psychology* (pp. 87–126). Hillsdale, NJ: Erlbaum.

Emmons, R. A. (1990). Motives and life goals. In S. Briggs, R. Hogan, & W. Jones (Eds.), *Handbook of personality psychology.* Orlando, FL: Academic Press.

Emmons, R. A., & King, L. A. (1988). Conflict among personal strivings: Immediate and long-term implications for psychological and physical well-being. *Journal of Personality and Social Psychology, 54,* 1040–1048.

Emmons, R. A., & King, L. A. (1989). Personal striving differentiation and affective reactivity. *Journal of Personality and Social Psychology, 56,* 478–484.

Emmons, R. A., & McAdams, D. P. (1991). Personal strivings and motive dispositions: Exploring the links. *Personality and Social Psychology Bulletin, 17,* 648–654.

Epstein, S. (1983). A research paradigm for the study of personality and emotions. In M. M. Page & R. A. Dienstbier (Eds.), *Nebraska Symposium on Motivation, 1982.* Lincoln: University of Nebraska Press.

Epstein, S. (1990). Cognitive-experiential self-theory. In L. A. Pervin (Ed.), *Handbook of personality: Theory and research* (pp. 165–192), New York: Guilford Press.

Erber, R., & Erber, M. W. (1992, July). *On remembering your favorite things: Mood-incongruent recall and mood regulation.* Presented at the Joint Meeting of the European Association of Experimental Social Psychology and the Society for Experimental Social Psychology, Leuven/Louvain-la-Neuve, Belgium.

Erdelyi, M. H. (1985). *Psychoanalysis: Freud's cognitive psychology.* New York: Freeman.

Erdelyi, M. H. (1990). Repression, reconstruction, and defense: History and integration of the psychoanalytic and experimental frameworks. In J. L. Singer (Ed.), *Repression and dissociation* (pp. 1–31). Chicago: University of Chicago Press.

Erikson, E. (1964). *Childhood and society.* New York: W. W. Norton & Company, Inc.

Evans, K. (1993). *Intimacy in T.A.T stories, dreams, memories, and personal strivings.* Unpublished undergraduate honors thesis, Department of Psychology, Connecticut College, New London, CT.

Feather, N. (1975). *Values in education and society.* New York: Free Press.

Feather, N. (1982). *Expectations and actions: Expectancy-value models in psychology.* Hillsdale, NJ: Erlbaum.

Fenichel, O. (1927/1953). *The economic function of screen memories.* Collected Papers, Vol. 1 (pp. 113–116). New York: Norton.

Fine, R. (1990). *Love and work: The value system of psychoanalysis.* New York: Continuum.

Fisher, C. (1956). Dreams, images, and perception: A study of unconscious-preconscious relationships. *Journal of the American Psychoanalytic Association, 5,* 5–60.

Fitzgerald, F. S. (1920/1975). *This side of paradise.* Iowa City, IA: Windhover Press.

Fitzgerald, F. S. (1925/1988). *The great Gatsby.* New York: Cambridge University Press.

Fitzgerald, J. M. (1980). Sampling autobiographical memory reports in adolescence. *Developmental Psychology, 16,* 675–676.

Fitzgerald, J. M. (1981). Autobiographical memory reports in adolescence. *Canadian Journal of Psychology, 35,* 69–73.

Fluegel, J. C. (1917). A quantitative study of feeling and emotion in everyday life. *British Psychological Society, 24,* 408.

Fluegel, J. C. (1925). A quantitative study of feeling and emotion in everyday life. *British Journal of Psychology, General Section, 15,* 318–355.

Forgas, J. P. (1991). *Emotion and social judgments.* New York: Pergamon Press.

Forgas, J. P., Bower, G .H., & Moylan, S. J. (1990). Praise or blame? Affective influence on attributions for achievement. *Journal of Personality and Social Psychology, 59,* 809–819.

Frank, J .D. (1974). *Persuasion and healing.* New York: Schocken Books.

Freud, S. (1894/1962). The neuro-psychoses of defence. In J. Strachey (Ed.), *The complete psychological works of Sigmund Freud, standard edition* (vol. 3). London: Hogarth.

Freud, S. (1899/1973). Screen memories. In J. Strachey (Ed.), *The complete works of Sigmund Freud, standard edition* (vol. 18). London: Hogarth.

Freud, S. (1901/1973). Childhood memories and screen memories. In J. Strachey (Ed.), *The complete works of Sigmund Freud, standard edition* (vol. 6). London: Hogarth.

Freud, S. (1910/1973). Leonardo da Vinci and a memory of his childhood. In J. Strachey (Ed.), *The complete works of Sigmund Freud, standard edition* (vol. 11). London: Hogarth.

Freud, S. (1914/1973). Remembering, repeating, and working-through. In J. Strachey (Ed.), *The complete works of Sigmund Freud, standard edition* (vol. 12). London: Hogarth.

Freud, S. (1917/1973). A childhood recollection from 'Dichtung und Warheit. In J. Strachey (Ed.), *The complete works of Sigmund Freud, standard edition* (vol. 17). London: Hogarth.

Freud, S. (1920/1973). Beyond the pleasure principle. In J. Strachey (Ed.), *The complete works of Sigmund Freud, standard edition* (vol. 18). London: Hogarth.

Freud, S. (1926/1959). Inhibitions, symptoms and anxiety. Trans. J. Rickman. In J. Strachey (Ed.), *The complete works of Sigmund Freud, standard edition* (vol. 20). London: Hogarth.

Freud, S. (1938). Constructions in analysis. *International Journal of Psychoanalysis*, 19, 377–387.

Galambos, J. A., Abelson, R. P., & Black, J. B. (Eds.), (1986). *Knowledge structures*. Hillsdale, NJ: Erlbaum.

Galton, F. (1892). Psychometric experiments. *Brain*, 2, 149–162.

Galton, F. (1911). *Inquiries into human faculty and its development*. 2nd ed. New York: E. P. Dutton.

Gangestad, S. W. (1989). The evolutionary history of genetic variation: An emerging issue in the behavioral genetic study of personality. In D. M. Buss & N. Cantor (Eds.), *Personality psychology: Recent trends and emerging directions* (pp. 320–332). New York: Springer-Verlag.

Gardiner, J. M. (1990). A new psychology of memory? *Contemporary Psychology*, 35, 215–218.

Gendlin, E .T. (1979). *Focusing*. New York: Bantam Books.

Gergen, K. (1985). The social constructionist movement in modern psychology. *American Psychologist*, 40, 266–275.

Gergen, K., & Gergen, M. (1988). Narrative and the self as relationship. In L. Berkowitz (Ed.) *Advances in experimental social psychology* (vol. 21, pp. 17–55). New York: Academic Press.

Gibbons, F. X., Carver, C. S., Scheier, M. F., & Hormuth, S. E. (1979). Self-focused attention and the placebo effect: Fooling some of the people some of the time. *Journal of Experimental Social Psychology*, 15, 263–274.

Gilbert, G. M. (1938). The new status of experimental studies on the relationship of feeling to memory. *Psychological Bulletin*, 35, 26–35.

Gilligan, C. (1982). *In a different voice*. Cambridge, MA: Harvard University Press.

Gilligan, S. G., & Bower, G. H. (1984). Cognitive consequences of emotional arousal. In C. Izard, J. Kagan, & R. Zajonc (Eds.), *Emotions, cognitions, and behavior* (pp. 547–588). New York: Cambridge University Press.

Gleick, J. (1987). *Chaos: Making a new science*. New York: Viking Press.

Gordon, K. (1925). The recollection of pleasant and unpleasant odors. *Journal of Experimental Psychology*, 8, 225–239.

Greenacre, P. (1949). A contribution to the study of screen memories. *Psychoanalytic Study of the Child*, 3/4, 73–84.

Greenberg, G. (1992). *A hermeneutic analysis of the codependence literature*. Unpublished doctoral dissertation. Department of Psychology, Saybrook Institute, San Francisco, CA.

Greenwald, A. (1980). The totalitarian ego: Fabrication and revision of personal history. *American Psychologist, 35*, 603–618.

Greenwald, A., & Banaji, M. (1989). The self as a memory system: Powerful, but ordinary. *Journal of Personality and Social Psychology, 57*, 41–54.

Greenwald, A. & Pratkanis, A. (1984). The Self. In R. S. Wyer & T. K. Srull (Eds.), *Handbook of social cognition* (vol. 3, pp. 129–178). Hillsdale, NJ: Erlbaum.

Hanawalt, N. G. & Gebhardt, L. (1965). Childhood memories of single and recurrent incidents. *Journal of Genetic Psychology, 107*, 85–89.

Hansen, R. D., Hansen, C. H., & Crano, W. D. (1989). Sympathetic arousal and self attention: The accessibility of interoceptive and exteroceptive arousal cues. *Journal of Experimental Social Psychology, 25*, 437–499.

Hartmann, H. (1939). *Ego psychology and the problem of adaptation*. New York: International Universities Press.

Hayden, J. O. (1977). *William Wordsworth: The poems* (vol. 1). New Haven, CT: Yale University Press.

Hayden, R. (1975). Those winter sundays. In *Angle of ascent: New and selected poems* (p. 113). New York: Liveright Publishing Corporation.

Head, H. (1926). *Aphasia and kindred disorders of speech*. London: Macmillan.

Herman, J. L. (1992). *Trauma and recovery*. New York: Basic Books.

Hermans, H. J. M., Kempen, H. J. G., & van Loon, R. J. P. (1992). The dialogical self: Beyond individualism and rationalism. *American Psychologist, 47*, 23–33.

Hess, E. H. (1975). *The tell-tale eye*. New York: Litton.

Higgins, E. T. (1987). Self-discrepancy: A theory relating self and affect. *Psychological Review*, 94, 319–340.

Higgins, E. T. (1989). Continuities and discontinuities in self-regulatory and self-evaluative process: A developmental theory relating self and affect. *Journal of Personality, 57*, 407–444.

Hoffman, M., & Birch, C. (1991). *Amazing grace*. New York: E. P. Dutton.

Holmes, D. S. (1970). Differential change in affective intensity and the forgetting of unpleasant personal experiences. *Journal of Personality and Social Psychology, 15*, 234–239.

Holmes, D. S. (1974). Investigations of repression: Differential recall of material experimentally or naturally associated with ego threat. Psychological Bulletin, *81, 632–653.*

Holmes, D. S. (1990). The evidence for repression: An examination of 60 years of research. In J. L. Singer (Ed.), *Repression and dissociation: Implications for personality theory, psychopathology, and health* (pp. 85–102). Chicago: University of Chicago Press.

Howard, G. S. (1991). Cultural tales: A narrative approach to thinking, cross-cultural psychology, and psychotherapy. *American Psychologist, 46*, 187–197.

Howes, D. H., & Solomon, R. L. (1951). Visual duration threshold as a function of word probability. *Journal of Experimental Psychology, 41*, 401–410.

Huba, G., Singer, J. L., Aneshensel, C., & Antrobus, J. S. (1983). *Short imaginal processes inventory*. Port Huron, MI: Research Psychology Press.

Hull, C. (1943). *Principles of behavior.* New York: Appleton-Century-Crofts.

Hyland, M. (1987). Control theory interpretation of psychological mechanisms of depression: Comparison and integration of several theories. *Psychological Bulletin, 102,* 109–121.

Ingram, R. E. (1990). Self-focused attention in clinical disorders: Review and a conceptual model. *Psychological Bulletin,* 107, 156–176.

Inhelder, B., & Piaget, J. (1958). *The growth of logical thinking from childhood to adolescence.* New York: Basic Books.

Isen, A. M. (1985). The asymmetry of happiness and sadness in effects on memory in normal college students. *Journal of Experimental Psychology: General, 114,* 388–391.

Isen, A. M., Shalker, T. E., Clark, M., & Karp, L. (1978). Affect, accessibility of material in memory and behavior: A cognitive loop? *Journal of Personality and Social Psychology, 36,* 1–12.

Izard, C. E. (1979). *Human emotions.* New York: Plenum.

Izard, C. E. (1991). *The psychology of emotions.* New York: Plenum.

Jaeck, L. M. (1990). *Marcel Proust and the text as macrometaphor.* Toronto: University of Toronto Press.

Janoff-Bulman, R. (1992). *Shattered assumptions: Towards a new psychology of trauma.* New York: Free Press.

Johnson, M. K., & Sherman, S. J. (1990). Constructing and reconstructing the past and the future in the present. In E. T. Higgins & R. M. Sorrentino (Eds.), *Handbook of motivation and cognition* (vol. 2, pp. 482–526). New York: Guilford.

Jung, C. G. (1919). *Studies in word association: Experiments in the diagnosis of psychopathic conditions carried out at the psychiatric clinic at the University of Zurich.* New York: Moffat, Yard.

Kanfer, R., & Zeiss, A. M. (1983). Depression, interpersonal standard setting, and judgments of self-efficacy. *Journal of Abnormal Psychology, 92,* 319–329.

Kaplan, H. S. (1974). *The new sex therapy.* New York: Brunner-Mazel.

Kavanagh, D., & Bower, G. H. (1985). Mood and self-efficacy: Impact of joy and sadness on perceived capabilities. *Cognitive Therapy and Research, 9,* 507–525.

Kelly, G. A. (1955). *The psychology of personal constructs* (vol. 1). New York: Norton.

Kennedy, H. K. (1971). Problems in reconstruction in child analysis. *Psychoanalytic Study of the Child, 26,* 386–402.

Kenrick, D. T. (1989). A biosocial perspective on mates and traits: Reuniting personality and social psychology. In D. M. Buss, & N. Cantor (Eds.), *Personality psychology: Recent trends and emerging directions* (pp. 308–319). New York: Springer-Verlag.

Kernberg, O. F. (1976). *Object-relations theory and clinical psychoanalysis.* New York: Jason Aronson, Inc.

Kihlstrom, J. F. (1981). Personality and memory. In N. Cantor & J. F. Kihlstrom (Eds.), *Personality, cognition, and social interaction* (pp. 123–149). Hillsdale, NJ: Erlbaum.

Kihlstrom, J. F. (1989). On what does mood-dependent memory depend? *Journal of Social Behavior and Personality, 4,* 23–32.

Kihlstrom, J. F., Barnhardt, T. M., & Tatary, D. J. (1992). The psychological unconscious: Found, lost and regained. *American Psychologist, 47,* 788–791.

Kihlstrom, J. F., & Cantor, N. (1984). Mental representations of the self. In L. Berkowitz (Ed.), *Advances in experimental social psychology* (vol. 17). New York: Academic Press.

Kihlstrom, J. F., & Harackiewicz, J. M. (1982). The earliest recollection: A new survey. *Journal of Personality, 50*, 134–148.

Kihlstrom, J. F., & Hoyt, I. P. (1990). Repression, dissociation, and hypnosis. In J. L. Singer (Ed.), *Repression and dissociation: Implications for personality theory, psychopathology, and health* (pp. 181–208). Chicago: University of Chicago Press.

Klein, G. S. (1956). Perception, motives, and personality: A clinical perspective. In J. L. McCary (Ed.), *Psychology of personality* (pp. 121–199). New York: Logos Press.

Klein, G. S. (1970). *Perception, motives, and personality.* New York: Alfred A. Knopf.

Klein, G. S. & Schlesinger, H. (1949). Where is the perceiver in perceptual theory? *Journal of Personality, 18*, 32–47.

Klinger, E. (1978). Modes of normal conscious flow. In K. S. Pope and J. L. Singer (Eds.), *The stream of consciousness: Scientific investigations into the flow of human experience.* New York: Plenum.

Klinger, E., Barta, S. G., & Maxeiner, M. E. (1981). Current concerns: Assessing therapeutically relevant motivation. In P. C. Kendall, & S. Hollon (Eds.), *Assessment strategies for cognitive-behavioral interventions* (pp. 161–195). New York: Academic Press.

Koffka, K. (1935). *Principles of gestalt psychology.* New York: Harcourt.

Kohut, H. (1971). *The analysis of the self.* New York: International Universities Press.

Kolodner, J. L. (1983). Reconstructive memory: A computer model. *Cognitive Science, 7*, 281–328.

Kolodner, J. L. (1984). *Retrieval and organizational strategies in conceptual memory: A computer model.* Hillsdale, NJ: Erlbaum.

Kris, E. (1956a). The personal myth: A problem in psychoanalytic technique. *Journal of the American Psychoanalytic Association, 4*, 653–681.

Kris, E. (1956b). The recovery of childhood memories in psychoanalysis. *Psychoanalytic Study of the Child, 11*, 54–88.

Kuiken, D. (Ed.) (1989). Mood and memory: Theory, Research, and Applications. *Journal of Social Behavior and Personality, 4*, 1–192.

Kuiper, N. A., & Derry, P. A. (1982). Depressed and non-depressed content self-reference in mild depressives. *Journal of Personality, 50*, 67–80.

Langer, E. J. (1975). The illusion of control. *Journal of Personality and Social Psychology, 32*, 311–329.

Langs, R. J. (1965a). Earliest memories and personality: A predictive study. *Archives of General Psychiatry, 12*, 379–390.

Langs, R. J. (1965b). First memories and characterological diagnosis. *Journal of Nervous and Mental Disease, 141*, 318–320.

Langs, R. J. (1967). Stability of earliest memories under LSD-25 and placebo. *Journal of Nervous and Mental Disease, 144*, 171–184.

Langs, R. J., & Reiser, M. (1960). *A manual for the scoring of earliest memories, revised.* New York: Albert Einstein College of Medicine.

Langs, R. J., Rothenberg, M. B., Fishman, J. R., & Reiser, M. F. (1960). *Archives of General Psychiatry, 3*, 523–534.

Larsen, R. (1989). A process approach to personality psychology: Utilizing time as a facet of data. In D. Buss & N. Cantor (Eds.), *Personality psychology: Recent trends and emerging directions*. New York: Springer-Verlag.

Last, J. M., & Bruhn, A. R. (1983). The psychodiagnostic value of children's earliest memories. *Journal of Personality Assessment, 47*, 597–603.

Last, J. M., & Bruhn, A. R. (1985). Distinguishing child diagnostic types with early memories. *Journal of Personality Assessment, 49*, 187–192.

Lazarus, R. (1982). Thoughts on the relations between emotion and cognition. *American Psychologist, 37*, 1019–1024.

Lazarus, R. (1984). Thoughts on the relations between emotion and cognition. In K. R. Scherer & P. Ekman (Eds.), *Approaches to emotion* (pp. 247–257). Hillsdale, NJ: Erlbaum.

Lazarus, R. (1991a). *Emotion and adaptation*. New York: Oxford University Press.

Lazarus, R. (1991b). Progress on a cognitive-motivational-relational theory of emotion. *American Psychologist, 46*, 819–834.

Leeper, R. W. (1948). A motivational theory of emotions to replace "Emotions as disorganized response." *Psychological Bulletin, 55*, 5–21.

Lettieri, R. J. (1983). Consciousness, self-deception, and psychotherapy: An analogue study. *Imagination, Cognition, and Personality, 3*, 83–97.

Leventhal, H., & Scherer, K. (1987). The relationship of emotion to cognition: A functional approach to a semantic controversy. *Cognition and Emotion, 1*, 3–28.

Levitt, E. E. (1967). *The psychology of anxiety*. Indianapolis: Bobbs–Merrill.

Linton, M. (1986). Ways of searching and the contents of memory. In D. C. Rubin (Ed.), *Autobiographical memory*. New York: Cambridge University Press.

Linville, P. (1985). Self-complexity and affective extremity: Don't put all of your eggs in one cognitive basket. *Social Cognition, 3*, 94–120.

Linville, P. W. (1987). Self-complexity as a cognitive buffer against stress-related illness and depression. *Journal of Personality and Social Psychology, 52*, 663–676.

Little, D. (1983). Personal projects: A rationale and method for investigation. *Environment and Behavior, 15*, 273–309.

Little, D. (1989). Personal projects analysis: Trivial pursuits, magnificent obsessions, and the search for coherence. In D.M. Buss & N. Cantor (Eds.), *Personality psychology: Recent trends and emerging directions*. New York: Springer-Verlag.

Lloyd, G. G., & Lishman, W. A. (1975). Effect of depression on the recall of pleasant and unpleasant experiences. *Psychological Medicine, 5*, 173–180.

Loevinger, J. (1976). *Ego development: Conceptions and theories*. San Francisco: Jossey-Bass.

Loftus, E. F., & Klinger, M. R. (1992). Is the unconscious smart or dumb? *American Psychologist, 47*, 761–765

Luria, A. R. (1932). *The nature of human conflict*. New York: Liveright.

Macht, M. L., Spear, N. E., & Levis, D. J. (1977). State-dependent retention in humans induced by alternatives in affective state. *Bulletin of the Psychonomic Society, 10*, 415–418.

Madigan, R. J., & Bollenbach, A. K. (1982). Effects of induced mood on retrieval of personal episodic and semantic memories. *Psychological Reports, 50*, 147–157.

Mandler, G. (1975). *Mind and emotion*. New York: Wiley.

Mandler, G. (1984). *Mind and body: Psychology of emotion and stress.* New York: Norton.

March, J. F., & Simon, H. A. (1958). *Organizations.* New York: Wiley.

Marcia, J. E. (1980). Identity in adolescence. In J. Adelson (Ed.), *Handbook of adolescent psychology* (pp. 159–187). New York: Wiley.

Markus, H. R., & Kitayama, S. (1991). Culture and the self: Implications for cognition, emotion, and motivation. *Psychological Review, 98,* 224–253.

Maslow, A. H. (1954). *Motivation and personality.* New York: Harper & Row.

Maslow, A. H. (1968). *Toward a psychology of being.* (2nd Ed.). New York: D. Van Nostrand.

Masson, J. M. (1984). *The assault on truth: Freud's suppression of the seduction theory.* New York: Farrar, Straus, & Giroux.

Matlin, M., & Stang, D. (1978). *The Pollyanna principle: Selectivity in language, memory and thought.* Cambridge, MA: Schenkman.

Matt, G. E., Vasquez, C., & Campbell, W. K. (1992). Mood-congruent recall of affectively toned stimuli: A meta-analytic review. *Clinical Psychology Review, 12,* 227–255.

Mayer, J. D., Gaschke, Y. N., Braverman, D. L., & Evans, T. W. (1992). Mood-congruent judgment is a general effect. *Journal of Personality and Social Psychology, 63,* 119–132.

Mayer, J. D., & Salovey, P. (1988). Personality moderates the interaction of mood and cognition. In K. Fiedler & J. Forgas (Eds.), *Affect, cognition, and social behavior* (pp. 87–99). Gottingen, Germany: Hogrefe.

Mayman, M. (1968). Early memories and character structure. *Journal of Projective Techniques and Personality Assessment, 32,* 303–316.

Mayman, M., & Faris, M. (1960). Early memories as expressions of relationship paradigms. *American Journal of Orthopsychiatry, 30,* 507–520.

McAdams, D. P. (1980). A thematic coding system for the intimacy motive. *Journal of Research in Personality, 14,* 413–432.

McAdams, D. P. (1982). Experiences of intimacy and power: Relationships among social motives and autobiographical memory. *Journal of Personality and Social Psychology, 42,* 292–302.

McAdams, D. P. (1984). Scoring manual for the intimacy motive. *Psychological Documents, 14,* (2613), 7.

McAdams, D. P. (1987). A life-story model of identity. In R. Hogan & W. H. Jones (Eds.), *Perspectives in personality* (vol. 2, pp. 15–50). Greenwich, CT: JAI Press.

McAdams, D. P. (1988). *Power, intimacy, and the life story: Personological inquiries into identity.* New York: Guilford Press.

McAdams, D. P. (1989). The development of narrative identity. In D. Buss & N. Cantor (Eds.), *Personality psychology: Recent trends and emerging directions* (pp. 160–174). New York: Springer-Verlag.

McAdams, D. P. (1990a). Unity and purpose in human lives: The emergence of identity as the life story. In A. I. Rabin, R. A. Zucker, R. A. Emmons, & S. Frank (Eds.), *Studying persons and lives,* (pp. 148–200). New York: Springer.

McAdams, D. P. (1990b). *The person: An introduction to personality psychology.* San Diego: Harcourt Brace Jovanovich.

McAdams, D. P., Lensky, D. B., Daple, S. A., & Allen, J. (1988). Depression and the organization of autobiographical memory. *Journal of Social and Clinical Psychology, 7,* 332–349.

McClelland, D. C. (1985). How motives, skills, and values determine what people do. *American Psychologist, 40*, 812–825.

McClelland, D. C. (1985). *Human motivation*. Glenview, IL: Scott-Foresman.

McDougall, W. B. (1930). Autobiography. In C. Murchison (Ed.), *A history of psychology in autobiography*. Worcester, MA: Clark University Press.

McGeogh, J. A., & Irion, A. L. (1952). *The psychology of human learning*. New York: Longman.

McGuire, W. J., & McGuire, C. V. (1988). Content and process in the experience of self. In L. Berkowitz (Ed.), *Advances in experimental social psychology* (vol. 21, pp. 97–144). New York: Academic Press.

Meehl, P. E. (1973). Why I do not attend case conferences. In P. E. Meehl (Ed.), *Psychodiagnosis: Selected papers* (pp. 225–302). New York: Norton.

Meichenbaum, D. (1977). *Cognitive-behavior modification: An integrative approach*. New York: Plenum.

Meltzer, H. (1930). The present status of experimental studies on the relationship of feeling to memory. *Psychological Review, 53*, 173–203.

Merton, R. K. (1957). *Social theory and social structure*. Glencoe, IL: Free Press.

Miller, M. L. (1956). *Nostalgia: A psychoanalytic study of Marcel Proust*. Boston: Houghton Mifflin.

Miller, N. E., & Dollard, J. (1941). *Social learning and imitation*. New Haven, CT: Yale University Press.

Miller, N., Galanter, E., & Pribram, K. (1960). *Plans and the structure of behavior*. New York: Holt.

Mischel, W. (1968). *Personality and assessment*. New York: John Wiley and Sons.

Mischel, W., Ebbesen, E. E., & Zeiss, A. (1976). Determinants of selective memory about the self. *Journal of Consulting and Clinical Psychology, 44*, 92–103.

Mischel, W., & Peake, P. K. (1983). Analyzing the construction of consistency in personality. In M. M. Page & R. A. Dienstbier (Eds.), *Nebraska Symposium on Motivation, 1982*. Lincoln: University of Nebraska Press.

Moffitt, K. H. (1991). *Linking personal past, present, and future: Self-defining memories, affect, and strivings*. Master's thesis, Department of Psychology, Connecticut College, New London, CT.

Moffitt, K. H., Nelligan, D., Carlson, M., Vyse, S., & Singer, J. A. (August, 1992). *Depression and memory narrative type*. Paper presented at the annual meeting of the American Psychological Association, Washington, D.C.

Moffitt, K. H., & Singer, J. A. (1993). Continuity in the life story: Self-defining memories, affect, and approach/avoidance personal strivings. *Journal of Personality*, in press.

Moffitt, K. H., Zittel, C., & Singer, J. A. (1993). *Agency and communion in self-defining memories and personal strivings*. Unpublished manuscript, Department of Psychology, Connecticut College, New London, CT.

Moore, K. (1992). A day of glory. *Sports Illustrated* (Dec. 28) 74.

Moore, R. G., Watts, F. N., & Williams, J. M. G. (1988). The specificity of personal memories in depression. *British Journal of Clinical Psychology, 27*, 275–276.

Moretti, M. M. & Shaw, B. F. (1989). Automatic and dysfunctional cognitive processes in depression. In J. S. Uleman & J. A. Bargh (Eds.), *Unintended thought* (pp. 383–421). New York: Guilford Press.

Mosak, H. H. (1958). Early recollections as a projective technique. *Journal of Projective Techniques*, 22, 302–311.

Murray, H. A. (1938). *Explorations in personality*. New York: Oxford University Press.

Natale, M. (1978). Effect of induced elation and depression on internal/external locus of control. *Journal of Psychology, 100*, 315–321.

Natale, M., & Hantas, M. (1982). Effect of temporary mood states on selective memory about the self. *Journal of Personality and Social Psychology, 42*, 927–934.

Neisser, U. (1967). *Cognitive psychology*. Englewood Cliffs, NJ: Prentice–Hall.

Neisser, U. (1978). Memory: What are the important questions? In M. M. Gruneburg, P. E. Morris, & R. N. Sykes (Eds.), *Practical aspects of memory* (pp. 3–24). London: Academic Press.

Neisser, U. (Ed.) (1982). *Memory observed*. San Francisco: Freeman.

Neisser, U. (1986). Nested structure in autobiographical memory. In D. C. Rubin (Ed.), *Autobiographical memory* (pp. 71–81). New York: Cambridge University Press.

Neisser, U. & Winograd, E. (Eds.) (1988). *Remembering reconsidered: Ecological approaches to the study of memory*. Cambridge, MA: Cambridge University Press.

Niedenthal, P. M. (1990). Implicit perception of affective information. *Journal of Experimental Social Psychology, 26*, 505–527.

Niedenthal, P. M. (1993). *Affective reactions in social perception*. Manuscript under review.

Niedenthal, P. M., & Cantor, N. (1986). Affective responses as guides to category-based inferences. *Motivation and Emotion, 10*, 217–232.

Nietzsche, F. (1886/1966). *Beyond good and evil*. New York: Random House, Vintage Books.

Ogilvie, D. (1987). The undesired self: A neglected variable in personality research. *Journal of Personality and Social Psychology, 52*, 379–385.

Olson, H. A. (Ed.) (1979). *Early recollections*. Springfield, IL: Charles C. Thomas.

Ortony, A., Clore, G. L., & Collins, A. (1988). *The cognitive structure of emotion*. New York: Cambridge University Press.

Palfai, T. P., Salovey, P. (1992). The influence of affect on self-focused attention: Conceptual and methodological issues. *Consciousness and Cognition, 1*, 306–339.

Palys, T. S., & Little, D. (1983). Perceived life satisfaction and the organization of personal project systems. *Journal of Personality and Social Psychology, 44*, 1221–1230.

Pan, S. (1926). The influence of context upon learning and recall. *Journal of Experimental Psychology, 9*, 468–491.

Parrott, W. G., & Sabini, J. (1990). Mood and memory under natural conditions: Evidence for mood incongruent recall. *Journal of Personality and Social Psychology, 59*, 321–336.

Paul, I. H. (1959). Studies in remembering: The reproduction of connected and extended verbal material. In G. S. Klein (Ed.), *Psychological issues* (pp. 1–152). New York: International Universities Press,.

Pear, T. H. (1922). *Remembering and forgetting*. New York: Dutton.

Pervin, L. A. (1983). The stasis and flow of behavior: Toward a theory of goals. In M. M. Page & R. A. Dienstbier (Eds.), *Nebraska Symposium on Motivation, 1982*. Lincoln: University of Nebraska Press.

Pervin, L. A. (1985). Personality: Current controversies, issues, and directions. *Annual Review of Psychology, 36,* 83–114.

Pervin, L. A. (1989). Goal concepts in personality and social psychology: A historical introduction. In L. A. Pervin (Ed.), *Goal concepts in personality and social psychology.* Hillsdale, NJ: Erlbaum.

Piaget, J. (1926/1955). *The language and thought of the child.* New York: Harcourt Brace Jovanovich.

Poetzl, O. (1917). The relationship between experimentally induced dream images and indirect vision. *Psychological Issues, 2,* monograph 7.

Polkinghorne, D. E. (1988). *Narrative knowing and the human sciences.* New York: State University of New York Press.

Postman, L., & Brown, O. R. (1952). The perceptual consequences of success and failure. *Journal of Abnormal and Social Psychology, 47,* 213–221.

Potts, R., Camp, C., & Coyne, C. (1989). The relationship between naturally occurring dysphoric moods, elaborative encoding, and recall performance. *Cognition and Emotion, 3,* 197–205.

Privette, G. (1983). Peak experience, peak performance, and flow: A comparative analysis of positive human experiences. *Journal of Personality and Social Psychology, 45,* 1361–1368.

Privette, G., & Landsman, T. (1983). Factor analysis of peak performance: The full use of potential. *Journal of Personality and Social Psychology, 44,* 195–200.

Proust, M. (1913/1930). *Remembrance of things past, vol.1 (Swann's way).* Trans. by C. K. Scott Moncrieff. New York: Albert & Charles Boni.

Proust, M. (1927/1932). *Remembrance of things past, vol. 7 (The past recaptured).* Trans. by C. K. Scott Moncrieff. New York: Albert & Charles Boni.

Publilius Syrus (100 B.C./1961). Sententiae. In J. W. Duffy and A. M. Duffy (Eds.), *Minor Latin poets.* Cambridge, MA: Harvard University Press.

Pyszczynski, T., & Greenberg, J. (1987). Self-regulatory preservation and the depressive self-focusing style: A self-awareness theory of reactive depression. *Psychological Bulletin,* 102, 122–138.

Rapaport, D. (1942). *Emotions and memory.* Baltimore: Williams and Wilkins.

Rapaport, D. (Ed.). (1951). *Organization and pathology of thought.* New York: Columbia University Press.

Rapaport, D. (1959). A historical survey of psychoanalytic ego psychology. *Psychological Issues, 1,* 5–17.

Rapaport, D., Gill, M. M., & Schafer, R. (1945–1946). *Diagnostic psychological testing,* vols. 1 & 2. Chicago: Year Book Publishers.

Ratliff, M. M. (1938). The varying function of affectively toned olfactory, visual, and auditory cues in recall. *American Journal of Psychology, 1,* 695–701.

Read, S. J., & Miller, L. C. (1989). Inter-personalism: Toward a goal-based theory of persons in relationships. In L. A. Pervin (Ed.), *Goal concepts in personality and social psychology.* Hillsdale, NJ: Erlbaum.

Reis, H. T., & Stiller, J. (1992). Publication trends in JPSP: A three-decade review. *Journal of Personality and Social Psychology, 18,* 465–472.

Reiser, B. J. (1983). Contexts and indices in autobiographical memory. *Cognitive science technical report #24.* New Haven, CT: *Cognitive Science Program,* Yale University.

Reiser, B. J., Black, J. B., & Abelson, R. P. (1985). Knowledge structures in the organization and retrieval of autobiographical memories. *Cognitive Psychology, 17,* 89–137.

Reiser, B. J., Black, J. B., & Kalamarides, P. (1986). Strategic memory search processes. In D. C. Rubin (Ed.), *Autobiographical memory* (pp. 100–121). New York: Cambridge University Press.

Reyher, J. (1967). Hypnosis in research on psychopathology. In J. E. Gordon (Ed.), *Handbook of clinical and experimental hypnosis.* New York: Macmillan.

Riger, S. (1992). Epistemological debates, feminist voices: Science, social values, and the study of women. *American Psychologist, 47,* 730–740.

Robinson, J. A. (1976). Sampling autobiographical memory. *Cognitive Psychology, 8,* 578–595.

Robinson, J. A. (1980). Affect and retrieval of personal memories. *Motivation and Emotion, 4,* 149–174.

Robinson, J. A. (1986). Autobiographical memory: A historical prologue. In D. C. Rubin (Ed.), *Autobiographical memory.* New York: Cambridge University Press.

Robinson, J. A. & Swanson, K. L. (1990). Autobiographical memory: The next phase. *Applied Cognitive Psychology, 4,* 321–335.

Rokeach, M. (1973). The nature of human values. New York: Free Press.

Rorschach, H. (1921/1942). *Pyschodiagnostik.* Trans. by Hans Huber Verlag. Bern: Bircher.

Roseman, I. J. (1984). Cognitive determinants of emotional states. In P. Shaver (Ed.), *Review of Personality and Social Psychology* (vol. 5, pp. 11–36). Beverly Hills, CA: Sage.

Roseman, I. J., Spindel, M. S., & Jose, P. E. (1990). Appraisals of emotion-eliciting events: Testing a theory of discrete emotions. *Journal of Personality and Social Psychology, 59,* 899–915.

Rosenhan, D. L., & Seligman, M. E. P. (1989). *Abnormal Psychology* (2nd ed.). New York: Norton.

Rosenthal, R. (1966). *Experimenter effects in behavioral research.* New York: Appleton-Century-Crofts.

Ross, M. (1989). Relation of implicit theories to the construction of personal histories. *Psychological Review, 96,* 341–357.

Ross, M., & Conway, M. (1986). Remembering one's own past: The construction of personal histories. In R. M. Sorrentino & E. T. Higgins (Eds.), *Handbook of motivation and cognition* (pp. 122–144). New York: Guilford Press.

Ross, M., & Holmberg, D. (1990). Recounting the past: Gender differences in the recall of events in the history of a close relationship. In J. M. Olson & M. P. Zanna (Eds.), *Self-inference processes: The Ontario symposium* (pp. 135–152). Hillsdale, NJ: Erlbaum.

Rubin, D. C. (1982). On the retention function for autobiographical memory. *Journal of Verbal Learning and Verbal Behavior, 21,* 21–38.

Rubin, D. C. (Ed.) (1986). *Autobiographical memory.* New York: Cambridge University Press.

Rubin, D. C., Wetzler, S. E., & Nebes, R. D. (1986). Autobiographical memory across the life span. In D. C. Rubin (Ed.), *Autobiographical memory.* New York: Cambridge University Press.

Ryan, E. R. (1970). *Object relations and ego coping style in early memories.* Unpublished master's thesis, University of Michigan.

Ryan, E. R., & Bell, M. D. (1984). Changes in object relations from psychosis to recovery. *Journal of Abnormal Psychology, 93*, 209–215.

Sackeim, H.A. (1983). Self-deception, self-esteem, and depression: The adaptive value of lying to oneself. In J. Masling (Ed.), *Empirical studies of psychoanalytical theories* (vol. 1, pp. 101–157). Hillsdale, NJ: Analytic Press.

Sackeim, H. A., & Gur, R. C. (1979). Self-deception, other-deception, and self-reported psychopathology. *Journal of Consulting and Clinical Psychology, 47*, 213–215.

Sacks, O. (1992). The last hippie. *New York Review of Books, 39*, 53–62.

Salaman, E. (1970). *A collection of moments: A study of involuntary memories.* London: Longman.

Salaman, E. (1970/1982). A collection of moments. In U. Neisser (Ed.), *Memory observed* (pp. 49–63). San Francisco: Freeman.

Salovey, P. (1986). The effects of mood and focus of attention on self-relevant thoughts and helping intention. *Dissertation Abstracts International*, 1987–1988, 48, 3121–B.

Salovey, P. (1991) (Ed.). *The psychology of jealousy and envy.* New York: Guilford Press.

Salovey, P. (1992). Mood-induced self-focused attention. *Journal of Personality and Social Psychology, 62*, 699–707.

Salovey, P., & Birnbaum, D. (1989). Influence of mood on health-relevant cognition. *Journal of Personality and Social Psychology, 57*, 539–551.

Salovey, P., & Mayer, J. D. (1990). Emotional intelligence. *Imagination, Cognition, and Personality, 9*, 185–211.

Salovey, P., & Rodin, J. (1985). Cognitions about the self. In P. Shaver (Ed.), *Self, situations and social behavior* (pp. 143–166). Beverly Hills, CA: Sage.

Salovey, P., & Rosenhan, D. L. (1989). Mood states and prosocial behavior. In H. Wagner & A. Manstead (Eds.), *Handbook of social psychophysiology* (pp. 371–391). Chichester, Eng.: Wiley.

Salovey, P., Sieber, W. J., Smith, A. F., Turk, D. C., Jobe, J. B., & Willis, G. B. (1992). Laboratory research on reporting chronic pain episodes in health surveys. *National Center for Health Statistics, Vital and Health Statistics*, Series 6, #6.

Salovey, P., & Singer, J.A. (1989). Mood congruency effects in childhood versus recent autobiographical memories. *Journal of Social Behavior and Personality, 4*, 99–120.

Salovey, P., & Singer, J. A. (1991). Cognitive behavior modification. In F. H. Kanfer & A. P. Goldstein (Eds.), *Helping people change: A textbook of methods* (4th ed., pp. 361–395). New York: Pergamon Press.

Salovey, P., & Turk, D. C. (1991). Clinical judgment and decision-making. In C. R. Snyder & D. R. Forsyth (Eds.), *Handbook of social and clinical psychology: The health perspective* (pp. 416–437). New York: Pergamon Press.

Sampson, E. E. (1978). Scientific paradigms and social values: Wanted—A scientific revolution. *Journal of Personality and Social Psychology, 36*, 1332–1343.

Sarbin, T. R. (1986). *Narrative psychology: The storied nature of human conduct.* New York: Praeger.

Scarr, S. (1985). Constructing psychology: Making facts and fables for our times. *American Psychologist, 40*, 499–512.

Schachtel, E. (1947). On memory and childhood amnesia. *Psychiatry, 10*, 1–26.

Schachter, S., & Latane, B. (1964). Crime, cognition, and the autonomic nervous system. In D. Levin (Ed.), *Nebraska Symposium on Motivation.* Lincoln: University of Nebraska Press.

Schacter, S., & Singer, J. E. (1962). Cognitive, social, and physiological determinants of emotional state. *Psychological Review, 62,* 379–399.

Schafer, R. (1983). *The analytic attitude.* New York: Basic Books.

Schaffer, L. F., Gilman, B., & Schoen, M. (1940). *Psychology.* New York: Harper & Brothers.

Schank, R. C. (1982). *Dynamic memory: A theory of reminding and learning in computers and people.* New York: Cambridge University Press.

Schank, R. C. (1990). *Tell me a story.* New York: Scribners.

Schank, R. C., & Abelson, R. P. (1977). *Scripts, plans, goals, and understanding.* Hillsdale, NJ: Erlbaum.

Scheff, T. J. (1966). *Being mentally ill: A sociological theory.* Chicago: Aldine.

Scheier, M. F., & Carver, C. S. (1977). Self-focused attention and the experience of emotion: Attraction, repulsion, elation, and depression. *Journal of Personality and Social Psychology, 35,* 625–636.

Scheier, M. F., Carver, C. S., & Gibbons, F. X. (1981). Self-focused attention and reactions to fear. *Journal of Research in Personality, 15,* 1–15.

Scherer, K. (1984). *On the nature and function of emotion: A component process approach.* In K. Scherer & P. Ekman (Eds.), Approaches to emotion (pp. 293–318). Hillsdale, NJ: Erlbaum.

Scherer, K. (1986). Vocal affect expression: A review and a model for future research. *Psychological Bulletin, 99,* 143–165.

Schrecker, P. (1913/1973). Individual psychological significance of first childhood recollections. *Journal of Individual Psychology, 29,* 146–156.

Schwartz, G. E., Weinberger, D. A., & Singer, J. A. (1981). Cardiovascular differentiation of happiness, sadness, anger, and fear following imagery and exercise. *Psychosomatic Medicine, 43,* 343–364.

Schwarzer, R. (1984). The self in anxiety, stress, and depression: An introduction. In R. Schwarzer (Ed.), *The self in anxiety, stress, and depression.* Amsterdam: North Holland.

Secord, P. F., & Backman, C. W. (1965). An interpersonal approach to personality. In B. Maher (Ed.), *Progress in experimental personality research* (vol. 2, pp. 91–125). New York: Academic Press.

Sedikides, C. (1992a). Changes in the valence of the self as a function of mood. In M. S. Clark (Ed.) *Emotion and social behavior* (pp. 271–311). Newbury Park, CA: Sage.

Sedikides, C. (1992b). Mood as a determinant of attentional focus. *Cognition and Emotion, 6,* 129–148.

Shapiro, D. (1965). *Neurotic styles.* New York: Basic Books.

Shattuck, R. (1963). *Proust's binoculars.* New York: Random House.

Sheffield, F., Wulff, J. J., & Backer, R. (1951). Reward value of copulation without sex drive reduction. *Journal of Comparative and Physiological Psychology, 44,* 3–8.

Shevrin, H. (1988). Unconscious conflict: A convergent psychodynamic and electrophysiological approach. In M. J. Horowitz (Ed.), *Psychodynamics and cognition.* Chicago: University of Chicago Press.

Shevrin, H. (1990). Subliminal perception and repression. In J. L. Singer (Ed.), *Repression and dissociation: Implications for personality theory, psychopathology, and health.* (pp. 103–119). Chicago: University of Chicago Press.

Showers, C., & Cantor, N. (1985). Social cognition: A look at motivated strategies. *Annual Review of Psychology, 36*, 275–305.

Simon, H. A. (1967). Motivational and emotional controls of cognition. *Psychological Review, 74*, 29–39.

Simon, H. A. (1982). Comments. In M. S. Clark and S. T. Fiske (Eds.), *Affect and cognition* (pp. 333–342). Hillsdale, NJ: Erlbaum.

Singer, J. A. (1990a). Affective responses to autobiographical memories and their relationship to long-term goals. *Journal of Personality, 58*, 535–563.

Singer, J. A. (1990b). Rediscovering motivation in cognitive theories of personality. [Review of L.A. Pervin (Ed.) Goal concepts in personality and social psychology.] *Imagination, Cognition, and Personality, 9*, 265–7.

Singer, J. A. (1992). Challenges to the integration of the psychoanalytic and cognitive perspectives on the self. *Psychological Inquiry, 3*, 59–61.

Singer, J. A., & Moffitt, K. H. (1991–1992). An experimental investigation of specificity and generality in memory narratives. *Imagination, Cognition, and Personality, 11*, 233–257.

Singer, J. A., & Salovey, P. (1988). Mood and memory: Evaluating the network theory of affect. *Clinical Psychology Review, 8*, 211–251.

Singer, J. A. & Singer, J. L. (1992). Transference in psychotherapy and daily life: Implications of current memory and social cognition research. In J. W. Barron, M. N. Eagle, & D. L. Wolitzky (Eds.) *Interface of Psychoanalysis and psychology* (pp. 516–538). Washington, D.C.: American Psychological Association.

Singer J. A., Zittel, C. Tyson, A., Kirmmse, J. (August, 1993). *Earliest memories of racial/ethnic difference and prejudice.* Paper presented at the annual meeting of the American Psychological Association, Toronto, Ontario.

Singer, J. L. (1966). *Daydreaming.* New York: Random House.

Singer, J. L. (1974a). Daydreaming and the stream of thought. *American Scientist, 6*, 417–425.

Singer, J. L. (1974b). *Imagery and daydream methods in psychotherapy and behavior modification.* New York: Academic Press.

Singer, J. L. (1975). Navigating the stream of consciousness: Research in daydreaming and related inner experience. *American Psychologist, 30*, 727–738.

Singer, J. L. (1984). The private personality. *Personality and Social Psychology Bulletin, 10*, 332–349.

Singer, J. L. (1988). Psychoanalytic theory in the context of contemporary psychology: The Helen Block Lewis memorial address. *Psychoanalytic Psychology, 5*, 95–125.

Singer, J. L. (1990a). *Repression and dissociation: Implications for personality theory, psychopathology, and health.* Chicago: University of Chicago Press.

Singer, J. L. (1990b). Preface: A fresh look at repression, dissociation, and the defenses as mechanisms and as personality style. In J. L. Singer (Ed.), *Repression and Dissociation* (pp. xi–xxiv). Chicago: University of Chicago Press.

Singer, J. L., & Bonanno, G. A. (1990). Personality and private experience: Individual variations in consciousness and in attention to subjective phenomena. In L. Pervin (Ed.), *Handbook of personality* (pp. 419–444). New York: Guilford Press.

Singer, J. L., & Kolligan, J. (1987). Personality: Developments in the study of private experience. *Annual Review of Psychology, 38*, 533–574.

Singer, J. L., & Salovey, P. (1991). Organized knowledge structures in personality: Schemas, self-schemas, prototypes, and scripts. In M. Horowitz (Ed.), *Person schemas* (pp. 33–79). Chicago: University of Chicago Press.

Skinner, B. F. (1938). *The behavior of organisms*. New York: Appleton-Century–Crofts.

Smelser, N. J., & Erikson, E. H. (Eds.) (1980). *Themes of work and love in adulthood*. Cambridge, MA: Harvard University Press.

Smith, C. P., (Ed.), (1992). *Motivation and personality: Handbook of thematic content analysis*. New York: Cambridge University Press.

Smith, W. W. (1921). Experiments on memory and affective tone. *British Journal of Psychology, 11*, 236–250.

Snyder, M. (1981). "Seek and ye shall find. . . ." In E. T. Higgins, C. P. Herman, & M. P. Zanna (Eds.), *Social cognition: The Ontario symposium on personality and social psychology* (pp. 277–303). Hillsdale, NJ: Erlbaum.

Snyder, M., & Swann, W. B., Jr. (1978). Hypothesis-testing processes in social interaction. *Journal of Personality and Social Psychology, 36*, 1202–1212.

Snyder, M., & White, P. (1982). Moods and memories: Elation, depression, and the remembering of events in one's life. *Journal of Personality, 50*, 149–167.

Soseki, N. (1914/1957). *Kokoro*. South Bend, IN: Regnery–Gateway.

Spence, D. P. (1982). *Narrative truth and historical truth: Meaning and interpretation in psychoanalysis*. New York: Norton.

Spence, D. P. (1988). Passive remembering. In U. Neisser & E. Winograd, *Remembering reconsidered: Ecological and traditional approaches to the study of memory* (pp. 311–325). New York: Cambridge University Press.

Spence, D. P. (1990). *The Freudian metaphor*. New York: Norton.

Spencer, H. (1873). *Principles of psychology*. New York: Appleton.

Strauman, T. J., & Higgins, E. T. (1987). Automatic activation of self-discrepancies and emotional syndromes: When cognitive structures influence affect. *Journal of Personality and Social Psychology, 53*, 1004–1014.

Sullivan, E. B. (1927). Attitude in relation to learning. *Psychological Monographs, 36*, 1–149.

Sullivan, M. J. L., & Conway, M. (1989). Negative affect leads to low-effort cognition: Attributional processing for observed social behavior. *Social Cognition, 7*, 315–337.

Swann, W. B. (1983). Self-verification: Bringing social reality into harmony with the self. In J. Suls & A. G. Greenwald (Eds.), *Social psychological perspectives on the self* (vol. 2, pp. 33–66). Hillsdale, NJ: Erlbaum.

Swann, W. B. (1985). *The self as architect of social reality*. In B. Schlenker (Ed.), *The self and social life* (pp. 100–125). New York: McGraw-Hill.

Swann, W. B. (1987). Identity negotiation: Where two roads meet. *Journal of Personality and Social Psychology, 53*, 1038–1051.

Swann, W. B., & Hill, C. A. (1982). When our identities are mistaken: Reaffirming self-conceptions through social interaction. *Journal of Personality and Social Psychology, 43*, 59–66.

Swann, W. B., & Predmore, S. C. (1985). Intimates as agents of social support: Sources of consolation or despair. *Journal of Personality and Social Psychology, 49*, 1609–1617.

The Remembered Self

Swann, W. B., & Read, S. J. (1981a). Acquiring self-knowledge: The search for feedback that fits. *Journal of Personality and Social Psychology, 41*, 1119–1128.

Swann, W. B., & Read, S. J. (1981b). Self-verification processes: How we sustain our self-conceptions. *Journal of Experimental Social Psychology, 17*, 351–370.

Swir, A. (1989). Poems on my father and my mother (Trans. by C. Milosz & L. Nathan). *The American Poetry Review*, (Jan-Feb), 23–26.

Tait, W. D. (1913). The effect of psycho-physical attitudes on memory. *Journal of Abnormal Psychology, 8*, 10–37.

Tate, E. (1991). About the play and playwright. *Long Wharf Theatre production of Betrayal* (pp. 11–13), New Haven, CT.

Taylor, S. E. (1989). *Positive illusions: Creative self-deception and the healthy mind.* New York: Basic Books.

Taylor, S. E., & Brown, J. D. (1988). Illusion and well-being: A social psychological perspective on mental health. *Psychological Bulletin, 103*, 193–210.

Taylor, S. E., & Crocker, J. (1981). Schematic bases of social information processing. In E. T. Higgins, C. P. Herman, & M. P. Zanna (Eds.), *Social cognition: The Ontario symposium* (vol. 1, pp. 89–134). Hillsdale, NJ: Erlbaum.

Teasdale, J. D., & Fogarty, S. J. (1979). Differential effects of induced mood on retrieval of pleasant and unpleasant memories from episodic memory. *Journal of Abnormal Psychology, 88*, 248–257.

Teasdale, J. D., & Rezin, V. (1978). The effects of reducing frequency of negative thoughts on the mood of depressed patients—tests of a cognitive model of depression. *British Journal of Clinical Psychology, 17*, 65–74.

Teasdale, J. D., & Russell, M. L. (1983). Differential effects of induced mood on the recall of positive, negative, and neutral words. *British Journal of Clinical Psychology, 22*, 163–171.

Teasdale, J. D., & Taylor, R. (1981). Induced mood and accessibility of memories: An effect of mood state or of induction procedure? *British Journal of Clinical Psychology, 20*, 39–48.

Teasdale, J. D., Taylor, R., & Fogarty, S. J. (1980). Effects of induced elation-depression on the accessibility of memories of happy and unhappy experiences. *Behavior Research and Therapy, 18*, 339–346.

Thody, (1988). *Marcel Proust.* New York: St. Martin's Press.

Thorndike, E. L. (1927). The law of effect. *American Journal of Psychology, 39*, 212–222.

Tolman, E. C. (1917). Retroactive inhibition as affected by conditions of learning. *Psychological Monographs, 25*, 1–50.

Tolman, E. C. (1932). *Purposive behavior in animals and men.* New York: Appleton-Century-Crofts.

Tolman, E. C., & Johnson, I. (1918). A note on association-time and feeling. *American Journal of Psychology, 29*, 187–195.

Tomkins, S. S., (1962). *Imagery, affect, consciousness*, vol. 1. New York: Springer.

Tomkins, S. S. (1963). *Imagery, affect, consciousness*, vol. 2. New York: Springer.

Tomkins, S. S. (1979). Script theory: Differential magnification of affects. In H. E. Howe and R. A. Dienstbier (Eds.), *Nebraska symposium on motivation*, vol. 26 (pp. 201–236). Lincoln: University of Nebraska Press.

Tomkins, S. S. (1987). Script theory. In J. Aranoff, A. I. Rabin, & R. A. Zucker (Eds.), *The emergence of personality* (pp. 147–216). New York: Springer.

Tomkins, S. S. (1991). *Imagery, affect, consciousness*, vol. 3. New York: Springer.

Tulving, E. (1972). Episodic and semantic memory. In E. Tulving & W. Donaldson (Eds.), *Organization of memory* (pp. 381–403). New York: Academic Press.

Tulving, E. (1983). *Elements of episodic memory*. New York: Oxford University Press.

Turk, D. C., & Salovey, P. (1988). *Reasoning, inference, and judgment in clinical psychology*. New York: The Free Press.

Ucros, C. G. (1989). Mood state-dependent memory: A meta-analysis. *Cognition and Emotion, 3*, 139–167.

Underwood, B., Froming, W. J., & Moore, B. S. (1980). Mood, attention, and altruism: A search for mediating variables. *Developmental Psychology, 13*, 541–542.

Valenstein, E. S. (1973). *Brain control*. New York: Wiley.

Vargas Llosa, M. (1990). *The storyteller*. New York: Penguin.

Wahler, R. G., & Afton, A. D. (1980). Attentional processes in insular and noninsular mothers: Some differences in their summary reports about child problem behaviours. *Child Behaviour Therapy, 2*, 25–41.

Washburn, M. F., Giang, F., Ives, M., & Pollock, M. (1925). Memory revival of emotions as a test of emotional and phlegmatic temperaments. *American Journal of Psychology, 36*, 456–459.

Watts, F. N., & Cooper, Z. (1989). The effects of depression on structural aspects of the recall of prose. *Journal of Abnormal Psychology, 98*, 150–153.

Webster's new international dictionary of the english language (2nd ed., unabridged). (1952). Springfield, MA: G. & C. Merriam.

Wegner, D. (1989). *White bears and other unwanted thoughts*. New York: Viking Press.

Wegner, D., & Giuliano, T. (1980). Arousal-induced attention to self. *Journal of Personality and Social Psychology, 38*, 719–726.

Weinberger, D. (1989). *Social-emotional adjustment in older children and adults: I. Psychometric properties of the Weinberger Adjustment Inventory*. Unpublished manuscript, Department of Psychology, Stanford University.

Weinberger, D. (1990). The construct validity of the repressive coping style. In J. L. Singer (Ed.), *Repression and dissociation* (pp. 337–386). Chicago: University of Chicago Press.

Weiner, B. (1982). The emotional consequences of causal attributions. In M. S. Clark and S. T. Fiske (Eds.), *Affect and cognition*. Hillsdale, NJ: Erlbaum.

Weiner, B. (1985). An attributional theory of achievement motivation and emotion. *Psychological Review, 92*, 548–573.

Weiner, B., Russell, D., & Lerman, D. (1979). The cognition-emotion process in achievement-related contexts. *Journal of Personality and Social Psychology, 40*, 650–663.

Welkowitz, J., Cohen, J., & Ortmeyer, D. (1967). Value system similarity: Investigation of patient-therapist dyads. *Journal of Consulting Psychology, 31*, 48–55.

Wessman, A. E., & Ricks, D. F. (1966). *Mood and personality*. New York: Holt, Rinehart, & Winston.

Westen, D. (1991). Social cognition and object relations. *Psychological Bulletin, 109,* 429–455.

Westen, D. (1992). The cognitive and the psychoanalytic self: Can we put ourselves together. *Psychological Inquiry, 3,* 1–13.

White, H. (1980). The value of narrativity in the representation of reality. *Critical Inquiry, 7,* 5–28.

White, R. W. (1959). Motivation reconsidered: The concept of competence. *Psychological Review, 66,* 297–333.

Whitman, R. M., Kramer, M., & Baldrige, B. (1963). What dream does the patient tell? *Archives of General Psychiatry, 8,* 277–282.

Whitman, W. (1892/1958). *Leaves of grass.* New York: Signet Classics.

Wicker, F. W., Lambert, F. B., Richardson, F. C., & Kahler, J. (1984). Categorical goal hierarchies and classification of human motives. *Journal of Personality, 52,* 285–305.

Williams, J. M. G., & Broadbent, K. (1986). Autobiographical memory in suicide attempters. *Journal of Abnormal Psychology, 95,* 144–149.

Williams, J. M. G., & Dritschel, B. H. (1988). Emotional disturbance and the specificity of autobiographical memory. *Cognition and Emotion, 2,* 221–234.

Williams, J. M. G., & Scott, J. (1988). Autobiographical memory in depression. *Psychological Medicine, 18,* 689–695.

Williams, J. M. G., Watts, F. N., McLeod, C., & Matthews, A. (1988). *Cognitive psychology and emotions disorders.* Chichester, Eng.: Wiley.

Williams, T. (1945/1970). *The glass menagerie.* New York: New Directions.

Wine, J. D. (1971). Text anxiety and direction of attention. *Psychological Bulletin, 76,* 92–104.

Witkin, H. A. (1950). Individual differences in ease of perception of embedded figures. *Journal of Personality, 19,* 1–15.

Witkin, H. A., Lewis, H. B., Hertzman, M., Machover, K., Meissner, P. B., and Wapner, S. (1954). *Personality through perception.* New York: Harper.

Wohlgemuth, A. (1923). The influence of feeling on memory. *British Journal of Psychology, General Section, 13,* 405–416.

Wood, J. V., Saltzberg, J. A., & Goldsamt, L.A. (1990). Does affect induce self-focused attention? *Journal of Personality and Social Psychology, 58,* 899–908.

Woodworth, R. S. (1940) *Psychology, 4th edition.* New York: Henry Holt.

Wordsworth, W. (1798/1977). Lines composed a few miles above Tintern Abbey, on revisiting the banks of the Wye during a tour. In J.O. Hayden (Ed.), *William Wordsworth: The poems* (vol. 1) (pp. 357–362). New Haven, CT: Yale University Press.

Wright, J., & Mischel, W. (1982). Influence of affect on cognitive social learning person variables. *Journal of Personality and Social Psychology, 43,* 901–914.

Young, P. T. (1936). *Motivation of behavior.* New York: Wiley.

Young, P. T. (1943). *Emotion in man and animal: Its nature and relation to attitude and motive.* New York: Wiley.

Zajonc, R. B. (1980). Feeling and thinking: Preferences need no inferences. *American Psychologist, 35,* 151–175.

Zajonc, R. B. (1984). On the primacy of affect. *American Psychologist, 39*, 117–123.

Zirkel, S., & Cantor, N. (1990). Personal construal of a life task: Those who struggle for independence. *Journal of Personality and Social Psychology, 58*, 172–185.

Zuckerman, M., & Lubin, B. (1985). *Manual for the multiple affect adjective check list—revised.* San Diego, CA: Edits.

Index